# Southern Odyssey

# Southern Odyssey

SELECTED WRITINGS BY

## Sherwood Anderson

EDITED BY

Welford Dunaway Taylor

and Charles E. Modlin

THE UNIVERSITY OF GEORGIA PRESS *Athens and London*

Published by the University of Georgia Press
Athens, Georgia 30602
Works by Sherwood Anderson © 1997 by Charles E. Modlin
and Hilbert H. Campbell, Trustees, Sherwood Anderson
Literary Estate Trust
All other text © 1997 by Welford Dunaway Taylor
and Charles E. Modlin
All rights reserved
Designed by Kathi Dailey Morgan

Set in Berkeley Old Style by G & S Typesetters, Inc.
Printed and bound by Maple-Vail Book Manufacturing Group, Inc.
The paper in this book meets the guidelines for permanence
and durability of the Committee on Production Guidelines
for Book Longevity of the Council on Library Resources.

Printed in the United States of America

01  00  99  98  97   C   5   4   3   2   1

*Library of Congress Cataloging in Publication Data*

Anderson, Sherwood, 1876–1941.
    [Southern odyssey]
    Southern odyssey: selected writings by Sherwood Anderson   /
  edited by Welford Dunaway Taylor and Charles E. Modlin.
       p.    cm.
  Includes bibliographical references and index.
  ISBN 0-8203-1899-X (alk. paper)
    1. Southern States—Social life and customs—1865–    —Anecdotes.
2. Southern States—History—1865–1951—Anecdotes.
3. Southern States—Social conditions—1865–1945—Anecdotes.
4. Anderson, Sherwood, 1876–1941—Views on Southern States.
I. Taylor, Welford Dunaway.   II. Modlin, Charles E.   III. Title.
F209.6.A53   1997
818'.91203—dc20       96-30789

*British Library Cataloging in Publication Data available*

*For Margie and Carole*

# Contents

# Preface

Although Sherwood Anderson's contact with the South spanned many years, it is not generally recognized as a separate, distinctive segment of his life and work. There are several plausible explanations for this. Some of his shorter writings on southern subjects were published in obscure or now-defunct magazines and are therefore easily overlooked. But even items appearing in better-known venues, such as *Scribner's* or *Vanity Fair,* have fallen victim to the short-lived fame common to publications in periodicals. Although a limited amount of this material has been included in collections of his work, first by Anderson and subsequently by other editors,[1] none of these volumes has had a primarily southern emphasis.

More to the point, perhaps, is the fact that Anderson's residence in the South began at a time when supporters and detractors alike were alleging the decline of his creative abilities. *Dark Laughter* (1925), his first novel containing southern elements, received a mixed critical response. Even staunch admirers maintained that it signalled a falling off, while his erstwhile protégé and friend, Ernest Hemingway, made it the butt of a ruthless parody. While it is true that *Dark Laughter* became a best-seller, in the minds of some of his contemporaries it cast a shadow over Anderson's subsequent work. Some still believe that his later efforts fail to measure up to such early successes as *Winesburg, Ohio* (1919), *The Triumph of the Egg* (1921), and *Horses and Men* (1923).

Nevertheless, during the past three decades more attention has been paid Anderson's southern experience in the form of reprintings of older works and newly formed collections.[2] But even after reading all these, plus the nonfiction collections *Perhaps Women* (1931), *No Swank* (1934),

*Puzzled America* (1935), and *Home Town* (1940), one still falls short of realizing the full range of Anderson's writing about the South. For one reason, the nonfiction volumes emphasize broader issues, some of which just happen to subsume the southern subjects. For another, a substantial body of material has remained unedited and unpublished. We have surveyed all the published writings from this period—fiction, essays, memoirs, letters, newspaper files—as well as manuscripts.[3]

This book has evolved from the two-fold belief that Anderson's southern phase—his final phase, as it turned out—is deserving of study apart from other, better known segments of his life and work. During his last sixteen years he produced a body of material relating to the region that is unique in variety, perspective, and vividness of expression. Indeed, a few of his sketches featuring southern subjects qualify as iconographic depictions of a region struggling with the burdens of prohibition, the depression, and racial division, along with vestiges of the Civil War and its aftermath. More important, the best of this work recalls the early Anderson, whose fictional pioneering changed the way American authors structured their stories and expanded the latitude for candid expression of their observations.

Although we have attempted to avoid relying too heavily on well-known material, we have at times rejected a lesser known text in favor of a familiar one, particularly when the latter was the better written. Still, our primary objective has been to locate unpublished texts, to rediscover others that appeared in obscure places, and to consider variant drafts whenever possible. For, as his numerous editors can attest, Anderson frequently recycled passages and entire texts, often revising substantially in subsequent printings.

Throughout the selection process we sought texts that define something of the substance of the South as Anderson perceived it. Moreover, we have sought material that tells something of Anderson's attitudes toward the South which, coupled with his remarkable ability to express the essence of a subject, allows us to see the region in an unprecedented way. Finally, we have selected with a view toward identifying those texts that might qualify for a place in the vast permanent chronicle of the modern South. We believe that Anderson offers a unique statement to this larger record, a statement comparable to the one that his best fiction makes about human nature. This volume is therefore an attempt to create an inclusive, representative, and rounded collection of writings—a reader with the southern focus that former collections have lacked. Viewed within this southern context, certain selections that might have seemed negligible in former settings take on new meaning and relevance.

A few long selections have been edited down in order to emphasize their southern content. Editorial omissions are indicated with bracketed ellipses. Anderson occasionally used ellipses in his own text to indicate pauses, not omissions. Obvious errors have been silently corrected, and occasional punctuation has been adjusted as needed for clarity. Interpolations appear in brackets.

Selections are arranged in five chapters, each having a thematic title. Their chronological sequencing follows the design of Anderson's developing southern experience—discovery, settling in the southern highlands, the journalistic venture, involvement in southern labor issues, and the depression and post–depression South. However, all are linked by certain common threads, two of which deserve comment. One is Anderson's fascination with individual people, whether for their uniqueness or as representatives of a larger issue. As he often stated late in his life, he made no claims to being a theorist or thinker on a grand scale. Rather, he maintained that the true gauge of collective problems was to be found in the particular—"thinking in the small," he called it. Thus, the unemployed woman hitchhiker to whom he gives a ride ("Hard-Boiled") and who recounts to him a story of violence, abuse, and poverty, is emblematic of the depression era in the South. A few days before his death Anderson was visited in his hotel room by a young friend, who told him of a trip he was planning to the South Seas—in search of people worth writing about. Anderson replied approvingly yet reminded his young visitor that "Of course, there's a wonderful story in the old man who brought you up in the elevator."[4]

A second unifying principle is less obvious but equally important. As a product of the nineteenth century, which produced a number of conflicting theories concerning the rationale for human existence, Anderson came to regard life not as a detailed blueprint but as "a loose, flowing thing," in which one must find one's way and thus determine the shape and meaning of his or her existence. In other words, he saw life as a journey, a quest for discovery and meaning. Because the final segment of Anderson's own long, meandering pilgrimage carried him through the South during a crucial period in its history, we have termed this experience—appropriately, we think—an odyssey.

# Acknowledgments

For assistance in preparing this volume, we thank the staff of the Newberry Library, most especially Margaret Kulis and Diana Haskell; Mary Vick of the Interlibrary Loan Department of the Boatwright Library, University of Richmond; Tanya Reece and Jenny Bay of Virginia Polytechnic Institute and State University; and Kathy Zacher of the University of Richmond.

# Introduction

Sherwood Anderson's initial contact with the South was vicarious. It was part of the folklore of his youth, a place of which he had read and heard and that obviously excited his imagination. While rural Ohio in the 1870s and 1880s celebrated its native sons who had fought in the Union army, it nonetheless retained a romanticized image of the antebellum South. Anderson's father, Irwin W. Anderson, a Civil War veteran and a member of the Grand Army of the Republic, claimed a proud (though largely fanciful) southern heritage. Anderson later made frequent mention of the stories he heard from his father and other Civil War veterans, and he nourished an ongoing (though unfulfilled) desire to write a book about the war. It was perhaps this perception that prompted Anderson, late in life, to suggest to a friend that "the one desire of my whole life I have dreamed most about, yearned the most for, . . . [is] I wish I might have been born a southern gentleman and have lived my life as one."[1]

As it was, his early life took a very different form. Most of his youth was spent in Clyde, Ohio, a small town near Lake Erie, which he left in the mid-1890s before finishing high school. Moving to Chicago, he worked as a laborer until he enlisted for service in the Spanish-American War (1898–99). Then, after completing high school at the Wittenburg Academy, he returned to Chicago, this time to work as a copywriter in an advertising agency. After marrying in 1904 (the first of four marriages), he returned to Ohio to begin a business career. Gradually becoming disillusioned in this role, and inclining ever more decidedly in the direction of writing, he finally suffered a nervous breakdown in the autumn of 1912. Shortly thereafter he returned to Chicago, where he divided his energies between advertising and literature. After placing several early stories in experimental "little" magazines of the period, Anderson published his first novel, *Windy McPherson's Son,* which appeared in 1916. In 1919, he published *Winesburg, Ohio,* a collection of stories structured as a novel, and the most accomplished and influential work of his career.

In the meantime, he had several random contacts with the South. During the summer and autumn of 1898 he had trained in Tennessee and Alabama before embarking with his infantry company for Cuba. Anderson married Cornelia Lane in May 1904, and the couple spent their honeymoon in Oakdale, Tennessee. As an advertising copywriter, and later as an independent businessman, he had clients in Kentucky whom he visited. Therefore, when he was seeking a quiet, unhurried place to complete the novel *Poor White* in the spring of 1920, he had a general idea of what the South might offer. Seeking a locale that afforded respite from urban living and his advertising responsibilities, he chose Mobile, Alabama, and a little later Fairhope, farther south on the Gulf Coast. He found both to be leisurely and quaint, the sort of atmosphere he could enjoy and in which he could work and could explore his inner self. The main themes of his letters from this period are self-discovery and artistic growth. They are accentuated by vivid color images of the snow-white beach, the "strange purple" of the sea, the lemon yellow of the native clay. He had brought a box of paints and spoke excitedly of having produced four watercolors that "stand up and remain beautiful. . . . One feels as though the doors to the spiritual house were slowly coming open."[2] It was apparently his first attempt at painting.

It is fair to say that no other natural setting ever affected him in this way. In addition to fostering inner growth, he was actively exploring life in his newly discovered surroundings. He cruised on fishing boats, revelled in the singing and dancing of the black residents, slept on the sand, and swam alone in the Gulf. He visited with the plain folk of the region and excitedly recounted their life stories. The overall effect of these experiences is impossible to calculate. He had, in effect, discovered a new world—vast, varied, rich in materials that fired his imagination and inspired his pen. But more significant, he had made an inward voyage into depths of his being he had not known existed.

Over the next five years he would return to the South for further exploration and for the same benefits that had rewarded his initial stay. The literary effects of these experiences would not be seen until 1925, after he had moved to New Orleans and just prior to his decision to locate permanently in the mountains of southwestern Virginia. But his odyssey into this strange new world, begun on the Gulf Coast of Alabama in the early months of 1920, would continue. Until the end he would explore its endless permutations, the while continuing his journeyings inward, an Odysseus questing for the Syracuse of his dreams.

By the time Sherwood Anderson came to the South to live in 1924, he had achieved the essential reputation that would assure him a place in the annals of American fiction. Though having little formal education, he possessed extraordinary talent and an irrepressible urge for self-expression. The primitive-like voice of his most successful fiction was derived not from literary models, but rather echoed the nonbookish argot of middle America. Nor did the structure of his stories draw on the patterns established by Poe, O. Henry, or the predictable fiction of popular magazines. Rather, his short stories, often called plotless, relied more on a probing impressionism than action. But the quality that perhaps best defines both his fiction and nonfiction is a curious and intense interaction with his subject. "I think I am rather primitive," he observed in one of his most illuminating introspections. "Between myself and nature there is, I'm sure, something always going on that is not a common experience."[3] This uncommon gift became a benchmark of Anderson's writings on the "nature" of the South. A journal entry from 1932 shows this process at its most intense:

> I was on the court house steps—drawn back into a hidden place where I could look out when darkness came. The town [Marion, Virginia] was like an absorbing book and I wanted to make a book called "Saturday Night." It was one of the times when a whole volume writes itself swiftly within you.
> There was, as it happened, a sort of band concert given by an organization called the Moose—in the court house auditorium. Very humble people for the most part must belong to it. They came quite close to me, passing in, light falling on them, workers and farmers with their families.
> Lovers. Girls in little thin dresses. Families marked by disease, what a procession. I was so excited that I trembled. It was one of the times when I, very lonely, . . . upset, . . . a bit tired perhaps—when

I was most open to impressions. It was one of the moments that will be remembered all my life. What I most hate about this idea of death is that I shall perhaps never be able to distill into work the essence of all such moments.[4]

While it would be false to suggest that the years Anderson spent in the South were filled with such moments (What artist could sustain such peaks of excitement?), he engaged his adopted world in diverse ways. The most successful of these culminated in such artistic epiphanies as the one described above.

Anderson's southern-related writings range broadly—from objective journalism to fiction. However, even at these extremities the forms are never pure for, being by nature a fiction writer, he cared little for the line separating the actual from the imaginary. As he admitted to a literary confidante in 1920, "Yesterday I started to write you a letter. I intended to tell you something about a very strange old woman here. Then the old woman became an old man and the letter became a story."[5] Thus, even in "They Elected Him," an ostensibly factual journalistic profile of the victor in a then-recent U.S. Senate race, Anderson succumbs to his fiction writing instincts with fanciful characterizations of his subject as a young student and of his father as a community doctor. Conversely, numerous "stories," such as "Virginia Justice," contain identifiable characters, settings, and situations.

Between the objective and the imaginary poles lie subgenres that intermix these elements in various ways. However, once he became sensitized to certain pressing social issues facing the South—expanding industrialism, labor unrest, unemployment—Anderson delivered a number of speeches in which the artist persona is uncharacteristically supplanted by the polemicist. Usually, though, he sidestepped partisan positions, thereby avoiding their attendant responsibilities. Though his private convictions were decidedly liberal—even radical at times—he generally strove to keep a neutral public stance. This was prompted in part by practicality. In late October 1927 he purchased two weekly newspapers in Marion, Virginia, one of which (*The Marion Democrat*) was Democratic; the other (*The Smyth County News*), Republican. As both nurtured strong partisan traditions, he sought to avoid even an appearance of favoritism. He was able to accomplish this by hiring editorialists from each camp, thus leaving himself the freedom of a centrist, yet one who was capable of aiming (usually) friendly jibes in either direction.

Anderson's motive involved more than simply a desire to maintain neutrality. It was, rather, a means of establishing latitude, a space in which he might effect an intermingling of creativity and traditional journalism. An editorial position, such as his campaign to have the city turn a dumping ground into a park, might be leavened with humor or gentle irony. News events, such as court sessions ("God and the Machine Age"), are often as satirical as they are factual. Feature articles (e.g., "In the Rich Valley") are characteristically autobiographical and tend to be more straightforward. However, if there is a signature genre among Anderson's journalistic writings, it is the impressionistic sketch. The subjects of these range from a former Confederate soldier ("A Veteran") to such simple, seemingly routine matters as driving up the Shenandoah Valley on a spring day ("A Traveler's Notes: The Shenandoah Valley"). Whatever his topic, it has more often than not been subjected to some degree of the personal interaction he described in the incident on the courthouse steps. The result is that it is transformed into his own unmistakable reality. The best of these leave a distinctive and lasting impression.

There are several stories, particularly among the pieces set in the Virginia highlands, that follow along the lines of the exemplum, a narrative intended to illustrate a principle or truth. This genre was an ideal one for Anderson, who was fascinated by unique qualities of character and behavior in people. "A Sentimental Journey" exemplifies the highlander's irrepressible ties to the native soil. Portions of "I Build A House" illustrate the mixture of generosity and wry sharpness that Anderson perceived in his new neighbors.

Presenting the following texts as candidates for canonization as southern writings raises an obvious question: Was Anderson a southern writer? Perhaps the answer should start with a further question: Was he a midwestern writer before he began writing about the South? Aside from such elements as setting and language, which arguably reflect a midwestern character, the work of Anderson's presouthern period is not "regional" in the strict sense of the term—any more than, say, James Joyce's *Dubliners* is "Irish," or Anton Chekov's stories are "Russian." All fiction, even that dealing with the most universal themes, is dependent upon place to a greater or lesser degree. But Anderson's characters often interact with forces that were not unique to the Midwest or even to the United States in general.

Moreover, Anderson himself disdained the restrictions implied by labels. "I would like always to be a guest in the world," he proclaims in a newspaper account of a trip to New York, "in Chicago, New York, London, Marion, in my own house. I do not want to say definitely that I will never stay anywhere, be anything. I am an author now, a newspaper man. Tomorrow I may be a soldier, a tramp. What does it matter?"[6]

There is, however, an important difference between his earlier depictions of place and those of the southern phase. In the former period he was finding his way. Though keenly aware of such limitations as his provincial upbringing and negligible formal education, his instincts correctly led him to people who put little store by such matters. His associates were frequently individuals involved in reforming the way that art in its various forms expressed modern life. Having no loyalties to well-established or traditional forms of expression, Anderson was free to make his own way and to find his own voice. This he ultimately did in *Winesburg, Ohio,* and in many of the stories that followed. He made similar, if less successful, attempts in several of the novels.

By 1925, when presented with a new array of regional subjects, his approach was fortified by this mass of experience. Having lived in Cleveland, Chicago, the West, and the South, he was no longer a provincial. He had made one trip to France and England and would revisit France late in 1926. In addition to enhancing his own perspective, such a background must have seemed like worldliness itself to many of the untravelled southerners he met. His experiences would afford him the ability to maintain a certain distance, along with the skill for trenchant interpretation. However, Anderson wore his sophistication lightly. His friends in Marion ranged from wealthy captains of industry to bellhops at the Hotel Marion. Throughout his life he practiced the common touch.

Sherwood Anderson was therefore not a regional author—midwestern, southern, or any other variety. This does not mean that he was not absorbed by the regions in which he lived, or that he was not accepted as part of their communities. What it does say is that unless he is assuming the familiar, semisatirical pose of the small-town journalist, or the skillfully wrought mask of his fictional reporter, Buck Fever, Anderson essentially spoke as a free agent and in the mature literary voice that had become his trademark. With the exception of the obvious journalistic stylizations mentioned above, he employed his own literary persona, whatever the degree of empathy he felt for his subject. It is particularly notable when he is writing of individuals with pronounced southern accents. In these instances he repeatedly admits to self-consciousness in trying to reproduce their dialect and will almost invariably paraphrase their speech in his own stylistic terms.

If, therefore, the identifying mark of indigenous regional writing is dialect or localized speech patterns, the texts that follow do not represent "southern" writing and, more important, Sherwood Anderson is not a "southern" author. He is, however, one of the many visitor-explorers who have become captivated by the South and recorded their responses while retaining their other-world identity, and the South should be proud to claim him, along with the written record of his southern experiences.

# Chronology

1876   Born September 13 in Camden, Ohio, third of seven children of Irwin M. and Emma Smith Anderson.

1884   Family moves to Clyde, Ohio.

1895   Emma Smith Anderson dies.

1896   Moves to Chicago, works as laborer.

1898–99   Serves in U.S. Army during Spanish-American War, trains in the South, and is stationed in Cuba after war.

1899   Works during summer with threshing crew near Clyde; in fall enrolls in college preparatory program at Wittenberg Academy, Springfield, Ohio.

1900   Completes studies, moves to Chicago, becomes copywriter for advertising firm.

1902   Begins writing a series of essays published over a three-year period in *Agricultural Advertising*.

1904   Marries Cornelia Lane; honeymoon trip to Tennessee and St. Louis World's Fair.

1906   Moves to Cleveland to become head of mail-order business.

1907   Moves to Elyria, Ohio, becomes head of mail-order paint company; birth of first son, Robert Lane Anderson.

1908   Birth of second son, John Sherwood Anderson.

1911   Birth of daughter, Marion Anderson.

1912   Abruptly walks out of office on November 28, shows up four days later in Cleveland in confused mental state.

1913   Returns to Chicago in February, lives on South Side near artists' and writers' colony, resumes copywriting; spends winter with his family at cabin in Ozark Mountains in Missouri.

1914 Returns to Chicago and advertising; publishes first story, "The Rabbit-Pen," in July.

1915 Begins writing *Winesburg, Ohio* stories in fall.

1916 *Winesburg, Ohio* stories begin to appear in periodicals; divorced from Cornelia Lane Anderson; spends summer at Upper Lake Chateaugay, New York, marries Tennessee Mitchell there; *Windy McPherson's Son* (novel).

1917 Returns to Upper Lake Chateaugay in summer; *Marching Men* (novel).

1918 Lives in New York City during fall; *Mid-American Chants* (poetry).

1919 *Winesburg, Ohio* published in May.

1920 Spends winter and spring in Mobile and Fairhope, Alabama; in fall moves to Palos Park, near Chicago; *Poor White* (novel).

1921 Visits Europe during summer; *The Triumph of the Egg* (stories); receives first *Dial* award for outstanding contributions to American literature.

1922 Lives in New Orleans during winter; moves to New York in August.

1923 Moves to Reno, Nevada, in February; *Many Marriages* (novel) and *Horses and Men* (stories).

1924 Divorced from Tennessee Mitchell Anderson; marries Elizabeth Prall; moves to New Orleans in July; lecture tour in fall and winter; *A Story Teller's Story* (memoir).

1925 Spends part of summer in Troutdale, Virginia; lecture tour in fall and winter; *Dark Laughter* (novel).

1926 Buys farm near Troutdale, moves there and builds house; leaves for Europe in December; *Sherwood Anderson's Notebook* (essays and notes) and *Tar: A Midwest Childhood* (fictionalized autobiography).

1927 Returns from Europe in March; buys two weekly newspapers in Marion, Virginia, becomes editor and publisher; *A New Testament* (poetry).

1929 Begins to turn over newspaper work to son, Robert; travels to Florida, New York State, and Washington, D.C.; *Hello Towns!* (newspaper selections).

1930 Travel throughout South.

1931 Travel, mostly in the South; transfers ownership of newspapers to Robert; *Perhaps Women* (essays).

1932  Lecture tour in spring; divorced from Elizabeth Prall Anderson; to Amsterdam in August to attend peace conference; *Beyond Desire* (novel).

1933  Spends winter in Kansas City; marries Eleanor Copenhaver; to New York City in fall; *Death in the Woods* (stories).

1934  Travel for *Today* magazine; to Media, Pennsylvania, in spring to help prepare dramatic version of *Winesburg, Ohio,* at Hedgerow Theatre; *No Swank* (essays).

1935  Spends much of winter at Brownsville and Corpus Christi, Texas; *Puzzled America* (essays).

1936  Trip to Southwest during winter; *Kit Brandon: A Portrait* (novel).

1937  To Corpus Christi in winter; attends writers' conference at Boulder, Colorado, in August; *Plays, Winesburg and Others* (collection).

1938  Trip to Southwest and Mexico in winter.

1939  Lectures at Olivet College, Michigan, in January and July; to California in fall.

1940  Lives in New York City much of year; *Home Town* (prose sketches with photographs).

1941  Begins trip to South America February 28; becomes ill on ship, dies of peritonitis, March 8, at Colón, Panama; buried at Marion, Virginia, on March 26.

# Southern Odyssey

# 1 Discovering the South

Although Sherwood Anderson professed to be fascinated by the grandiose antebellum South of myth and romance, his first extended stay in the region bore little resemblance to such notions. Writing from Mobile, Alabama, in January 1920, he made only passing reference to the "many fine houses" in that "sleepy old place,"[1] but described his own quarters as a room with a low ceiling and a fireplace. A few weeks later he was down the coast in Fairhope, living in a fisherman's shack a few feet from the bay and enjoying the out-of-doors. His accounts of the entire sojourn contain expressions of commonplace endemic experiences—the intense colors of the soil and water, the white beaches, the fishing villages, the natives, the African Americans and their singing. Two years later—the interim having been spent mainly in Chicago and on a European tour—he returned to the South, this time to the French Quarter of New Orleans, where he enjoyed being among the "Italians, French Creoles and Negroes, [who] are charmingly unambitious, basically cultured and gentle."[2]

When he returned to New Orleans in the summer of 1924, he chose again to live in the French Quarter. However, this time there were differences. He had come not merely to explore, but to settle—or so he thought. Soon after arriving, he began to make friends in the artistic community of this "Southern European" city. Many of his writings from this period center on New Orleans, which he viewed as a colorful and pleasant alternative to the frenzied life of mainstream America that he had encountered in such large northern cities as Chicago and New York.

New Orleans furnished the material for numerous sketches, for parts of *Dark Laughter,* for several notes in *Sherwood Anderson's Notebook* (1926), and even for a modernist poem;[3] however, by early summer 1926 Anderson had left New Orleans for good. He had bought a farm in the mountains of southwestern Virginia in 1926, and a grand new house now awaited him. It would be his home for the rest of his life and the base from which he would launch his broad-ranging explorations of the South. Thus, "The South," the final selection in "Discovering the South," has Anderson speaking about such sweeping issues as the role of the African American and differences in regional perception. "What the South needs most now is the artist—not visiting artists—its own," he asserts toward the end of the piece. He was by then on his way to achieving just that status.

## New Orleans, the *Double Dealer,* and the Modern Movement in America

Anderson's initial stay in New Orleans was brief but productive. He arrived in late January 1922 with the partially finished manuscript of the novel *Many Marriages* (1923) in hand. By mid-February he had written fifty thousand new words and the end was in sight. However, he usually balanced his work with other activities. He enjoyed walking in various parts of the city, meeting new people, and making friends. Some of these friends were connected with the *Double Dealer* (1921–26),[4] a local entry to the field of avant-garde "little magazines" that were cropping up in various parts of the country. Anderson's work had appeared in several of these publications in the past—for example, the *Little Review* and *Poetry* in Chicago and the *Seven Arts* in New York—and he applauded their aims. He published several items in the *Double Dealer* in 1922 and again in 1924 and 1925. The article below appeared in March 1922. The "modern spirit" that Anderson perceived in the diverse culture of New Orleans amounted to a kind of commonsense approach to living in an America where "fact [had become] dominant, submerging the imaginative life." But here, in this "lip of America," he sensed a natural, leisurely atmosphere where "fact is made secondary to the desire to live, to love, and to understand life."

[ . . . ]

When I came from New York to New Orleans, a few weeks ago, there was an oyster shucking contest going on in Lafayette Square, in the heart of the city. It was for the oyster opening championship of the world. Mike Algero, a handsome Italian, won it. I took that in and then went for a long walk on the docks, extending for miles along the Mississippi river front, looking at Negro laborers at work. They are the only laborers I have ever seen in America who know how to laugh, sing and play in the act of doing hard physical labor. And the man who thinks that, man for man, they do not achieve more work in a day than a white laborer of the North is simply mistaken.

That was a day for me.

By that time and by the time I had taken a ride through the "Vieux Carré," the old French Creole town, and had gone, in the evening, to see a bang-up Negro prize fight out under the stars in an open air arena—

Well, you see, I went back to my room and wrote a letter to a friend declaring New Orleans the most cultural city I had yet found in America.[5]

"Blessed be this people. They know how to play. They are truly a people of culture."

That was the substance of what I wrote to my friend.

Really, you see, we Americans have always been such a serious, long-faced people. Some one must have told us long ago that we had to make ourselves world-saviours or something like that. And it got under our skin. Every long-jawed, loose-mouthed politician in the country began to talk about our saving the human race. We got unnecessarily chesty. The grand manner got to be the vogue. It sticks to us.

What is the matter with us anyway? What are we bluffing ourselves about?

Does not a real culture in any people consist first of all in the acceptance of life, life of the flesh, mind and spirit? That, and a realization of the inter-dependence of all these things in making a full and a flowering life.

What I think is that the Modern Spirit in America really means something like a return to common sense. I am sure that even such serious representatives of the Anglo-Saxon race as H. G. Wells or Oswald Garrison Villard[6] aren't after all so much fussed about the destinies of the English and American peoples. I am sure any man is at bottom more concerned with what he is to have for dinner, how he is to spend his evening, explain himself to his friends, or perhaps even with the anticipation of the woman he hopes to hold in his arms, than he is with the destiny of any nation.

"Where can a man get six bottles of good wine? I have some friends coming to my house to dinner."

"I am a working man and my wife is going to have another kid. What kind of tobacco is that you are smoking? The bird I got this stuff from stuck me with something that bites my tongue like the devil."

I proclaim myself an American and one of the Moderns. At the present moment I am living in New Orleans, I have a room in the "Vieux Carré" with long French windows, through which one can step out upon a gallery, as wide as the sidewalk below. It is charming to walk there, above the street and to look down at others hustling off to work. I do not love work too much. Often I want to loaf and I want others to loaf with me, talk with me of themselves and their lives.

It happens that I have a passion for writing stories about people and there is a kind of shrewdness in me too. If I can understand people a little better perhaps they in turn will understand me. I like life and haven't too much of it to live. Perhaps if I take things in a more leisurely way I shall find more friends and lovers.

I sit in my room writing until the world of my imagination fades. Then I go out to walk on my gallery or take my stick and go walk in the streets.

There are two girls walking in Saint Peter Street. A man has stopped at a street crossing to light a pipe. A quiet, suggestive life stirs my imagination.

There is an old city here, on the lip of America, as it were, and all about it has been built a new and more modern city. In the old city a people once lived who loved to play, who made love in the moonlight, who walked under trees, gambled with death in the dueling field.

These people are pretty much gone now, but their old city is still left. Men here call it the "Vieux Carré."

And that I think charming too. They might have called it uptown or downtown.

And to me it is altogether charming that almost all of the old city still stands. From my window, as I sit writing, I see the tangled mass of the roofs of the old buildings. There are old galleries with beautiful hand-wrought railings, on which the people of the houses can walk above the street, or over which the housewife can lean in the morning to call to the vegetable man pushing his cart along the roadway below.

What colors in the old walls and doors of these buildings. Yellows fade into soft greens. There is a continual shifting interplay of many colors as the sunlight washes over them.

I go to walk. It is the dusk of evening and men are coming home from work. There are mysterious passageways leading back into old patios.

My beloved put in his hand by the hole in the door,
And my bowels were moved for him.
I rose up to open to my beloved;
And my hand dropped with myrrh,
And my fingers with liquid myrrh,
Upon the handle of the bolt.
I opened to my beloved;
But my beloved had withdrawn himself and was gone.[7]

I am in New Orleans and I am trying to proclaim something I have found here and that I think America wants and needs.

There is something left in this people here that makes them like one another, that leads to constant outbursts of the spirit of play, that keeps them from being too confoundedly serious about death and the ballot and reform and other less important things in life.

The newer New Orleans has no doubt been caught up by the passions of our other American cities. Outside the "Vieux Carré" there is no doubt a good deal of the usual pushing and shoving so characteristic of American civilization. The newer New Orleans begs factories to come here from other cities. I remember to have seen page advertisements, pleading with factory owners of the North to bring their dirt and their noise down here, in the pages of the *Saturday Evening Post,* if I remember correctly.

However, I am sure these people do not really mean it. There are too many elements here pulling in another direction, and an older and I believe more cultural and sensible direction.

At any rate there is the fact of the "Vieux Carré"—the physical fact. The beautiful old town still exists. Just why it isn't the winter home of every sensitive artist in America, who can raise money enough to get here, I do not know. Because its charms aren't known, I suppose. The criers-out of the beauty of the place may have been excursion boomers.

And so I proclaim New Orleans from my own angle, from the angle of the Modern. Perhaps the city will not thank me, but anyway it is a truly beautiful city. Perhaps if I can bring more artists here they will turn out a ragtag enough crew. Lafcadio Hearn[8] wasn't such a desirable citizen while he lived in the "Vieux Carré."

However, I address these fellows. I want to tell them of long quiet walks to be taken on the levee in back-of-town, where old ships, retired from service, thrust their masts up into the evening sky. On the streets here the crowds have a more leisurely stride, the Negro life issues a perpetual challenge to the artists, sailors from many lands come up from the water's edge and idle on the street corners, in the evening soft voices, speaking strange tongues, come drifting up to you out of the street.

I have undertaken to write an article on the Modern Spirit and because I am in New Orleans and have been so completely charmed by life in the "Vieux Carré" I may have seemed to get off the track.

I haven't really. I stick to my pronouncement that culture means first of all the enjoyment of life, leisure and a sense of leisure. It means time for a play of the imagination over the facts of life, it means time and vitality to be serious about really serious things and a background of joy in life in which to refresh the tired spirits.

In a civilization where the fact becomes dominant, submerging the imaginative life, you will have what is dominant in the cities of Pittsburgh and Chicago today.

When the fact is made secondary to the desire to live, to love, and to understand life, it may be that we will have in more American cities a charm of place such as one finds in the older parts of New Orleans now.

There has been a good deal of talk about the solid wall of preferred prejudices and the sentimentalities of the South and there may be a good deal of truth in the charge of southern intellectual backwardness.

Perhaps the South has only been waiting for the Modern Spirit, to assert itself to come into its own. It is, I believe, coming into its own a little through such efforts as the publication of *The Double Dealer,* a magazine devoted to the Arts, in New Orleans.

And, as I am supposed to be proclaiming the Modern Spirit, I repeat again that it means nothing to me if it does not mean putting the joy of living above the much less subtle and I think altogether more stupid joy of growth and achievement.

# From *Dark Laughter,* Chapter 10

Bruce Dudley, the protagonist of *Dark Laughter* (1925), follows a leisurely and circuitous course from Chicago, where the novel opens, to
Old Harbor, Indiana (his hometown), where most of the action is set.
These travels take him through New Orleans, where he spends several
months. Fleeing a loveless marriage and the pressures of living in a
metropolis, he finds the temper of the old Mississippi River city much
to his liking. The chapter treating his stay in New Orleans is dominated
both by the lithe body of the black woman he can see from the window of his room and by the relaxed, insouciant pace of life around
him. Both stand in marked contrast to the life he has known in Chicago. The woman and her lover embody sex at an elemental level,
something Bruce has not known in the repressive atmosphere of his
marriage. Though Bruce is an artist by inclination, the lassitude evoked
by the woman and by her race in general in such matters—that is, the
"slow dance"—is a revelation.

Anderson has been criticized for borrowing from James Joyce's *Ulysses* in *Dark Laughter.* Some of its acquired mannerisms, such as inte-
rior monologues, caused Ernest Hemingway to target the novel with
a parody, *The Torrents of Spring* (1926). However, there can be little
doubt that Bruce Dudley's response to New Orleans closely mirrors Anderson's own. What Bruce observes and feels in the passage below later
helps him to appreciate the character Sponge Martin, the earthy trades-
man with whom he works at the wheel factory in Old Harbor. The
primitive, liberating "dark laughter" of the African American celebrates
the breakdown of his resistance when he is lured into an affair with the
wife of the conventional factory owner.

Heat! Bruce Dudley had just come down river. June, July, August, September in New Orleans. You can't make a place something it won't be. It
was slow work getting down river. Few or no boats. Often whole days
idling about in river towns. You can take a train and go where you please,
but what's the hurry?

Bruce at that time, when he had just left Bernice and his newspaper job, had something in mind that expressed itself in the phrase—"What's your hurry?" He sat in the shade of trees by the river-bank, got a ride once on a barge, rode on little local packets, sat in front of stores in river towns, slept, dreamed. People talked with a slow drawling speech, niggers [9] were hoeing cotton, other niggers fished for catfish in the river.

The niggers were something for Bruce to look at, think about. So many black men slowly growing brown. Then would come the light brown, the velvet-browns, Caucasian features. The brown women tending up to the job—getting the race lighter and lighter. Soft southern nights, warm dusky nights. Shadows flitting at the edge of cotton-fields, in dusky roads by sawmill towns. Soft voices laughing, laughing.

Oh, ma banjo dog,
Oh, ho, ma banjo dog.

. . . . .

An' I ain't go'na give you
None of ma jelly roll.

. . . . .

So much of that sort of thing in American life. If you are a thinking man—and Bruce was—you make half acquaintances—half friendships—Frenchmen, Germans, Italians, Englishmen, Jews. The middle western intellectual circles along the edge of which Bruce had played—watching Bernice plunge more boldly in—were filled with men not American at all. There was a young Polish sculptor, an Italian sculptor, a French dilettante. Was there such a thing as an American? Perhaps Bruce was the thing himself. He was reckless, afraid, bold, shy.

If you are a canvas do you shudder sometimes when the painter stands before you? All the others lending their color to him. A composition being made. Himself the composition.

Could he ever really know a Jew, a German, a Frenchman, an Englishman?

And now a nigger.

Consciousness of brown men, brown women, coming more and more into American life—by that token coming into him too.

More willing to come, more avid to come than any Jew, German, Pole, Italian. Standing, laughing—coming by the back door—with shuffling feet, a laugh—a dance in the body.

Facts established would have to be recognized sometime—by individuals—when they were on an intellectual jag perhaps—as Bruce was then.

In New Orleans, when Bruce got there, the long docks facing the river. On the river just ahead of him when he came the last twenty miles, a small houseboat fitted up with a gas engine. Signs on it. "JESUS WILL SAVE." Some itinerant preacher from up river starting south to save the world. "THY WILL BE DONE." The preacher, a sallow man with a dirty beard, in bare feet, at the wheel of the little boat. His wife, also in bare feet, sitting in a rocking-chair. Her teeth were black stumps. Two children in bare feet, lying on a narrow deck.

The docks of the city go around in a great crescent. Big ocean freighters coming in bringing coffee, bananas, fruits, goods, taking out cotton, lumber, corn, oils.

Niggers on the docks, niggers in the city streets, niggers laughing. A slow dance always going on. German sea-captains, French, American, Swedish, Japanese, English, Scotch. The Germans now sailing under other flags than their own. The Scotch sailing under the English flag. Clean ships, dirty tramp ships, half-naked niggers—a shadow-dance.

How much does it cost to be a good man, an earnest man? If we can't produce good earnest men, how are we ever going to make any progress? You can't ever get anywhere if you aren't conscious—in earnest. A brown woman having thirteen children—a different man for every child—going to church too, singing, dancing, broad shoulders, broad hips, soft eyes, a soft laughing voice—getting God on Sunday night—getting—what—on Wednesday night?

Men you've got to be up and doing if you want progress.

William Allen White, Heywood Broun—passing judgment on the arts—why not—Oh, ma banjo dog—Van Wyck Brooks, Frank Crowninshield, Tallula Bankhead, Henry Mencken, Anita Loos, Stark Young, Ring Lardner, Eva Le Gallienne, Jack Johnson, Bill Haywood, H. G. Wells write good books, don't you think? [10] The Literary Digest, The Dial Book of Modern Art, Harry Wills.[11]

They dance south—out of doors—whites in a pavilion in one field, blacks, browns, high browns, velvet-browns in a pavilion in the next field—but one.

We've got to have more earnest men in this country.
Grass growing in a field between.
Oh, ma banjo dog!

Song in the air, a slow dance. Heat. Bruce had some money then. He might have got a job, but what was the use? Well, he might have gone uptown and tackled the New Orleans *Picayune,* or the *Item* or *States* [12] for a job. Why not go see Jack McClure, the ballad-maker—on the *Picayune?* [13] Give us a song, Jack—a dance—the gumbo drift. Come, the night is hot. What was the use? He still had some of the money he had slipped into his pocket when he left Chicago. In New Orleans you can get a loft in which to sleep for five dollars a month if you know how. You know how when you don't want to work—when you want to look and listen—when you want your body to be lazy while your mind works. New Orleans is not Chicago. It isn't Cleveland or Detroit. Thank God for that!

Nigger girls in the streets, nigger women, nigger men. There is a brown cat lurking in the shadow of a building. "Come, brown puss—come get your cream." The men who work on the docks in New Orleans have slender flanks like running horses, broad shoulders, loose heavy lips hanging down—faces like old monkeys sometimes—bodies like young gods—sometimes. On Sundays—when they go to church, or to a bayou baptizing, the brown girls do sure cut loose with the colors—gaudy nigger colors on nigger women making the streets flame—deep purples, reds, yellows, green like young corn-shoots coming up. They sweat. The skin colors brown, golden yellow, reddish brown, purple-brown. When the sweat runs down high brown backs the colors come out and dance before the eyes. Flash that up, you silly painters, catch it dancing. Song-tones in words, music in words—in colors too. Silly American painters! They chase a Gauguin shadow to the South Seas. Bruce wrote a few poems. Bernice had got very far away in, oh such a short time. Good thing she didn't know. Good thing no one knows how unimportant he is. We need earnest men—got to have 'em. Who'll run the show if we don't get that kind? For Bruce—for the time—no sensual feeling that need be expressed through his body.

Hot days. Sweet Mama!

Funny business, Bruce trying to write poems. When he had that job on the newspaper, where a man is supposed to write, he never wanted to write at all. Southern white men writing songs—fill themselves first with Keats and Shelley.

I am giving out of the richness of myself to many mornings,
At night, when the waters of the seas murmur I am murmuring.

I have surrendered to seas and suns and days and swinging ships.
My blood is thick with surrender.

It shall be let out through wounds and shall color the seas and
the earth.
My blood shall color the earth where the seas come for the night kiss
and the seas shall be red [14]

What did that mean? Oh, laugh a little, men! What matters what
it means?
Or again—

Give me the word.
Let my throat and my lips caress the words of your lips.

Give me the word.
Give me three words, a dozen, a hundred, a history.
Give me the word. [15]

A broken jargon of words in the head. In old New Orleans the narrow
streets are filled with iron gates leading away, past damp old walls, to
cool patios. It is very lovely—old shadows dancing on sweet old walls,
but some day it will all be torn away to make room for factories.

Bruce lived for five months in an old house where rent was low, where
cockroaches scurried up and down the walls. Nigger women lived in the
building across the narrow street.

You lie naked on the bed on hot summer mornings and let the slow
creeping river-wind come, if it will. Across the street, in another room, a
nigger woman of twenty arises at five and stretches her arms. Bruce rolls
and looks. Sometimes she sleeps alone but sometimes a brown man
sleeps with her. Then they both stretch. Thin-flanked brown man. Nigger girl with slender flexible body. She knows Bruce is looking. What
does it matter? He is looking as one might look at trees, at young colts
playing in a pasture.

Bruce got out of his bed and went away along a narrow street to another street near the river where he got coffee and a roll of bread for five
cents. Thinking of niggers! What sort of business is that? How come?
Northern men so often get ugly when they think of niggers, or they get
sentimental. Give pity where none is needed. The men and women of the
South understand better, maybe. "Oh hell, don't get fussy! Let things

flow! Let us alone! We'll float!" Brown blood flowing, white blood flowing, deep river flowing.

A slow dance, music, ships, cotton, corn, coffee. Slow lazy laughter of niggers. Bruce remembered a line he had once seen written by a Negro. "Would white poet ever know why my people walk so softly and laugh at sunrise?"

Heat. The sun coming up in a mustard-colored sky. Driving rains that came, swirled over a half-dozen blocks of city streets and in ten minutes no trace of moisture left. Too much wet warmth for a little more wet warmth to matter. The sun licking it up, taking a drink for itself. One might get clear-headed here. Clear-headed about what? Well, don't hurry. Take your time.

Bruce lay lazy in bed. The brown girl's body was like the thick waving leaf of a young banana plant. If you were a painter now, you could paint that, maybe. Paint a brown nigger girl in a broad leaf waving and send it up North. Why not sell it to a society woman of New Orleans? Get some money to loaf a while longer on. She wouldn't know, would never guess. Paint a brown laborer's narrow suave flanks onto the trunk of a tree. Send it to the Art Institute in Chicago. Send it to the Anderson Galleries in New York.[16] A French painter went down to the South Seas.[17] Freddy O'Brien went down.[18] Remember when the brown woman tried to ravage him and he said how he escaped? Gauguin put a lot of pep in his book but they trimmed it for us. No one cared much, not after Gauguin was dead anyway. You get a cup of such coffee for five cents and a big roll of bread. No swill. In Chicago, morning coffee at cheap places is like swill. Niggers like good things. Good big sweet words, flesh, corn, cane. Niggers like a free throat for song. You're a nigger down South and you get some white blood in you. A little more, and a little more. Northern travelers help, they say. Oh, Lord! Oh, my banjo dog! Do you remember the night when that Gauguin came home to his little hut and there, in the bed, was the slender brown girl waiting for him? Better read that book. "Noa-Noa," they call it. Brown mysticism in the walls of a room, in the hair—of a Frenchman, in the eyes of a brown girl. Noa-Noa. Do you remember the sense of strangeness? French painter kneeling on the floor in the darkness, smelling the strangeness. The brown girl smelling the strangeness. Love? What ho! Smelling strangeness.

Go softly. Don't hurry. What's all the shooting about?

A little more white, a little more white, graying white, muddy white, thick lips—staying sometimes. Over we go!

Something lost too. The dance of bodies, a slow dance.

Bruce on a bed in a five-dollar room. Away off, broad leaves of young banana plants waving. "D'you know why my people laugh in the morning? Do you know why my people walk softly?"

Sleep again, white man. No hurry. Then along a street for coffee and a roll of bread, five cents. Sailors off ships, bleary-eyed. Old nigger women and white women going to market. They know each other, white women, nigger women. Go soft. Don't hurry!

Song—a slow dance. A white man lying still on docks, in a five-dollar-a-month bed. Heat. No hurry. When you get that hurry out of you the mind works maybe. Maybe song will start in you too.

Lord, it would be nice with Tom Wills down here. Shall I write him a letter? No, better not. After a while, when cool days come, you mosey along up North again. Come back here some day. Stay here some day. Look and listen.

Song—dance—a slow dance.

## Letter to William Faulkner

For much of the period that he lived in New Orleans, Sherwood Anderson saw much of an aspiring young writer from northern Mississippi named William Faulkner. They had been introduced by Anderson's new wife, Elizabeth Prall, who had known Faulkner in New York. One of the products of their numerous conversations about literature was a spirited *jeu d'esprit* in which they exchanged narratives about a character named Al Jackson and his family. Written in the satirical, hyperbolic vein of Old Southwestern humor, the narratives are unique in the work of both authors in that each assumes the persona of a tall-tale raconteur. A descendant of Old Hickory, Al Jackson has retreated to the swamps of Louisiana after the Battle of Chalmette and has started raising sheep. The animals adapt to their watery environment by learning to swim and eventually develop scales. Claude, Al's brother, spends so much time in the water trying to get the sheep out that he too develops fish eyes and scales. He eventually becomes a shark with a particular fondness for terrorizing pretty blonde women.

As the tales unfolded, the more outlandish they became. One of

Faulkner's installments, or at least a part of it, can be found in his novel *Mosquitoes* (1927), where the tale is narrated by Dawson Fairchild, an avuncular writer who tends to pontificate. Fairchild is obviously modeled after Anderson, and he spins a yarn about Claude Jackson. Anderson's "letter" reproduced below is evidently a sequel to this, as it refers to the fact that "you dragged that in about Claude."

The evolution of the exchange has been studied in some detail;[19] however, unanswered questions remain. The following text appeared initially in the first collected edition of Anderson's letters.[20] It was probably written in 1925, well before the quarrel between Anderson and Faulkner in March 1926, which effectively ended their friendship.[21]


Dear Bill:

I'm mighty glad you also have run into the Jackson family, or at least a man who knows something about them. I've been on their trail for a year now and have heard a lot of news about their doings, but haven't met a Jackson yet. What I want specially is to meet Al himself. The whole country around here is full of stories about him. Are they true? I wonder. You know, I am a professional writer, and if I could ever get this Al Jackson's story straight, get a firsthand interview with him with pictures and all, I'd have a gold mine. Wouldn't wonder if I'd find some big magazine hungry for it. Who wouldn't want to know all about Al Jackson?

I'm sorry you dragged that in about Claude. There was Elenor Jackson too, Al and Claude's sister. I've heard stories about her, not here but over in Mississippi, but if you ever hear any of them, don't tell me. I've always thought of Al as one of the purest and cleanest American men I ever heard of, and I do wish the rest of his family were more like him. He ought to be pure and clean. He's been in the water so much.

But let me tell you how I picked up my own line on the Jacksons. Funny about Al. You meet a man over in Arkansas or Texas or up in Mississippi, and even as far west as Topeka or Denver or, say, in Baltimore, who tells you something about him, and then you go on for days and weeks and months and never meet a man or woman or child who ever heard of Al Jackson's people at all. One day in New York I counted. I met eight hundred and forty-two people between nine twenty-six in the morning and four-eighteen in the afternoon, and not one of them knew a word about Al. I had a boy with me to count.

I first heard of Al and his folks on a train. There was a fellow sitting in the seat beside me, name of Flu Balsam. He used to be a water man himself and claimed he had herded fish under Al for almost two years.

He was a blind kind of man from getting so much water in his eyes, but I never noticed anything special about his legs. He could walk on them all right.

This Flu, it seems, had been herding cows over in Texas, but had lost his horse. He was a nervous, erratic kind of a man with a tin ear got from the kick of a horse, and if he had web feet, like they say so many of the fishherds get, I couldn't notice. He had on congress shoes.[22]

About his losing his horse. It seems he couldn't sleep much nights, and so he traded his horse to an easygoing, restful kind of a Texan, and an expert sleeper, for a night's sleep. The fellow was to come around about seven in the evening to get the horse, and Flu was to get his sleep, and so Flu got the horse out in front of his house early and stood holding him, all ready to rush off to bed, but the fellow didn't show up till almost four in the morning.

And so this Flu Balsam lost his horse and his sleep too and of course couldn't herd cows any more; so he says he went fishherding with Al Jackson. That's what he says. He also said that Al brands all his fish by cutting a notch in their tails. Did you hear anything about that?

But to get back to Al. Here's another I heard. I was in a town over in Alabama and was standing on a station platform, and they had a bull in a crate, shipping him somewhere. I was watching the bull and knocking flies off his nose when a man came up, and we had a talk.

Of course we talked of Al. Nowadays all this country is ringing with stories of Al. He's the biggest man in the fish industry all right.

This new man looked honest enough. Of course he was southern, but I don't think he was a fishherd himself. You can always tell them by their congress shoes, and his were laced.

What he told me was that he was a traveling man selling congress shoes down here in Louisiana and in all these coast states, and he says about all his trade is among Al's fishherds. He says a fishherd wants to go out into society now and then, same as any other man, or get him a girl or a wife or something, and anything else but congress shoes hurt his feet. On account of having the webs that way, he says.

As I say, he was an honest-looking kind of man with a mustache and a glass eye, and he looked southern and talked that way too.

What he says and what I started to write you about was for you not [to] get yourself mixed up. He says that Al Jackson's people have nothing at all to do with the Stonewalls or the Andrews, not for me to get that notion into my head, so I didn't.

He says Al Jackson's people were straight slave-running folks. They used to have a boat, he says, and all they did was to run black ivory in.

There was one of them, he said, old Spearhead Jackson, who was a terror. Once he was coming over from Africa with a load of niggers on board, and night was coming on when a Britisher got after him. The Britisher kept closing up and closing up; so this old Spearhead had three niggers brought up and threw them into the sea.

The Britisher stopped, of course, to pick them up, being so humane and not in the business himself, and then he came on again, and so Spearhead had to throw out three more and then two, and just as darkness was coming on, he chucked out six. Fifteen good niggers gone and they worth all of eight hundred dollars apiece. "Do you wonder we hated the British in them days?" the man said who was talking to me. But old Spearhead made his getaway in the dark.

Later and after the war they had him up in the Tchufuncta country shooting what stray niggers he could find floating around loose at two dollars a head. Rather a comedown for him. It may have been up there that you heard about him. A branch of the Jacksons settled somewhere up there.

---

## A Meeting South

In light of what we know of the natures of Anderson and Faulkner, "A Meeting South" appears to be a blending of fact and personal mythologizing. David, the young southern poet the narrator meets and takes a liking to is of course a thinly disguised William Faulkner. This diminutive man, a lover of Shelley and Keats (both were favorites of Faulkner), a large bottle of corn whiskey concealed in his pocket, seems true to the original. However, David also tells about his family's plantation in Alabama; his pronounced limp (from an aviation accident in England during World War I); his wartime adventures in France; his aristocratic

English ancestry. All of this was Faulknerian fabrication. Faulkner had trained for the Royal Air Force in Canada but never completed his instruction, as the war ended and he was discharged. Before returning to Mississippi, he bought an officer's uniform and a swagger stick and affected a limp when he got off the train in Oxford. He would later invent many stories of daredevil adventures in an imaginary flight career.

It is therefore questionable whether Anderson, himself an inveterate self-mythologizer, actually believed the fables spun by his friend or whether he saw them for what they were but admired the skill with which they were crafted.[23] Or perhaps he simply found them appropriate for telling an interesting story of his own. In any case, taking his friend to see "Aunt Sally" (in reality "Aunt Rose"), a former madam, is an episode colored with the authentic hues of the New Orleans demimonde that Anderson knew.

He told me the story of his ill fortune—a crack-up in an airplane—with a very gentlemanly little smile on his very sensitive, rather thin lips. Such things happened. He might well have been speaking of another. I liked his tone and I liked him.

This happened in New Orleans, where I had gone to live. When he came, my friend, Fred, for whom he was looking, had gone away, but immediately I felt a strong desire to know him better and so suggested we spend the evening together. When we went down the stairs from my apartment I noticed that he was a cripple. The slight limp, the look of pain that occasionally drifted across his face, the little laugh that was intended to be jolly but did not quite achieve its purpose, all these things began at once to tell me the story I have now set myself to write.

"I shall take him to see Aunt Sally," I thought. One does not take every caller to Aunt Sally. However, when she is in fine feather, when she has taken a fancy to her visitor, there is no one like her. Although she has lived in New Orleans for thirty years, Aunt Sally is Middle Western, born and bred.

However, I am plunging a bit too abruptly into my story.

First of all I must speak more of my guest, and for convenience's sake I shall call him David. I felt at once that he would be wanting a drink and in New Orleans—dear city of Latins and hot nights—even in prohibition times such things can be managed. We achieved several and my own head became somewhat shaky but I could see that what we had taken had not affected him. Evening was coming, the abrupt waning of the day and the quick smoky soft-footed coming of night, characteristic of the semi-tropic city, when he produced a bottle from his hip pocket. It was so large that I was amazed. How had it happened that the carrying of so large a bottle had not made him look deformed? His body was very small and delicately built. "Perhaps, like the kangaroo, his body has developed some kind of a natural pouch for taking care of supplies," I thought. Really he walked as one might fancy a kangaroo would walk when out for a quiet evening stroll. I went along thinking of Darwin and the marvels of prohibition. "We are a wonderful people, we Americans," I thought. We were both in fine humor and had begun to like each other immensely.

He explained the bottle. The stuff, he said, was made by a Negro man on his father's plantation somewhere over in Alabama. We sat on the steps of a vacant house deep down in the old French Quarter of New Orleans—the Vieux Carré—while he explained that his father had no intention of breaking the law—that is to say, in so far as the law remained reasonable. "Our nigger just makes whiskey for us," he said. "We keep him for that purpose. He doesn't have anything else to do, just makes the family whiskey, that's all. If he went selling any, we'd raise hell with him. I dare say Dad would shoot him if he caught him up to any such unlawful trick, and you bet, Jim, our nigger I'm telling you of, knows it too.

"He's a good whiskey-maker, though, don't you think?" David added. He talked of Jim in a warm friendly way. "Lord, he's been with us always, was born with us. His wife cooks for us and Jim makes our whiskey. It's a race to see which is best at his job, but I think Jim will win. He's getting a little better all the time and all of our family—well, I reckon we just like and need our whiskey more than we do our food."

Do you know New Orleans? Have you lived there in the summer when it is hot, in the winter when it rains, and through the glorious late fall days? Some of its own, more progressive, people scorn it now. In New Orleans there is a sense of shame because the city is not more like Chicago or Pittsburgh.

It, however, suited David and me. We walked slowly, on account of his bad leg, through many streets of the Old Town, Negro women laughing all around us in the dusk, shadows playing over old buildings, children with their shrill cries dodging in and out of old hallways. The old city was once almost altogether French, but now it is becoming more and more Italian. It, however, remains Latin. People live out of doors. Families were sitting down to dinner within full sight of the street—all doors and windows open. A man and his wife quarreled in Italian. In a patio back of an old building a Negress sang a French song.

We came out of the narrow little streets and had a drink in front of the dark cathedral and another in a little square in front. There is a statue of General Jackson, always taking off his hat to northern tourists who in winter come down to see the city. At his horse's feet an inscription— "The Union must and will be preserved." We drank solemnly to that declaration and the general seemed to bow a bit lower. "He was sure a proud man," David said, as we went over toward the docks to sit in the darkness and look at the Mississippi. All good New Orleanians go to look at the Mississippi at least once a day. At night it is like creeping into a dark bedroom to look at a sleeping child—something of that sort—gives you the same warm nice feeling, I mean. David is a poet and so in the darkness by the river we spoke of Keats and Shelley, the two English poets all good southern men love.

All of this, you are to understand, was before I took him to see Aunt Sally.

Both Aunt Sally and myself are Middle Westerners. We are but guests down here, but perhaps we both in some queer way belong to this city. Something of the sort is in the wind. I don't quite know how it has happened.

A great many northern men and women come down our way and, when they go back North, write things about the South. The trick is to write nigger stories. The North likes them. They are so amusing. One of the best-known writers of nigger stories was down here recently and a man I know, a southern man, went to call on him. The writer seemed a bit nervous. "I don't know much about the South or southerners," he said. "But you have your reputation," my friend said. "You are so widely known as a writer about the South and about Negro life." The writer had a notion he was being made sport of. "Now look here," he said, "I don't claim to be a highbrow. I'm a business man myself. At home, up North, I associate mostly with businessmen and when I am not at work I go out to the country club. I want you to understand I am not setting myself up as a highbrow.

"I give them what they want," he said. My friend said he appeared angry. "About what now, do you fancy?" he asked innocently.

However, I am not thinking of the northern writer of Negro stories.

I am thinking of the southern poet, with the bottle clasped firmly in his hands, sitting in the darkness beside me on the docks facing the Mississippi.

He spoke at some length of his gift for drinking. "I didn't always have it. It is a thing built up," he said. The story of how he chanced to be a cripple came out slowly. You are to remember that my own head was a bit unsteady. In the darkness the river, very deep and very powerful off New Orleans, was creeping away to the gulf. The whole river seemed to move away from us and then to slip noiselessly into the darkness like a vast moving sidewalk.

When he had first come to me in the late afternoon, and when we had started for our walk together, I had noticed that one of his legs dragged as we went along and that he kept putting a thin hand to an equally thin cheek.

Sitting over by the river, he explained as a boy would explain when he has stubbed his toe running down a hill.

When the World War broke out he went over to England and managed to get himself enrolled as an aviator, very much, I gathered, in the spirit in which a countryman, in a city for a night, might take in a show.

The English had been glad enough to take him on. He was one more man. They were glad enough to take anyone on just then. He was small and delicately built but after he got in he turned out to be a first-rate flyer, serving all through the war with a British flying squadron, but at the last got into a crash and fell.

Both legs were broken, one of them in three places, the scalp was badly torn and some of the bones of the face had been splintered.

They had put him into a field hospital and had patched him up. "It was my fault if the job was rather bungled," he said. "You see it was a field hospital, a hell of a place. Men were torn all to pieces, groaning and dying. Then they moved me back to a base hospital and it wasn't much better. The fellow who had the bed next to mine had shot himself in the foot to avoid going into a battle. A lot of them did that, but why they picked on their own feet that way is beyond me. It's a nasty place, full of small bones. If you're ever going to shoot yourself don't pick on a spot like that. Don't pick on your feet. I tell you it's a bad idea.

"Anyway, the man in the hospital was always making a fuss and I got sick of him and the place too. When I got better I faked, said the nerves of my leg didn't hurt. It was a lie, of course. The nerves of my leg and of my face have never quit hurting. I reckon maybe, if I had told the truth, they might have fixed me up all right."

I got it. No wonder he carried his drinks so well. When I understood, I wanted to keep on drinking with him, wanted to stay with him until he got tired of me as he had of the man who lay beside him in the base hospital over there somewhere in France.

The point was that he never slept, could not sleep, except when he was a little drunk. "I'm a nut," he said smiling.

It was after we got over to Aunt Sally's that he talked most. Aunt Sally had gone to bed when we got there, but she got up when we rang the bell and we all went to sit together in the little patio back of her house. She is a large woman with great arms and rather a paunch, and she had put on nothing but a light flowered dressing-gown over a thin, ridiculously girlish, nightgown. By this time the moon had come up and, outside, in the narrow street of the Vieux Carré, three drunken sailors from a ship in the river were sitting on a curb and singing a song,

"I've got to get it,
You've got to get it,
We've all got to get it
In our own good time."

They had rather nice boyish voices and every time they sang a verse and had done the chorus they all laughed together heartily.

In Aunt Sally's patio there are many broad-leafed banana plants and a Chinaberry tree throwing its soft purple shadows on a brick floor.

As for Aunt Sally, she is as strange to me as he was. When we came and when we were all seated at a little table in the patio, she ran into her house and presently came back with a bottle of whiskey. She, it seemed, had understood him at once, had understood without unnecessary words that the little southern man lived always in the black house of pain, that whiskey was good to him, that it quieted his throbbing nerves, temporarily at least. "Everything is temporary, when you come to that," I can fancy Aunt Sally saying.

We sat for a time in silence, David having shifted his allegiance and taken two drinks out of Aunt Sally's bottle. Presently he rose and walked up and down the patio floor, crossing and re-crossing the network of delicately outlined shadows on the bricks. "It's really all right, the leg," he said, "something just presses on the nerves, that's all." In me there was a self-satisfied feeling. I had done the right thing. I had brought him to Aunt Sally. "I have brought him to a mother." She has always made me feel that way since I have known her.

And now I shall have to explain her a little. It will not be so easy. That whole neighborhood in New Orleans is alive with tales concerning her.

Aunt Sally came to New Orleans in the old days, when the town was wild, in the wide-open days. What she had been before she came no one knew, but anyway she opened a place. That was very, very long ago when I was myself but a lad, up in Ohio. As I have already said Aunt Sally came from somewhere up in the middle-western country. In some obscure subtle way it would flatter me to think she came from my state.

The house she had opened was one of the older places in the French Quarter down here, and when she had got her hands on it, Aunt Sally had a hunch. Instead of making the place modern, cutting it up into small rooms, all that sort of thing, she left it just as it was and spent her money rebuilding falling old walls, mending winding broad old stairways, repairing dim high-ceilinged old rooms, soft-colored old marble mantels. After all, we do seem attached to sin and there are so many people busy making sin unattractive. It is good to find someone who takes the other road. It would have been so very much to Aunt Sally's advantage to have made the place modern, that is to say, in the business she was in at that time. If a few old rooms, wide old stairways, old cooking ovens built into the walls, if all these things did not facilitate the stealing in of couples on dark nights, they at least did something else. She had opened a gambling and drinking house, but one can have no doubt about the ladies stealing in. "I was on the make all right," Aunt Sally told me once.

She ran the place and took in money, and the money she spent on the place itself. A falling wall was made to stand up straight and fine again, the banana plants were made to grow in the patio, the Chinaberry tree got started and was helped through the years of adolescence. On the wall the lovely Rose of Montana bloomed madly. The fragrant Lantana grew in a dense mass at a corner of the wall.

When the Chinaberry tree, planted at the very center of the patio, began to get up into the light it filled the whole neighborhood with fragrance in the spring.

Fifteen, twenty years of that, with Mississippi River gamblers and racehorse men sitting at tables by windows in the huge rooms upstairs in the house that had once, no doubt, been the town house of some rich planter's family—in the boom days of the forties. Women stealing in too in the dusk of evenings. Drinks being sold. Aunt Sally raking down the kitty from the game, raking in her share, quite ruthlessly.

At night, getting a good price too from the lovers. No questions asked, a good price for drinks. Moll Flanders[24] might have lived with Aunt Sally. What a pair they would have made! The Chinaberry tree beginning to be lusty. The Lantana blossoming—in the fall the Rose of Montana.

Aunt Sally getting hers. Using the money to keep the old house in fine shape. Salting some away all the time.

A motherly soul, good, sensible middle-western woman, eh? Once a racehorse man left twenty-four thousand dollars with her and disappeared. No one knew she had it. There was a report the man was dead. He had killed a gambler in a place down by the French Market and while they were looking for him he managed to slip in to Aunt Sally's and leave his swag. Some time later a body was found floating in the river and it was identified as the horseman but in reality he had been picked up in a wire-tapping haul in New York City and did not get out of his northern prison for six years.

When he did get out, naturally, he skipped for New Orleans. No doubt he was somewhat shaky. She had him. If he squealed there was a murder charge to be brought up and held over his head. It was night when he arrived and Aunt Sally went at once to an old brick oven built into the wall of the kitchen and took out a bag. "There it is," she said. The whole affair was part of the day's work for her in those days.

Gamblers at the tables in some of the rooms upstairs, lurking couples, from the old patio below the fragrance of growing things.

When she was fifty, Aunt Sally had got enough and had put them all out. She did not stay in the way of sin too long and she never went in too deep, like that Moll Flanders, and so she was all right and sitting pretty. "They wanted to gamble and drink and play with the ladies. The ladies liked it all right. I never saw none of them come in protesting too much. The worst was in the morning when they went away. They looked so sheepish and guilty. If they felt that way, what made them come? If I took a man, you bet I'd want him and no monkey-business or nothing doing.

"I got a little tired of all of them, that's the truth." Aunt Sally laughed. "But that wasn't until I had got what I went after. Oh pshaw, they took up too much of my time after I got enough to be safe."

Aunt Sally is now sixty-five. If you like her and she likes you she will let you sit with her in her patio gossiping of the old times, of the old river days. Perhaps—well, you see there is still something of the French influence at work in New Orleans, a sort of matter-of-factness about life—what I started to say is that if you know Aunt Sally and she likes you, and if, by chance, your lady likes the smell of flowers growing in a patio at night—really, I am going a bit too far. I only meant to suggest that Aunt Sally at sixty-five is not harsh. She is a motherly soul.

We sat in the garden talking, the little southern poet, Aunt Sally and myself—or rather they talked and I listened. The southerner's great-grandfather was English, a younger son, and he came over here to make his fortune as a planter, and did it. Once he and his sons owned several great plantations with slaves, but now his father had but a few hundred acres left, about one of the old houses—somewhere over in Alabama. The land is heavily mortgaged and most of it has not been under cultivation for years. Negro labor is growing more and more expensive and unsatisfactory since so many Negroes have run off to Chicago, and the poet's father and the one brother at home are not much good at working the land. "We aren't strong enough and we don't know how," the poet said.

The southerner had come to New Orleans to see Fred, to talk with Fred about poetry, but Fred was out of town. I could only walk about with him, help him drink his home-made whiskey. Already I had taken nearly a dozen drinks. In the morning I would have a headache.

I drew within myself, listening while David and Aunt Sally talked. The Chinaberry tree had been so and so many years growing—she spoke of it as she might have spoken of a daughter. "It had a lot of different sicknesses when it was young, but it pulled through." Someone had built a high wall on one side of her patio so that the climbing plants did not get as much sunlight as they needed. The banana plants, however, did very well and now the Chinaberry tree was big and strong enough to take care of itself. She kept giving David drinks of whiskey and he talked.

He told her of the place in his leg where something, a bone perhaps, pressed on the nerve, and of the place on his left cheek. A silver plate had been set under the skin. She touched the spot with her fat old fingers. The moonlight fell softly down on the patio floor. "I can't sleep except somewhere out of doors," David said.

He explained how that, at home on his father's plantation, he had to be thinking all day whether or not he would be able to sleep at night.

"I go to bed and then I get up. There is always a bottle of whiskey on the table downstairs and I take three or four drinks. Then I go out doors." Often very nice things happened.

"In the fall it's best," he said. "You see the niggers are making molasses." Every Negro cabin on the place had a little clump of ground back of it where cane grew and in the fall the Negroes were making their 'lasses. "I take the bottle in my hand and go into the fields, unseen by the niggers. Having the bottle with me that way, I drink a good deal and then lie down on the ground. The mosquitoes bite me some, but I don't mind much. I reckon I get drunk enough not to mind. The little pain makes a kind of rhythm for the great pain—like poetry.

"In a kind of shed the niggers are making the 'lasses, that is to say, pressing the juice out of the cane and boiling it down. They keep singing as they work. In a few years now I reckon our family won't have any land. The banks could take it now if they wanted it. They don't want it. It would be too much trouble for them to manage, I reckon.

"In the fall, at night, the niggers are pressing the cane. Our niggers live pretty much on 'lasses and grits.

"They like working at night and I'm glad they do. There is an old mule going round and round in a circle and beside the press a pile of the dry cane. Niggers come, men and women, old and young. They build a fire outside the shed. The old mule goes round and round.

"The niggers sing. They laugh and shout. Sometimes the young niggers with their gals make love on the dry cane pile. I can hear it rattle.

"I have come out of the big house, me and my bottle, and I creep along, low on the ground, 'til I get up close. There I lie. I'm a little drunk. It all makes me happy. I can sleep some on the ground like that when the niggers are singing, when no one knows I'm there.

"I could sleep here, on these bricks here," David said, pointing to where the shadows cast by the broad leaves of the banana plants were broadest and deepest.

He got up from his chair and went limping, dragging one foot after the other, across the patio and lay down on the bricks.

For a long time Aunt Sally and I sat looking at each other, saying nothing, and presently she made a sign with her fat finger and we crept away into the house. "I'll let you out at the front door. You let him sleep, right where he is," she said. In spite of her huge bulk and her age she walked across the patio floor as softly as a kitten. Beside her I felt awkward and uncertain. When we had got inside she whispered to me. She had some champagne left from the old days, hidden away somewhere in the old house. "I'm going to send a magnum up to his dad when he goes home," she explained.

She, it seemed, was very happy having him there, drunk and asleep on the brick floor of the patio. "We used to have some good men come here in the old days too," she said. As we went into the house through the kitchen door I had looked back at David, asleep now in the heavy shadows at a corner of the wall. There was no doubt he also was happy, had been happy ever since I had brought him into the presence of Aunt Sally. What a small huddled figure of a man he looked, lying thus on the brick, under the night sky, in the deep shadows of the banana plants.

I went into the house and out at the front door and into a dark narrow street, thinking. Well, I was, after all, a northern man. It was possible Aunt Sally had become completely southern, being down here so long.

I remembered that it was the chief boast of her life that once she had shaken hands with John L. Sullivan[25] and that she had known P. T. Barnum.[26]

"I knew Dave Gears. You mean to tell me you don't know who Dave Gears was? Why, he was one of the biggest gamblers we ever had in this city."

As for David and his poetry—it is in the manner of Shelley. "If I could write like Shelley I would be happy. I wouldn't care what happened to me," he had said during our walk of the early part of the evening.

I went along enjoying my thoughts. The street was dark and occasionally I laughed. A notion had come to me. It kept dancing in my head and I thought it very delicious. It had something to do with aristocrats, with such people as Aunt Sally and David. "Lordy," I thought, "maybe I do understand them a little. I'm from the Middle West myself and it seems we can produce our aristocrats too." I kept thinking of Aunt Sally and of my native state, Ohio. "Lordy, I hope she comes from up there, but I don't think I had better inquire too closely into her past," I said to myself, as I went smiling away into the soft smoky night.

―――――

# The South

Not until Anderson had moved from New Orleans to southwestern Virginia did he undertake to write on race relations in the South. He had of course written rather fancifully of southern blacks before, but never directly in terms of their interacting as a race with whites. In a sense it was an atypical subject for Anderson, in that it was a topic of vast proportions traditionally discussed in ideological terms. To him such an approach constituted "thinking in the large," a challenge he left to intellectuals and social theorists, preferring instead to approach issues of this magnitude intuitively and from the perspective of representative components. If the result in "The South" is somewhat impressionistic, rather than rationally derived, it is also Anderson at his most characteristic.

"The South" bears many of his familiar markings: a sympathetic feel for the region; observations of the rhythmic physicality of blacks going about their work; the naturalness of their approach to living; his many talks about the black race with southern white men. He goes to special pains to avoid theorizing and to downplay such conventional attitudes as the strict "moral" posture of northern whites and the arbitrary prejudicial barriers behind which southern whites hid their true feelings. But he does not skirt the formidable issue of miscegenation. His desire for a South in which the two races can frankly communicate their private feelings and actions to each other may seem idealistic, yet it is refreshingly free from the clichés of regional prejudice and conventional thinking.

"The South" was originally published in *Vanity Fair* 27 (September 1926): 49–50, 138, and reprinted in *Hello Towns!* 54–65.

The white race is one great family, the black another. In the Far East, the yellow men. Families of brown men, scattered over the Pacific—living on islands.

The American Pacific coast grew alarmed at the way yellow men pushed in and managed to squeeze them out.

Suppose you have, living in the family, in the house with you, a man or woman who wins your affection. There is a reason why you cannot sit with such a one at table, marry, make love with such a one.

Something strange—a strange kind of relationship between men and women—men and men—women and women.

Something tender—often brutal, often fine—making white men something they would not otherwise be—making black, brown, high-brown, velvet-brown men and women something they would not otherwise be.

I have had in mind, for some time now, trying to write several articles about sections of the country in which I have lived. No one will take what I say too seriously. It does not matter. Writing may clarify some of my own thoughts and feelings.

I am living in a valley between mountains cutting the North off from the South and can roll down either way. One roll into West Virginia, another into North Carolina. Of these particular places I shall say nothing. There has been in me always something calling from the North, a voice calling from the South. In regard to the Negro I am southern. I have no illusions about making him my brother.

I have just come from the far South, have been living there for two or three years. The heat and mosquitoes drove me out. Some of these days I shall drift back down there.

Southern nights, soft voices, New Orleans, Mobile, the Mississippi, live oaks, ships, forests—Negroes—always the Negroes—setting the tempo of life.

Here I find myself sitting at my desk, trying to write of the South—wanting to do it.

Liking Negroes—wanting them about—not wanting them too close. In me the southern contradiction so puzzling to the North.

To a man like myself—that is to say to the artist type of man living in America—there is something tremendously provocative in the American South, in all the life of the South. The South is to me not just a place—it is an idea—a background.

Laughter perhaps—leisure—a kind of warm joy in living.

Born in the Middle West—a youth spent as a wanderer and factory hand—after years of struggle, trying to be a successful man of affairs in industrial northern cities—I went south for the first time when I was well into middle life.

Something had drawn me south—something I had felt since boyhood. It may have been the reading of *Huckleberry Finn*—or the talk of my father.

He was a man southern bred and proud of it.[27]

All southern men, men whose people came from the South, tell you about it at once. The notion of a southern aristocracy persists. Whether or not it is justified is another matter. I have always had difficulty deciding just what an aristocrat is.

Innumerable Americans have had the experience of a first southern trip—by train . . .

The little miserable towns, the badly kept plantations, lean hogs in the streets of towns, lean white men, shabbiness.

Niggers.

Shiftlessness.

I got it all that first time south and landed at last in the old city of Mobile. This was in the month of February. I went to a hotel.

I did not intend to stay there. I had saved a little money and wanted to live cheaply, while I wrote a novel. We high-brow writers have to live low.

It rained—a soft patter of rain in the streets. I put my bags in my room, ate hastily and went out into the night—my first southern night.

For how many hours did I wander, sometimes in lighted streets where white men lived, sometimes in little dark Negro streets? At once I felt—how shall I explain? There was something friendly—in dark figures passing in dark streets, in buildings. Something friendly seemed to come up out of the warm earth under my feet.

In northern industrial towns at night, as you wander thus through streets of small houses, there is always something tense and harsh in voices coming out of houses. Something nervous—irritable—in people.

Life is too difficult. Everything moves too fast.

The tenseness was in my own voice, that first night in the South. I had gone south hoping to get it out.

Softness in voices, laughter, an easy careless swing to bodies of men and women. I walked in a soft cloud of words, not clearly caught, feeling warmth in sounds, in people.

There was a Negro ballad I had once heard Carl Sandburg sing, a ballad about the boll weevil.

"I like this place,
This'll be my home."

I went murmuring the song—not being a bold singer—have been murmuring it to myself these last four or five years—while I lingered in the South.

Being northern, I yet never went south without a feeling of gladness, never have turned back northward without some feeling of inner fear—of sadness.

I got the nigger craze. All northern men of the artist type who go south get it.

Well, for those of us who tell tales, sing songs, work in colors, in stone, the Negroes have something—something physical—rhythm—something we want to get into ourselves—our work.

I had not gone the length of wanting the Negro to replace the white. I hadn't even gone with Abe Lincoln who said "Just because I want to see justice done the black is no sign I want to sleep with him."[28] I wasn't thinking of justice.

Being in the South, what I most wanted was a decent sort of relationship with white southern men. In Mobile, New Orleans, Baton Rouge—other towns of the South—there is always a difficulty for the northern man to overcome.

It concerns the blacks.

You are in the South and would like to know—because you are a writer, interested in the life about you—something about the relationships of black, brown, yellow and white.

The Negro race in the South is so apparently getting lighter. How does that happen? What's going on? White blood constantly creeping in from somewhere.

Northern travelers can't do it all.

Many of the Negro women seen in the streets, in cities, on country roads, on river boats, about houses where you go to dine—splendid creatures.

People always whispering things. "Such and such a white man has a touch of the tar pot." It doesn't come in through white southern women. You know that.

I went walking with southern men, eating, drinking, talking with southern men.

Men are what the civilization in which they live makes them.

Be careful now.

A good deal of fear, everywhere in the South, of cheap, snap northern judgments. One of these fellows hot on justice goes south. He sees the Negroes doing all the work with their hands—sees them wearing ragged clothes, eating in fence corners like dogs, gets indignant.

He can tell you all about everything in ten days.

I did not want to do it like that. The Negro problem is the vast overshadowing problem of the South. No man questions that.

Try down there to associate with the Negro; sit with him, eat with him, talk with him.

You would learn nothing. A white man of the right sort will tell you everything better—more clearly. You would get nothing but the contempt of both whites and blacks. Chances are you would deserve it, too.

Some days I sat for hours on the docks—watching Negroes work. That wasn't for the Negroes' sake. It was for my own sake. The Negro had something I wanted. All sensible white men want it. There is a kind of closeness to nature, trees, rivers, the earth, more primitive men have that men less primitive are all seeking. We want to have the cake and eat it. I know I do.

I remember a morning. I went before daylight to conceal myself in a lumber pile, lay hidden all day, Negroes at work all about me.

Later many talks with southern white men. They began to open up a little—saw I hadn't come down there to tell them anything. Some grew immediately angry, flared up. Others got my point of view—seemed to like it.

Suppose strangers always coming into your house to tell you where to hang your pictures, how to place your chairs, how to treat others in your house.

In what bed to sleep. The South has had to stand a lot from the North—God knows.

Yes, it happens—boys in the country—in the cities—brown girls.

How are you going to help that?

To say it does not happen—constantly—is foolish. If it did not happen there would be no problem, and there is a problem. If the Negro were just an animal. He isn't. Often he is a tremendously attractive man—or, alas, woman.

If you think you, being northern, a puritan perhaps, would run your house better, be more truly what you call "moral," you're a fool.

I remember a brown man laughing. He was sweeping out my room in a house in the country. "White man and brown woman get the fun in this country. White woman and brown man get left."

Well, I have stressed the problem. I like to accept life as it comes up to me. Nothing in the life of the South shocks me. I would take my chances with southern white men and women. Given the same problem I could not handle it better.

It seems to me that what the South needs most now is the artist—not visiting artists—its own—but there is a difficulty.

The South needs southern expression of all phases of southern life in song, prose, painting, music. To get that it needs acceptance of itself, more frankness.

It needs to begin to escape the nonsense about spotless white womanhood, insisting too much upon a kind of purity that is humanly impossible. It needs most of all to wipe out fear of ugly puritanical northern judgments.

The South has got to cleanse itself of the fear of facing itself.

Not an easy job.

The southern problem—that of a race living so intimately with the white race—not living with it at all—fear of race mixture—is the hardest problem any section of the country has to face.

Having lived in the South I believe southern white men handle it as well as northern men ever could—perhaps better.

Chicago, talking of southern violence.

If you go on the theory that exact justice is a human possibility, everything is wrong. I do not subscribe to any such theory.

I have a notion that injustice has a place of its own in the scheme of life.

As for the Negro, I am sure he is better off in the South than in the North. There, at least, injustice is often tempered by real affection.

The land belongs to the blacks. White men own legally the railroads, the land, the boats on the rivers, the rivers, forests, swamps, but they are nigger boats, nigger rivers, nigger swamps, forests, railroads.

It can't be otherwise.

Any intelligent southern white would agree—laughing—"what of it?"

The Negro does the work, the dust of the fields and the water of the rivers and swamps run through his fingers. No white man anywhere has done what the Negro has done with the railroad.

Songs of railroads, dreams of railroads—voyages from town to town—a chicken for frying tucked under the arm.

"Have you got your ticket bought
O, Lord!
Have you got your ticket bought?"

Railroading into a nigger heaven.

The land is really the Negro's land because he works it, sings of it, loves it.

What of it?

The white man isn't going to let him take it away.

The white man of the South getting at his problem the best he can, perhaps. Having to put up with violent fools in his own race, having to be father to innumerable black children.

The blacks remain children.

In the country—in the South—in many households in cities, the conditions of slavery days not much changed.

A relationship between the races not frankly faced, but faced more than the North suspects.

All sorts of subtle angles—loyalty, tenderness, attempts at justice that do not show on the surface.

The Negro unbelievably cunning—"cute" is the word.

Getting for himself in the South—so much the whites do not get and that does not appear on the surface.

The South—the white South—getting bolder. Southern white life will yet express itself—really—in song, prose, painting, music.

The Negro contributing—doing too much of the contributing now. A second-rate Negro poet or artist always getting twice the credit of an equally able white man. That's northern sentimentality.

It is a difficult, delicate job to see the southern white man's angle and see it whole, but the northern man will have to do it if he wants to draw nearer the South.

To go black—think all the hope of future cultural development in the South is in the southern black, because he sings, dances, produces jazz—is hopelessness.

The puzzle remains—two races that when they meet to produce blood mixture must meet in secret, in shame.

The southern problem is the most difficult problem in America. The attitude of the North has never helped much.

I spent a few days at a southern plantation. There were several thousand acres—a village of blacks.

The seasons were long, land cheap.

Two white women owned and ran the place.

We came in the late afternoon and dined in a great room of the old house.

The management of such a house would drive a northern white woman crazy in a week.

The two southern women were handling it easily—naturally.

Delicious food—in vast abundance—dogs, cats, niggers—men, women and children.

Life squirming and writhing everywhere underfoot—nigger life, insect life, animal life.

The niggers worked the land on shares. The arrangement would be called "peonage" by a northern reformer.

Sure, all the niggers in debt to the two women, always in debt.

What grows on the place belongs to everyone on the place. The niggers eat, sleep, sing, make love, work some.

As we dined one of the women told me of hogs, chickens, eggs, turkeys always being carried off secretly to be consumed in some cabin.

She had to know her blacks.

If a man stole a hog, needing it—having children to feed, having been ill—having been a good nigger when times were better—she said nothing, laughed and let it go.

She had to know what nigger stole the hog and why.

She managed to let him know she knew without too many words.

There's a way.

Cunning, creeping life all about the two women. They did not dare be afraid.

I stayed four days and went back on "settlement" day.

That is the great day when the Negro squares up for his year's work.

Not much chance for the whites to cheat. If they do they lose their niggers.

The Negro won't go away physically.

Cheat him and he'll live on you all through the next year, doing no work.

He knows how.

Negroes aren't fools either. Trick niggers among them—but a trick Negro is like the trick white workman of the North.

The two women had to know their people.

Niggers on such southern plantations are taken out sometimes and whipped.

I saw a southern white woman whip a Negro man for trying to hit another Negro man with an axe.

It was about a Negro girl they both wanted.

The white woman knew what was coming. She was watching. She stepped in just in time to prevent a murder. Such things are not uncommon in the South.

The two women I visited knew every Negro man, every Negro woman and child on their place as a northern woman might know the children of her own body.

Plenty of southern white men of the same sort—on other plantations about.

The two white women were doing the job because their white men were all dead. Southern white families—the old ones—are dying out. That may be one reason why so many Negroes come north.

Just why the old white families are passing is another story. It may be simply the old South's passing, a new South being born. In southern cities the Negro labor doesn't sing any more. The South may have to industrialize, like the East, Mid-America, the Far West; southern city newspapers all say so.

And the dying out of the old families may be due to something else.

The thing not talked about except among intimates—never publicly—in the South.

A gradual loss of personal dignity in white men, due to a condition—thrust into relationships too complex and difficult for the generality of men to handle.

At the plantation I visited, the plantation run by two childless women, the last of their particular family, the problem was touched upon during our visit.

After dining one evening we sat on a wide gallery. There was talk of the old days. Always talk of old days in the South.

Then later a troop of black and brown women came up to the house to sing.

The old work songs, ballads about the life of the Negroes on the plantation, were taboo.

An idea had got abroad among the blacks that it was wicked to sing of work, of play. Only songs of a Baptist or Methodist God permitted.

A few wicked niggers, however. They stepped forward and sang of a wreck on the railroad that crossed the edge of the plantation some three miles from the house, of the year when the flu came and so many Negroes died.

I have seldom heard the miseries of flu so aptly described.

The wicked Negroes having a grand time—singing the ungodly songs—the good ones standing aside and enjoying the wickedness of the wicked.

Puritanism taking hold of the Negroes, too.

The two southern white women half heroic figures in my imagination. I got a slant on them the next day.

We drove to a small town, a southern market town and the half white Negroes were all about.

A girl with straight hair and blue eyes—the hair golden brown.

A young Negro man with Jewish features, plainly marked.

Traces of white blood everywhere—in blacks—making the blacks not blacks but browns.

I dared to suggest to the women—tentatively of course—well, I asked the question . . .

Very few of the Negroes of that section had ever been twenty miles from home. Few enough northern visitors came that way.

Young white men growing up—getting married—making a new white man's South as a new East, Far West and Mid-America is always being made.

The woman looked at me with a hard light in her eyes.

"It is true," she said. "It happens. I don't like it."

"One thing I know. You are a northern man and can't judge in such matters, but I am southern through and through." She smiled at me, deciding not to be angry.

"What you suggest happens but southern white men never have anything to do with the matter."

It was the South—all I know of the South. If you of the North lived there do you think you would do the job better?

Southern civilization began with a problem—a war was fought—the problem remains.

It cannot be solved now—in any way I know.

It can be faced.

Facing it may be the one thing needed for the flowering of a truly southern art, a truly southern contribution to an American civilization.

# 2 The Southern Highlands

"I myself came into Virginia from the South," Anderson wrote in his *Memoirs.* "I alighted in the Southwest corner of the state and felt at home there." The statement fairly conveys the quintessence of his southern experience. For all that coastal Alabama and New Orleans had impressed him, he realized that he could never settle in either place. Each had offered a pleasing contrast when he needed it. Each was a new ambiance offering intriguing possibilities for exploration. But the one was remote and primitive, the other unbearably hot in the summer and expensive. In the summer of 1925, Anderson, hard at work on *Tar, A Midwest Childhood,* sought an escape from New Orleans. By the rankest coincidence one of his correspondents had just heard from a friend who was seeking boarders in her southwestern Virginia home. This accidental intermediary, a daughter-in-law of Joel Chandler Harris, recommended the situation to Anderson and Elizabeth. The John Greears were a large family who had lost virtually everything but their farm in recent financial reverses. But the house, sitting some three thousand feet above sea level in a quiet mountain hamlet, sounded ideal to the Andersons. After spending much of July and part of August with the Greears, Anderson had at last found a home in the South.

Having explored the environs of Troutdale, Virginia, in a rented horse and buggy, he had bought a tract of land beside a bold mountain creek. Upon returning to New Orleans in mid-August he engaged his friend William Spratling, then an architecture professor at Tulane, to design a house for the site. "Ripshin," named for the creek, would become his permanent home. The following selections treat his settling in and explorations of the Virginia highlands and beyond.

# I Build a House

It is somewhat ironic that Anderson's most complete account of his first months as a citizen of southwestern Virginia was written some ten years after the fact and was not published in his lifetime. In the interim he had written extensively about his adopted region, often on topics less appealing than the one he treats in "I Build a House"; however, this essay was conceived as a chapter in his memoirs,[1] a project on which he worked intermittently during the mid-to-late 1930s. Although the structure is loose and the subtopics wide ranging, the narrative is rich in anecdote and contains colorful accounts of certain natives of Trout-dale, Virginia, and events connected with the building of Ripshin. The process of accommodation had its tense moments, to be sure, as many of the neighbors saw Anderson's presence as an intrusion that threatened the existing value system. On the whole, however, they soon came to "fellowship" with him, each side accepting the other, faults and all.

A few other participants in the events recounted in "I Build A House" left their own accounts. Perhaps the best known is that in *Miss Elizabeth,* the memoir of Elizabeth Prall Anderson. However, the reminiscences of Caroline Greear, the Andersons' landlady on their initial trip to Troutdale, offers a more candid and straightforward portrayal of their day-to-day lives during the first few weeks and is a unique source of biographical information on this period.[2]

A new, strange life again had begun for me.

I had been in New Orleans through a summer and winter. I had very little money. Having lived through one New Orleans summer, with its oppressive heat, I wanted, if possible, to avoid another.

I began to write letters to men I knew.

"Tell me, if you can, of some place to which I can go, where it is cool and where it doesn't cost much to live."

The letters brought me several suggestions, among others one from Julian Harris.[3] Julian was at that time running his newspaper at Columbus, Georgia. He had made a fine and courageous fight against the Ku Klux Klan and I was full of admiration for him. In his letter he spoke of a Mrs. Greear, at Troutdale, Virginia, and I have the impression that he said that Troutdale was a place to which his father Joel Chandler Harris had often gone fishing. I wrote to Mrs. Greear and received an answer. I could, she said, come to live in her family for a dollar a day.

"That will be for a room," I thought. I found in fact that it meant a room, my meals, my washing and mending. It meant living in a delightful family.

So I was here, where I am now, in the Southwest Virginia hill country. I had come by train to the town of Marion, where I later ran two newspapers, one Democratic and the other Republican, and from there had gone on to Troutdale by a lumber railroad.

The train, pulled by an engine geared to climb steep hills with the drive wheels apparently flying at a furious rate, sparks flying out often setting afire the neighboring woods, really crawled along at ten miles an hour.

It was a strange, a new sort of country to me. On all sides were the magnificent hills, in the Greear family a troop of boys. They all bore Biblical names, John, Joshua, David, Philip, Solomon. There was a corn field beyond a hillside apple orchard in a little hollow in the hills, and in the corn field a small one-room cabin that had not been occupied for years.

The cabin stood in the tall corn. It had no windows. For years the dust had blown in through the openings where the windows had been and through the open door. It was a foot thick on the floor.

The boys came with shovels and brooms. They cleared it out. They built in a rude table at which I could sit. They brought a chair from the house.

It was a long summer without rain in the hills and the daily train from down in the rich Holston Valley, down in the place of paved roads and prosperous farms, sent sparks into the dry woods. The engine of the train, built for hauling long trains of cars loaded with heavy logs, went slowly. It crawled painfully up wooded Troutdale mountain sides, throwing off a stream of sparks. The little lumber town of Troutdale was in decay. Now all the best of the timber had been cut out.

This town in the hills had tried valiantly to go on being a town; the merchants, men who had saved money working in the lumber camp, tried to establish an industry. There had been a little bank and my host, John Greear, had been the cashier.

So all of the money of the community had been put into the building of a factory and it had failed, impoverishing the little mountain village. From the Greear house I could see the remnants of the factory. All of it but a tall brick chimney had been torn away and beside the chimney lay a huge old iron boiler brown now with rust. The chimney that had furnished the power for the factory, seemed to leer at you as you went past it on the dirt road that led over the mountains to the prosperous land beyond.

I was in the corn field at work. I wrote a book there, a book of childhood I called *Tar*. I was alone there, often all morning at my table. It was cool up there in the hills, or at least it seemed cool after New Orleans, and the sunlight came in to me through the tall corn.

The corn had begun to wither in the long drought. When there was a breeze blowing there was a sharp rustling sound. My feet, as I sat writing, were on the warm earth of the little floorless cabin. The corn seemed to be talking to me.

"What an ideal place for an American writer," I thought. I grew lyrical.

"The corn, the corn, how significant in all American life," I thought. I thought of all the great corn fields of the Middle West, of how when I was a small boy I had often crept into them at the edge of my own Ohio town.

I used to crawl in there and lie under the corn. It was warm and close in there. On the ground, under the tall corn, pumpkins grew. There was the singing of the insects. Little insects flew about my head or crawled along the warm ground. Then also the corn fields had talked to me. Like Henry Wallace,[4] whom I was to know later, I became for the time, a kind of corn-field mystic.

I even tried what I had often thought of doing. When I had written a chapter of my book I went outside my cabin and read it aloud to the corn. It was all a little ridiculous but I thought, "No one knows."

And the corn did seem to talk back to me.

"Sure, you are all right. Go ahead," it seemed to say.

I had rented an old horse and buggy and in the afternoon drove by many dirt roads over the mountains.

The old horse went slowly. I had a book with me and, putting the reins on the dashboard, let the old beast take his own way. I might well have had with me a volume of George Borrow, *Lavengro* or the *Romany Rye*.[5] They were books I loved and always carried in my bags.

I kept meeting mountain men and women who turned to stare at me.

The mountaineers are like the gypsies described by Borrow. They look directly at you with a strange, fixed, somewhat disconcerting stare. For a long time after you begin to know them they say little. They are watching you.

"What sort of fellow is this?"

Sometimes, as I rode thus, often in forest roads, some mountain man appeared suddenly out of a path that led away into the deep bushes. There was an old bearded man sitting on a log with a rifle on his knees. It was not until I had lived in the mountains for several years that Dave, one of the Greear boys,[6] told me of how I was all that summer under suspicion.

"They were watching you, quite sure you were a revenuer," he said. He explained how people came to the Greear house asking. All of this was during the time of prohibition and the business of making moonshine was flourishing.

The mountain man was poor. He lived far from the railroad. His little patch of corn, often but three or four acres, would not support his family.

The mountain families were prolific. One of my neighbors, Will Pruitt, who became a friend after I built my own house in the hills, had nineteen children by one wife. He was still vigorous, still strong. He went out on horse-trading expeditions. The farm I later bought had on it a little frame tenant house and after I had built my own house the American sculptress Lucile Swan[7] once came to live in the tenant house.

She was young and beautiful. She bought and rode a great black horse and once Will stopped in the road.

"That woman," he said. "It's a good thing my old woman hasn't died yet. I'd never let that woman get out of this country."

But that came later. I was there in that corn field writing. Some of the mountain men had gone to the Greears to inquire.

"Why, he's a writer. He's writing a book."

It seemed like nonsense to them. One of the mountain men later told me about it.

"You didn't look like that to us," he said.

He told me of how they had sent men through the corn, creeping toward my cabin. It may be that they heard me, spouting there in the corn field. It may have saved me. They perhaps thought I was crazy.

"Well, it's a good thing you didn't get out of that old buggy and walk about much in the woods. We'd have plunked you," the man said to me.

"We thought dead sure you were a revenuer but we couldn't be sure.

There were two or three men drew a bead on you, but didn't shoot. You came out mighty lucky," he said.

In my wanderings with my old horse that summer I went often along a particular road out of the lumber town. It was a little winding road that followed the windings of a brook. It kept crossing and recrossing the brook by fords. I got into a little valley between the hills.

It was a sweet little valley in which there was one small farm, owned, I was told, by a widow woman. She had lost her man. He had gone off to the West Virginia mountains, to the coal mines, and had been killed there. There were two small brooks passing through the valley and beside one of the streams, crossed by a log bridge, was a mountain cabin in which the widow lived with her children.

She was a sturdy woman and was farming her own farm and doing the work of a man. Once I stopped at the house and the widow being absent I spoke to the children. They had come down to the bridge to stare at me.

"Does your mother want to sell this farm?" I asked.

It was a question. I had no money with which to buy a farm. I was indulging in a dream.

"If I had some money I'd buy this farm. I'd live here in these hills." The hunger may have come down into me from my father, who, I think, had been a North Carolina hill boy.[8]

"If I could just buy this farm. I could live, comfortably enough, in that little cabin, over there."

My dreams ran far ahead. Sometime I might write a book that would really sell. All of that country was full of beautiful building stone. I might some day build such a stone house as I had seen in England or France.

The children, frightened by my inquiry, ran away to hide but presently one of them, a young girl, came timidly back. She stood across the creek from me and shouted in a shrill voice.

"Yes, mother wants to sell. She wants to move to West Virginia," she screamed and ran away. It seemed a curious desire to me.

Fall came and I still lingered in the hills that were now covered by color. An old desire to be a painter came back to me but I did not surrender to it. I had finished my book and had written and sent off several short stories.

And then luck came my way. Two of the short stories sold and I had some money and one day, when I was again driving down through my little valley, a book in my hand, the old horse meandering along, the hills surrounding the valley covered with flowing color as though beautiful oriental carpets had been laid over them, I met a woman in the road.

Was it a woman or was it some kind of a monster? I reined in the horse and sat staring. The thing was coming down the hill toward me. It was a woman with a great brass kettle on her head, a kettle for making apple butter. I hailed the woman; she came out from under the kettle.

She was the coal miner's widow who owned the little farm in the valley below.

"Do you still want to sell your farm?"

"Yes, I want to move to West Virginia."

Again that strange desire. I bought the farm there in the road.

A number of things had happened. Chief of all was the fact that Horace Liveright[9] had made a go of *Dark Laughter*. It was the only novel of mine that ever sold in a big way, became what is called a best seller. The sales climbed up and up. I went on a visit to New York and saw my own face staring at me from the advertising pages of newspapers, on the walls of busses and subways.

I saw men and women sitting in busses and subways with my book in their hands. They were stenographers taking it with them to the office.

"Have you read *Dark Laughter*?"

It was all very strange. It was as exciting as a young girl about to go to her first dance. I wanted to go speak to the men and women holding my book in their hands. I was in the subway and got up and clinging to a strap stood over one such woman. She was at page 181 of my book. That would be where I told of the orgies at the Quat'z Arts Ball in Paris in the year after the ending of the first World War. I remembered the American newspaper woman who had as an adventure gone to the ball and was telling of it.

She had told much that I hadn't dared put in the book. I had put in enough. I stood, in the New York subway, looking down at the woman whose eyes were fixed on the pages of my book. She was reading rapidly.

Why, she was such a respectable-looking woman. She was well dressed.

"She will be the wife of a lawyer, or a doctor or perhaps a merchant," I thought. She would live somewhere in a respectable suburb. She went to church on Sunday, belonged to a woman's book club.

I was reconstructing the life of the woman reading my book. A few years before I had written a sort of fantasy of the flesh in a book I had called *Many Marriages* and there had been, as I have said, a storm of criticism.

That the adventures told of in the book could have happened to a respectable seeming American had seemed terrible to American readers.

"That was my mistake," I told myself as I stood over the respectable woman reading my book in the subway. In the book she was reading the adventures in sex were taking place in Paris and that made it all right. That, I thought, had had much to do with the success of the later book.

I returned to my Virginia farm in the mountains. Already, during the winter, the cabin by Ripshin Creek had been torn down and a log cabin to work in had been built on a nearby hilltop. It was to be a place in which I could work while the building of a new house went on.

For I had formed rather grand plans. Money was, for the first time, rolling in. I was what is called in the South, "nigger rich." I had determined to have a house of stone to stand near where Ripshin joined Laurel Creek. There was a fine old apple orchard at that spot and my house, when built, would be protected from storms by the surrounding hills.

There was plenty of stone everywhere about but, in all the mountain country, there were no workmen who had ever built a stone house.

However, they were all ready to try. I had got an old man named Ball to be my builder and he was full of confidence. Bill Spratling, who was then teaching architecture at Tulane University, in New Orleans, drew some plans for me. However, we could not use the plans much, as neither the builder Ball or myself could understand the blueprints.

"But never mind," Ball said. "We'll get along."

Ball was a huge old man of near seventy who had been a builder of sawmills and it was said also that, as a younger man, he had been a famous moonshiner. I had been told that he was somewhat dangerous when crossed but he was always gentle with me.

He went about boasting of his new position. He engaged to have lumber sawed. He employed neighboring hill farmers. He set men to hauling huge stone. He stood before the store at Troutdale boasting.

"I'm something now," he declared. "I've got into a new position in life. I'm secretary to that millionaire who has moved in here."

But I was no millionaire. I had got a few thousand as royalty on my book *Dark Laughter* and there was the hundred dollars that came every Monday from Horace Liveright.

I was intensely bothered by that. There I was. I was presumed to be a writer. "But a writer should be writing," I told myself.

And now Ball had engaged many of the neighboring hill farmers to work for me. I had built a small frame house in the valley below the hill on which my log cabin stood. It had been thrown up hastily. I thought, "When my stone house is built I'll use it as a garage."

I slept and ate down there but in the morning I arose and climbed faithfully up to my cabin on the hill. I sat at my desk by an open window and before me, stretching away, were the tops of other hills.

The hills running away into the distance were a soft blue. They were covered by forests and the trees were just coming into leaf. Here and there, on distant hillsides, were small cleared fields and men plowing. A mountain road climbed a distant hill and a man on horseback went slowly up the road.

It was all too grand. I sat in the cabin with my pen in hand and there were the blank sheets on the desk before me and down below, on Ripshin Creek, the materials for my house were being brought in.

Men were at work down there and there was I up there on that hill, my pen poised in my hand, no words coming to me.

I sprang up and went outside my cabin to look out.

"Why, I cannot write. It is too exciting down there. This is the great time in a man's life. We are all, at heart, builders. It is the dream of every man, at some time in his life, to build his own house.

"And so my house is to be built and I am to stay up here, writing words on paper. How silly."

But there was that hundred dollar check. It came every Monday morning.

Horace had said, "I will send it to you every week for five years. I'll take what you write."

"I'll not bother you," he said.

Yet each week the arrival of the check was a reminder that I was not and perhaps could not be a writer while my house was building.

"But I am under this obligation to Horace." I went again into my hilltop cabin. What really happened was that I never did write a word in that cabin. It may be that the view from the hilltop was too magnificent. It made everything I wrote seem too trivial. I had in the end, after my house was built, to move the cabin from the hill, tuck it away among the trees by the creek.

But I was still up there and down below the work on my house was under way. I had to give it up. I took a train to New York.

"Please, Horace, quit it."

"Quit what?" he asked.

"Quit sending me that money."

I tried to explain how it affected me.

"But," he said, "I have made enough on the one book—I am in the clear. Why should you worry?"

I had a hard time convincing him. He even became suspicious.

"Are you not satisfied with me as your publisher? Is that it?"

It seemed, as he said, impossible to him that a writer should refuse money.

"All right, I'll quit it, but I think you are a little crazy."

And so I was released. It is true that, when my house was half finished, I had to go lecturing. It was bad enough but it was better than having the checks come every Monday to remind me that I was a writer, not a builder.

And this suggests something to my mind. Do you, the reader, belong to some literary circle in your town or city? Do you attend lectures by novelists and poets? Would you like to know something of the financial standing of these men and women? If so, you do not need to go to Dun and Bradstreet. If they are lecturing it is a hundred to one they are broke.

We were hauling stones in from the creek for the walls of my house. We were taking stone from neighboring hillsides. Mountain men from all the surrounding hills and hollows were working for me. We sawed lumber, cut shingles, dug and laid stone walls. We built a dry kiln to dry our green lumber. Mr. Ball climbed like a squirrel over the rafters of the house. My brother Karl came and made a painting of the half-completed structure and a drawing of Ball.

Ball had his own way of life. He built heavily the stone walls eighteen inches thick, all the lumber seasoned oak.

"I'm going to build you a house that will stand here until Gabriel blows that trumpet," he said.

The small hill farmers proved to be wonderfully efficient workmen. When there was work to do on their own farms, wood to cut for their wives, corn to be cut and cultivated, or even perhaps a run of moon to be made for the West Virginia trade, they did not come.

Well, it was all right. While the money made from the sale of *Dark Laughter* held out I did not mind. Perhaps once a month old man Ball came to me. He had been, I had noticed for several days, growing a bit irritable. I thought of shootings and knifings among the hill men. There was his son Ezra working on the job. He had killed one man.

"I'm afraid," said the old man, "that I will have to lay the men off for a few days.

"I'm not feeling so well."

A slow grin spread over his old face.

"All right," I said. I knew what was coming. Marion Ball would hire a man who owned an old open-faced Ford to drive him about over the hills. He would load the car with a few gallons of local white moon, would sit sprawled on the back seat. He would drive from farmhouse to farmhouse stopping to invite men to drink with him. He would make his driver stop while he slept for an hour beside some hillside road. It was his great bragging time.

"I'm going to build that millionaire down there the finest house ever built in this country. They said I couldn't do it, that I was just a sawmill builder. Why, that fellow down there, that writer, he trusts me like a brother."

Ball's vacation lasted for perhaps three or four days and then he would reappear. He looked as fresh as a young boy.

"It rests me up to go on a bender now and then," he explained.

Old Man Ball had his own notion of me. I was more or less a child who had to be taken care of. There was a fireplace, upstairs in the house, for which a stone arch had to be cut. All of the mountain men, I had found out, were natural craftsmen. They loved stone laying. They had pride in the job they were doing.

An old man came down out of the mountain. He was driving a mule and sat in a broken-down wagon. Later I learned that his wife was dead and that his children had all moved out of the country. They had perhaps, as so many sons of mountain men did, gone off to the West Virginia coal mines. The old man lived alone in a mountain cabin somewhere back in the hills.

He stopped before my house and came to where Ball and I were standing in the yard. He was nearly bent double with disease. In truth the old man was slowly dying of cancer of the stomach.

"Do you need any stone cutters here?" he asked. He might have been Tom Wolfe's father in *Look Homeward, Angel*.[10] This man was also a gigantic old fellow.

"And are you a stone cutter?"

"Why, I have been a stone cutter for twenty-five years," he declared.

I looked at Old Man Ball. I had never heard of any stone cutters in the hills.

"Do you know this man?" I asked Ball. "Is he a stone cutter?"

Ball looked over my head at the sky.

"Why, I'll tell you, man and boy, I have lived in this country for fifty years and some of the best men I've ever known in this country have been liars," he said.

Ball laughed and the strange old man laughed with him.

"Well, I've heard of this building going on down here," he said. "You know, Marion, I ain't got long to live. I got cancer but I want a hand in building this house."

So he got a hand. Ball took him upstairs to where the fireplace was building.

"We want an arch over that fireplace.

"You cut the stones for the arch. If they are all right, if they fit and look all right, I'll give you five dollars. Otherwise you don't get a cent."

Ball went about his affairs and I went up to where the old man was puttering about. He had got some pieces of string and was taking measurements. He kept tying knots in the string. He muttered.

"I'll show him, damn him, I'll show him," he kept declaring.

He put the pieces of string in his pocket, went painfully down the temporary stairway we had rigged up and getting into his broken-down wagon, went away.

"So that," I thought, "is the last of him. He will be dead soon now."

Very soon, after three or four weeks, he did die and we built a coffin for him. We built several rude coffins for hill men and women while my house was building. We took a day off and all went up to the old man's cabin to bury him.

And then, after several more weeks, it was time to lay up the arch over the fireplace, and Old Man Ball came to me. We drove up to that other old man's empty cabin. Ball had had a hunch.

"We might as well go up there and see," he said. He had known well the old man who had died.

"You can't tell, that old fool may have cut them stone."

So we drove up a mountain road to the empty cabin and there the stones were. They were in a little shed back of the cabin and when we brought them down they made a perfect little arch for my fireplace. The old mountain man, with the cancer eating away at him, had sat up there, slowly and painfully cutting the stones. He had managed to get a chisel and a hammer. He must have worked slowly, no doubt having to rest for long periods. He had wanted a hand in building my house. He had wanted to show Old Man Ball. He had done a fine job.

It must have seemed a very magnificent house to all the neighborhood. Their own houses were, for the most part, small unpainted shacks, often of one, two, or three rooms.

The civilization about me was not a money civilization. There was little money coming in. Moon liquor was about the only cash crop. When a man needed a new pair of shoes for his wife, a new pair of overalls, he sold a calf. Many of the people would have nothing to do with liquor making. Often they were Primitive Baptists and devoutly religious. For the most part I found them trustworthy, good workmen and honest. If they were suspicious of strangers, slow to establish friendships, they were also, when once they had accepted you, very loyal.

One of the mountain men explained it all to me.

"We wait until we are sure we can fellowship with a man," he said.

The Primitive Baptists (sometimes called Hardshell Baptists) were also foot washers. They had several big meetings during the summer, meetings called the Big June, Big July, etc. They were really great folk gatherings, often several hundred people coming out of the hills and hollows, to gather about some church.

Whole families came, the young girls in their best dresses, the men shaved and bathed. They gathered in the road before the church and in nearby fields. All had brought food and everyone was invited to eat. Among the young men the moon bottle was passed back and forth.

It was a folk movement in which all joined. People came in wagons and on horseback. They came in Ford cars and afoot. It was a great day for courting, girl meeting boy. If there was some drunkenness it did not amount to much.

The Primitive Baptists had no paid preachers. Their preachers, like the members of the congregation, were farmers. Abe Lincoln once said that he liked a preacher who preached like a man fighting bees. He should have been there.

There was another folk meeting that was very curious. There were no Negroes in our section. For years before I came there to build my house, there had been a tradition that no Negro was to come to live in that neighborhood. It was all right for a Negro to come for a few hours but he was warned.

"Get out before dark. Do not let the sun go down on you in this neighborhood."

I was told that the prejudice against the Negro had sprung up because of labor trouble. When lumbering in that district was at its height there had been a strike and Negroes had been brought in to break it.

The mountain men had run them off with guns. It had set up a tradition.

And then, besides, my neighbors had before the Civil War never been slaveholders. Like the men of eastern Tennessee they had been Union men. Perhaps they felt that the Negro was in some way to blame for all the trouble and hardship brought on by the war. Some of the older men had been forced into a war they didn't understand. Government had long been to them a thing far off.

They got no benefit from it. Roads were poor and there were always government men interfering. They sent in men to stop their liquor making. They wanted to collect taxes.

"For what?"

What had government ever done for them?

There was this feeling about the Negro but there was a summer Sunday every year when it was set aside.

It was a Nigger Meeting Sunday. On that day the Negroes from all the low valley country to the north and south came to a neighboring high mountain top. They held services there. They preached and sang all day long.

And the Negro congregations came. They were on the mountain top with the white mountain men, women and children. All sang together. All together walked up and down in the road. On that day, Negroes and whites fellowshipped together.

Life in the hills was changing. In a few years after I came into the hills to live, a paved road was built over our hills. It passed through Troutdale. Big cars began running over the mountains. A garage was built and there were two or three bright shining filling stations. The people of the hills had long been snuff dippers but the younger generation stopped dipping. They went down into the valley town to the movies. A few radios were bought. In the road I saw a woman of twenty-five. She had been reading some woman's magazine, had bought a cheap model of a dress of the latest New York style. Her lips, her cheeks, and even her fingernails were painted but she still had a snuff stick protruding from a corner of her mouth. It was a new world came into the hills and I was a part of it.

There was an old woman lived on a side road near my house. She had a little farm, her man was dead and she with her young daughter worked the farm. She was something rare to me and often I went to visit her, to sit with her in the evening on the porch of her little unpainted mountain cabin. She was one who proved something to me. In the South I had been hearing much talk of aristocracy. I had not heard it among the mountain people but, when I went down into the more prosperous valley town where later I ran the local newspaper, I heard much of it. It seemed to me to be always connected with the former ownership of slaves, with the ownership of rich valley land and money in the bank. To tell the truth I had grown a little weary of the talk of southern aristocracy and had been asking myself a question.

"But what is an aristocrat?"

I thought I had found one in the hills. It was my little old woman neighbor. She had pride. She seemed to feel no one below her, no one above her. She was very poor. She worked hard. Her little thin bent old body was all hardened by toil. When I had first come into her neighborhood she had come to see me and what poise she had had.

She had heard I was a writer of books.

"Mr. Anderson," she said, "I guess we are glad enough to have you come in here and build your house. You do not seem to us an uppity man but I thought I had better come and warn you. They tell me you are a writer of books, but, Mr. Anderson, we cannot buy any books. We are too poor and besides, Mr. Anderson, there are a lot of us who cannot read and write."

It was a summer day and my neighbor, the little old woman, was going to the mill.

She was going to have corn ground for flour and went along the road past my new house half bent double with the load on her thin old shoulders.

I called her in.

"You are tired," I said. "Come and sit with me for a spell."

Now my house was half completed. Workers were scrambling up walls of stone.

We sat on a bench and I made a gesture with my hand.

"Tell me what you think of it," I said.

"Do you not think it is going to be a beautiful house?"

"Yes," she said. Her old eyes were looking steadily at me and again she said she did not think I was an uppity man.

"I guess we are glad enough to have you come in here and build your house," she said. She mentioned the fact that I was giving men work. They earned cash money working for me.

"But there is something else," she said. "We were all poor together in this neighborhood before you came."

So I had set up a new standard of life, had changed things, perhaps I was profoundly disturbing a way of life that had had its own values. I could not answer the old woman. I sat looking at the ground by my own feet. What she had said had sent a queer wave of shame down through my body.

There was another arch of stone to be built in my house. It was a puzzle to us. However, we laid it out in the yard in the apple orchard behind the uncompleted house and built a wooden frame for it.

As I have said we had no tools and there were no stone cutters so my neighbors began bringing stones and trying to fit them into the arch. A man at work on the house would keep his eyes open as he came over the hills from his own cabin. If he saw a stone he thought might fit into the arch he hoisted it to his shoulder and brought it along. We gradually got the arch quite complete, lying there on the ground in the orchard and then the question arose as to which one of the men was to lay it up.

There was a good deal of controversy. Nearly all the men wanted the job but, after a good deal of discussion, it was given to a man named Cornett.

He did a good job and we all laid off work to watch him. The arch went up perfectly and when it was quite completed I went away to lunch.

Something happened. Why, I dare say the man Cornett was proud of his accomplishment. He had got hold of a chisel, may have gone off to the valley town to buy it. He carved his name in large crude letters across the face of the keystone of the arch. He did it while I and all the others were at lunch and when I returned I was furious.

I began swearing in a loud voice. I shouted. Here was something, I thought, that we had all had a hand in doing and this man had slapped his name on it. The keystone had been specially selected. It had a beautiful face. It was ruined.

I kept on ranting and raving and all the other workmen gathered about. There were shy grins on many faces.

As for Cornett, he said nothing. He went out of the room into the yard and when I came out there he stood with his coat on and his lunch pail in his hand.

"I want to talk with you. Come on down the road with me," he said.

"He is going to give me a beating," I thought. We walked in silence along the road until we came to a bridge. I had begun to be ashamed of some of the things I had said to him. When he spoke he spoke quietly enough.

"I'll have to quit you," he said. "I can't work on your house any more."

He explained that it was because all of the others would have the laugh on him.

"All right, I made a mistake. Next Sunday, when none of the others are here, I'll come back and cut my name off the stone. But I'll tell you what you should have done—if you felt you had to bawl me out, you shouldn't have done it before the others. You should have taken me aside. Then I could have stayed on here."

The man Cornett stood on the bridge looking at me. After all he had done a fine job in laying up the arch.

"Let's see, you write books, don't you?" he asked. I said I did.

"Well, when you have written a book you sign it, you put your name on it, don't you?" he asked.

He had me there. I had nothing to say, and with a slow grin on his face he walked away.

We had got near to the end of our job. The walls were up and the roof was on my house but there was the question of getting it plastered.

And then a man came, from some distant town, who was a professional plasterer.

He was quite frank.

"I'll tell you," he said. "I am a good man at my job but I get drunk and when I get drunk I stay that way.

"You'd better keep liquor away from me," he said and so I called the men together.

It was agreed that no one would give him a drink.

"We'll wait until the job is done and then we'll give the fellow a real sendoff."

So the plastering was started and presently all was done except one room. I went away to town.

It was late afternoon when I came back and there was a scene I'll not forget. Ball later explained that they had all thought they could get a start on the celebration while they were doing the last room but the moon liquor they had secretly brought for the occasion must have been very potent.

The craftsman instinct in all the men had taken control of them. There was a scaffold in the room and one by one they had all climbed up onto it. As they did this they had kept taking drinks of the moon and the plaster was already, when I arrived, a foot deep on the floor. It was in their clothes, in their hair, in their eyes, but they did not mind.

One by one they kept climbing to the scaffold.

"Now you let me try it, Frank."

Several of the men had fallen from the scaffold and when I got there two of them were lying in the soft mess on the floor. They were shouting and singing. They were boasting of their skill.

"Come on, Anderson. You try your hand at it," they shouted when they saw me standing at the door of the room.

And so I went away. There was nothing else to do. I left them at their game and, on the next day, nothing being said, they all came back to clean up the mess they had made.

My house was my house. It is true that I had to go on a lecture tour to pay for having it finished and, when it was finished, I had to close it for two years, being unable to support living in it.[11] But there it was.

It was a place for my books. It was a place to come and to bring my friends. It was, I thought, a beautiful house and in building it I had got into a new relationship with my neighbors. They were John and Will and Pete and Frank to me, and I was Sherwood to them. I was no longer a man apart, a writer, a something strange to them. I was just a man, like themselves. I had a farm. I planted corn and kept cows. They had found out that I was far from the millionaire they had at first taken me to be and I had found my land.

---

## A Note on Story Telling

Among the neighbors living near Ripshin were two brothers, Felix and John Sullivan. Both worked for Anderson on the farm at various times and became his friends. Felix, whose natural storytelling ability Anderson admired, became the subject of several sketches. Three of these were published in *Vanity Fair* in 1929 and 1930, one of which is a longer version of the following text. Anderson was so impressed by Felix's skill as a raconteur that he encouraged him to write his stories down. Felix responded that he "wouldn't know how to commence," being uneducated; but Anderson told him that education wasn't necessary for a good writer. Anderson was also impressed with Felix's sense of humor, and may have modeled his fictional reporter, Buck Fever,[12] on him.

They happen everywhere. The best story tellers are often uneducated men. The stories of a man like Lincoln, when retold or put into print, are often pretty bad. The man's great reputation must have been founded on something more substantial than the occasional flashes of wit that remain in the tales repeated.

Men in the country who lead simple lives, who do not see newspaper funny strips or read humorous books, often tell me tales that are infinitely better than anything I see in print.

There is an old country builder, all his life a mountain man, who has, during the last year, told me four stories I have been trying ever since to get into words.

I want words that will convey just the flavor of his telling. I haven't found them yet.

One of the stories I watched grow. He and I stood in the road and there were two neighbor men on horseback. It was, I fancy, just the Abraham Lincoln sort of story telling.

It went well but he wasn't satisfied. I could see that.

Several days later I gave him another chance. Again four or five people were standing about. I laid the groundwork for the story—led up to it, that is to say, and made a faltering attempt to begin telling it myself. That was for bait.

I stopped. I could see his eyes shining, his lips moving. "You tell it. It's your story," I said.

Well, he did tell it, that time. He had been at work on it. All real story tellers are alike. The old man had been thinking of the attempt in the road. Nights, after he had gone to bed or when walking in country roads alone, he had been practicing. He had left a bit out here, added something there. His vocabulary was meager. It is amazing how little vocabulary has to do with story telling. One word can be made to serve many purposes. It must be fitted just so into the whole. The whole thing must have a design, form.

The old man told his story the second time magnificently.

All writers, I am sure, have an experience I am constantly having. There are certain people that feed me.

They appear at the most unexpected times and places.

There was a man, an Irishman,[13] used to work at a desk near my own when I was a copy writer in an advertising agency. God only knows how many stories I got from that man. He had the trick. What he did was to put his finger on the essential spot. I grew so ashamed after a time, having fed upon him so much, that I told him about it. "You should write the stories yourself," I told him. He tried. How he came out I don't know.

Not so well, I fancy.

He had read too much, had too much respect for stories in books.

Many good story tellers, when they take their pen in hand, become quite impossible.

What a writer has to learn, first of all, is not to have too much respect for the printed word just because it is the printed word. Such contempt is a very difficult thing to learn. Some people never learn it. You are a writer or you aren't.

A novel—a story.

Who cares for a novel because it is a novel?

Form is something to talk about. It isn't at all what critics, who write so much of "form," think it is. People who write about writing are very fond of playing with the word.

It is as intangible a thing as love. Did any one ever succeed in telling you what love was?

There is a certain advantage to be gained by what is called amateurishness. God knows, I, a story teller, do not care much about associations with writers. When a writer has begun to succeed a little he becomes a professional. The fun is out of the game. Such a man is too niggardly. He is always thinking of using all the material he can get his hands on. I have had professionals tell me a story quite openly and well. Such a man has, for the moment, forgotten himself. He has let go.

Then he remembers. I am another professional—or he thinks I am. I may be. God knows I hope not. Most of the praying I do is an appeal to God to help me escape professionalism. I have had such a man, after telling a story well, say to me, "Look here. That's mine. You can't have it."

The idea back of the remark made me a little ill.

If, just now, American writing is on the whole better than English writing, and I think it is, it is because it is more amateurish, more free, less professional.

What a writer wants is an escape from talk of writing. Thinking of it is all right.

Well, a man should think of writing. He should think of his story. He should hunt it day and night until he gets it, the soul, the very meat of his story.

Talking with other writers very likely only throws a man off. He gets on the subject of style. If you want to create a new method of writing prose, that's all right too, but it has nothing to do with the story itself.

What is the matter with James Joyce? None of the critics put their fingers on the spot when his *Ulysses* appeared.[14] The man is scientific, an experimenter. When he tries to tell a story he is a poor story teller, God knows.

On the whole, I find myself better off associating with farmers, working men, business men, painters—anyone except other writers. I can get what they have to say in their books.

And what stories I occasionally get from people, how beautifully told. People who lead rather isolated lives, like farmers, do it best. Perhaps they have more time to brood.

I remember a story I got last summer. It was told me by a man met on the road.

We were both on horseback and had stopped to gossip.

How he came to tell the story I can't remember. I wish I could tell it as he did. The story, his telling of it, lit up my whole day.

He was a man of about thirty, a farm hand. His name was Felix.

He had been in the war. He went in as a private and after he had joined was transferred, as he said, out of the National Army into the Regular Army. What that means I don't know.

Anyway there he was, a countryman, a rather heavy slow-speaking man thrown into a regiment where practically all the others were city men.

When they had got overseas they were stationed somewhere in the south of France. It was near the Italian border.

There was in the regiment an Italian-American from New York. He had been in America for nineteen years, had come here as a boy with an older brother and then he found himself with the American army near the Italian border, within some thirty-five miles of where his father lived.

He asked for a furlough, to pay a visit home, and they wouldn't give it to him.

There had been some kind of a general order. Felix, the farm hand who told me this story, said that in his opinion the head men of the army must have spent most of their time issuing general orders. There were so many of them.

The Italian-American, when they told him he couldn't go for a visit home, simply ran amuck.

"I'll go anyway," he said. "I warn you. If you want to keep me here you'd better lock me up."

What they decided to do was to let the man go for the visit home, but to have an American-born soldier go with him.

They chose Felix.

There was where Felix's best story telling came in. He described the walk over the Italian hills with the Italian-American. After they got outside the American lines the man spoke hardly a word of English and Felix had no Italian.

It did not matter. The American farm hand—he was from the hills of Virginia—got it all.

He felt the growing joy of the man, the feeling for his own hills. He said the man kept jumping and shouting in the road. He would walk for a mile singing at the top of his lungs.

They came to the house where the father lived. It was a little stone house in a valley. There was a hillside road leading down and in the road the man kept meeting people. They did not know him but he rushed at them shouting. He hugged and kissed men, women and children. You are to bear in mind he was dressed in the uniform of the American army. Felix said the people did not know the man but felt his joy. Felix felt it too.

It was enough for everyone.

At the door of the little stone house in the valley, when they came to it, the father and the son stood facing each other. The older man, the father, was almost deaf, he was almost blind.

However, he felt something. He just stood staring at the two men in the American uniforms. Minutes passed. Felix said he could hear nothing but the ticking of a clock in the house. A young woman came into the room where the old man was and stood with her arms crossed.

There was a gun hanging on pegs on the wall.

Suddenly the old Italian man grabbed the gun and, pushing the two young men out of the doorway, ran into the yard.

He began loading and shooting.

He shot a rooster, a goose, a pig, a goat, and then another pig.

All the time he laughed and shouted and screamed. Felix, the man from the mountains of Virginia, as I have said, knew no Italian and yet he knew just what was going on. He even knew the old man's words. As the old man loaded and shot off his gun, making a regular slaughter house out of the barnyard, he kept yelling.

"My son! My son! My son!"

"A feast! A feast! A feast!"

That, I thought, when Felix told me the incident, was story telling. Giving me, as he did, just the sense of that homecoming, the joy and wonder of it.

He did it with less words than any story teller I have ever heard. It was like Old Testament story telling.

And there was something else added. It concerned the woman who was the Italian-American soldier's sister. She had been a babe in arms when her brother left for America and did not, of course, remember him at all. His coming home couldn't have meant much to her, but her father's joy meant a lot.

Well, now she was a grown woman and married. Her husband, a poor laborer, was in the Italian army. They hadn't any possessions but she was living for the time in her father's house and he had given her a goose. He wanted it back to make a part of the feast for his son. He, the son and Felix had eaten up everything else on the place and had drunk all the wine.

She hung onto the goose because she wanted to give it to Felix as a present when he and her brother had to go back to the army. It was her way of expressing her thanks to him for bringing her brother home and making the old father so happy.

Felix said he carried the goose under his arm the whole thirty-five miles back to camp. It wobbled its long neck and hissed at everyone along the road but he hung onto it. When he got back to camp he made a pet of it and for a month or two it went waddling and hissing up and down the company street. Then, he said, the regiment had to move to another place and he put the goose into the company mess. He said the piece he got—a wing it was—didn't taste very good. He said he kept thinking of the Italian-American's sister. "I was kind of stuck on her," he said. "When I was carrying the goose home," he said, "over the Italian hills, I kept shutting my eyes and trying to imagine I had her instead of the goose held tight like that in my arms."

## Virginia Justice

In telling of his experiences in his new Virginia home, Anderson used both fiction and fanciful nonfiction. At times, however, the distinctions are blurred, as in his account of how minor civil disputes were adjudicated in rural Virginia at the time. Anderson is obviously Fred, who is spoken of in the third person. The name of Sam Hopkins, the sheriff, combines those of Sam Dillard, the sheriff of Marion, and Oliver Hopkins, the jailer. These were not the only changes. The account of the incident as related in *Miss Elizabeth* (139–41), has the trial ending with a very different result. The discrepancy between the two accounts illustrates the priority that Anderson habitually gave to imagination over fact.

An excellent tandem piece to "Virginia Justice" is "Country Squires." [15] Here Anderson goes into some detail about this form of jurisprudence in rural Virginia. He also describes two cases similar to the one in "Virginia Justice" in which ordinary citizens, given the title of "squire," were empowered to hear small civil cases. However, even as Anderson was writing these pieces, the system was being abolished. Under the new structure such cases were heard by a special trial judge who was paid by the state, thereby putting an end both to the fee system the squires had enjoyed and a unique form of entertainment for the people. "These squire courts," Anderson observed, "were our folk theatres, ourselves and our neighbors the actors. Their disappearance has taken something very colorful out of our lives." [16]

"Virginia Justice" first appeared in *Today* 2 (July 21, 1934): 6–7, 24.

Fred's place, at the edge of our town, is in a little valley in the hills. Fred is a small, quiet man. I am not putting down his real name. He is a well-known writer. A good many writers who go into the country to live are seeking what they call local color, but I do not believe Fred is up to anything of the sort. Once I asked him: "Did you come here just to live among us, or did you build your house and settle down here to write us up?"

He smiled. "I haven't run short of things to write about," he said. "Every man and woman I ever saw is a story. There are too many stories. A man is a fool who seeks materials. The thing is to know how to handle materials. That's something."

When Fred settled here, in our hills, among our Blue Ridge mountain people—hillbillies, I guess you'd call them—he was misunderstood. For one thing, everyone thought he was rich. These mountain people of ours aren't much like the mountain moonshiners you read about in magazine stories. It's true a good many of them can't read or write, but if you think they are stupid, just try to trade horses with one of them.

When Fred built his house, in his upland valley, a few miles out of town, half the mountain men for miles about worked for him. Old Jim Salt was boss on the job, when he wasn't drunk. Fred paid good wages, the best ever paid about here. That may have been a mistake. Folks thought he was easy.

They began laying for him, robbing him a little here, a little there. They thought he didn't know it, but the truth is that he didn't much mind. He isn't a man who has much money sense, and once when I spoke to him of the matter he said to me, "Pshaw! They haven't enough imagination to rob me much."

The little sharp tricks some of our mountain men worked on him only amused the man.

Once he talked to me a long time about money. It seemed to puzzle him. I guess he talked to me more openly than others in town because I've been a college professor. He may have thought I was more at home in his book world. He had a mountain man named Felix working for him. Felix was building a stone wall, and he is a great talker. Fred told me that he went and sat for an hour on the wall near where Felix was at work, and that Felix began spinning yarns. What Felix was really doing was loafing, but he told Fred a tale and Fred went into the house and wrote it down—"word for word as Felix told it," he said. "I got $300 for it and

I was paying Felix $2 a day. I guess if a man understood money, he'd understand a lot."

Fred had a neighbor named Tom Case, a one-eyed man. Tom's queer. He is both mean and generous. Catch him in one mood and he'll steal the fillings out of your teeth, but the next day when you meet him, he'll give you his shirt.

Tom's farm is in on the hillside, above the valley where Fred built his house, and after Fred moved in, Tom laid for him. Fred had bought himself an old saddle horse to ride about the country, and one day the horse got through a fence into Tom's corn field. It was an accident the first time, but Tom got roaring mad, or pretended to be mad, and went down to Fred's house, raving and swearing and demanding $10 damage. The horse hadn't done fifty cents worth of damage to the corn, but Fred gave him the ten.

So it happened again, and then a third time. We all thought Tom was letting the horse into the corn. It was a small hillside field, and there wasn't $5 worth of corn in it. Thirty dollars for Tom. "Pretty good, eh?" everyone said. We all knew well enough what Tom was doing, but in all of us there was something of the same feeling. "Well, he's a city man. He makes money easy." We might even have been a little jealous of Tom's easy picking.

And then Tom spoiled it. He went whole-hog on Fred. The horse got in the corn a fourth time and he wanted $25. Jake Wilson told me he wanted to get his roof fixed. "Roof fixed?" said Hardy Davidson. "He's after a new house and a new farm."

But he overreached that time. He raved and swore and declared he'd kill Fred, and he took Fred's horse and locked him in his barn. I've noticed that when a man is being dirty, mean and crooked with another, he begins to hate the other. Fred kept quiet when all this happened, and came into town and got the sheriff to go get his horse. He had decided to go to law with Tom, and put up a $100 bond to cover any possible damage Tom might get in court.

Tom was so sore he even threatened to shoot the sheriff when he went for the horse. Fred told me that, in the mood he was in, he was afraid Tom might starve the beast. The business about shooting the sheriff was bluff, of course. The sheriff just laughed and made Tom unlock the barn, and took the horse home. "You're a fool. You've spoiled your own racket," he said, and Tom, who was standing in the barnyard with a shotgun in his hand, danced with rage. Our sheriff, Sam Hopkins, says that when a man is going to shoot, he doesn't talk. "He just shoots," he says.

So there was to be a trial in a Virginia squire's court, and half the town and all the farmers and hill men for miles around turned out. It was a nice day, a Saturday in the fall after the corn was cut. The trial was on the Burleson road, at Squire Wills' house. Squire Wills sat with Squire Grey, from the Flat Ridge. These Virginia squires don't pretend to know much law, and they don't like lawyers around telling them what's what. Get a lawyer, and you lose your case, every time. That's why neither Fred nor Tom got one. The squires are elected, and there may be as many as a dozen in one county. They get $3 each for sitting in a case, and you can have as many as three sitting, if you want.

So we were all fixed for a big day, and we all went. These country courts are our theatre, here in the hills. The two squires, both old men, sat solemnly on the front porch of Squire Wills' house and we all gathered on the lawn in front, or in the road.

There was a good deal going on. It was a rare day in the fall, and the horse traders were out. Men and women had come in cars, and the mountain men on horses. There was a good deal of shouting and laughing, some at Tom, some at Fred.

Tom didn't speak to anyone but his brother from Floyd County, who had come over for the trial. The brother stood in the road, and Tom rode up and down on a big black horse. He had his shotgun with him, and he had been drinking a good deal of "mountain moon" and he was trying to intimidate both Fred and the judges.

It didn't work. So Tom stopped his horse near his brother and leaned over to whisper to him. We were all watching. After all, we thought, although Tom Case never had shot anyone, he might begin.

And then, after Tom had whispered to another man, and he to a third, and the third man had gone to whisper to Fred, who was sitting on the edge of the porch, and Fred shook his head, we all knew that, anyway, the trial wasn't going to be settled out of court. Fred told me afterward that Tom offered to settle for $12. "I wouldn't have settled for ten cents," Fred said.

He was beginning to get the spirit of the country, all right.

So then the trial began, and Fred got up and told how he had given Tom $10 three times and he said he might have done it this time but that Tom had been a hog. "I suggest," he said, "that the judges, or Tom and me, select three men and let them go down to Tom's place and look at that corn field. I'll still pay whatever they say is right," he said.

So that, of course, brought on something new. The two squires put their heads together and whispered and nodded, and finally said that Fred could choose a man, Tom another, and that the judges would choose a third.

Of course Tom objected. He swore, he raved, he rode his big horse up and down the road, he waved his gun, he whispered with his brother, and once one of the judges warned him.

"We could have you up for contempt of court, Tom," Squire Wills yelled, and everyone, even Tom and the other judge, had to laugh at that. They figured some lawyer must have been talking to Squire Wills.

Finally, anyway, Tom selected his Floyd County brother, and Fred chose me, and the judges named Jim Wilson, and we drove down to Tom's field. Tom's wife came out while we were looking over the corn. We couldn't see where there had been any damage done that you could notice . . . it's pretty hard to damage a hillside corn field much . . . and the wife said she was fair ashamed of Tom and had argued with him, but for us not to tell him what she said. We decided on $2 because we all thought Fred could spare it, but Tom's brother spoke up and said, "No, let's make it $3."

He laughed when he said it, and I said $3 would be all right. "Fred'll maybe write all this up and get his money back anyway," I said.

Then we came back and gave in our decision, and you should have heard Tom roar. He threw his gun on the ground and rode around, and shook his fist under first his brother's nose, then Jim's, and then mine, but, as we say in the hills, we didn't pay him no mind, and the judges gave out their decision and stuck Fred for the costs.

So then Fred got a little sore, the first time I ever saw him bothered much. He got up and protested. "Look here," he said, "I tendered this man $10. You all know I've got $30 invested in that corn field now, and you all know he was after $25 from me, and the judges you sent down there only found $3 damage." He turned to us referees. "Men," he said, "how much would the whole crop of corn in the field have been worth if my horse had never got in there? If he got in and wasn't put in."

"About $7," Jim Wilson said, and the whole crowd had to laugh.

What was wrong, of course, was with the judges. There was a little shed beside Squire Wills' house and he and Squire Grey went in there. They stayed for a while, conferring, I guess, and then Squire Grey came to the door and motioned for Fred to come in. He told me afterwards how it was. He said the squires told him that the costs of the trial would be $6. "Three dollars apiece," they said. "We don't want to stick you,

Fred, but Tom's mad. He won't pay," they said. They told Fred they thought it wouldn't be fair for them not to get their regular fees for such a big important trial, and Fred told them he thought so, too. "Only I don't want that Tom to get the best of me in this," he said.

Then Fred did some fast thinking. He told me afterward that he was prouder of that moment than of any other in his whole life.

"Look here," he said to the two Virginia squires, "I'll tell you what let's do. You go out there on the porch and announce that the cost of the trial is to be divided, fifty-fifty. I'll pay the $3 damage, and half the costs and that makes $6. You two keep it all. Tom won't get a red cent."

And so it was done, and I don't believe Tom quite understands it yet. He got some damage, and he didn't get it. He was madder than ever, but not at Fred now, but at the squires, and he swore he'd run them both out of the country.

So he got his gun, off the ground where he had thrown it, and rode off, swearing, and we all went on home. Afterwards, Fred told me of something else that happened. He said he didn't see Tom again for as much as two months, and that then, one day in the early winter, when it was raining, he was out for a walk in the rain and met Tom on his black horse, on a narrow mountain road. He said Tom stopped, and he stopped, and they both stood and stared at each other awhile, and then they both began to laugh and Tom got down off his horse.

Fred said they must have talked for two hours, friendly as the devil, about crops and weather and Democrats and Republicans and horses and who'd be a good man for county assessor, old Sylvester Sullivan being dead, but they never mentioned the trial at all.

And after that, Fred had Tom on his hands. He'd come down once a week looking for some work to do, and when Fred let him do a few chores, now and then, about the place, he wouldn't take a cent.

"I'm only doing this work because I believe in neighbors being good neighbors," Tom said.

---

## Jug of Moon

One of Anderson's best realized depictions of mountain people, "Jug of Moon" evokes the pathos of vibrant life contrasted with sudden death. Though not written until 1934, it reflects a fascination with the southern highlander that Anderson had shown from his first visit to Trout-dale in 1925. This is one of several sketches that he wrote primarily to explore the unique qualities of their character. (Other examples are "A Sentimental Journey," below, "A Mountain Dance," and "These Mountaineers."[17]) "Jug of Moon" employs the device of contrasting the colorful mountain man Billy Graves with two "outsiders" (Anderson and his sculptor friend). It was first published in *Today* 2 (September 15, 1934): 6–7, 23.

The hill people of Eastern and Middle America have begun to get into the public consciousness. The hill country runs across America, between the North and the South, taking in great chunks of Virginia, North Carolina, West Virginia, northern Georgia and Alabama, Tennessee, Kentucky and Missouri.

There have been plays, stories, magazine articles and books written about the hill people. Some of the writing has been intelligent and sensible and a lot of it has been foolish, some of it even hurtful.

There is this trick that so many writers have, of working always along broad lines. A tall lean mountain man stands at a still on a mountain side, with a rifle in his hand. He has just shot a Federal agent on the road below. Such things happen in the mountains, but not all mountain men are tall, lean and fierce, and few enough of them own rifles. It is again, as I have found in so many other levels of American life, a matter of just people. Mean ones, generous, tricky, fierce, gentle—there they are.

There still is, however, in the hill country, a way of life that is outside the tone of most America just now. The machine has not penetrated deeply into the hills. Hand weaving is still being done. Grain is still cut with a cradle. You may see oxen on the hill roads and in the fields, and when a man dies his neighbors come to his house and build his coffin in the yard before his door.

Although they call themselves southern, the hill men are not to be confused with the men of the great coastal plains, the "crackers," so called, of the hot plains of lower Georgia, South Carolina, Florida, Alabama and Mississippi. They are alike only in that the men of the plains are also poor.

In the hills there are a good many men and women who cannot read or write, and that is confusing. There are so many smart, learned men of the richer valley towns who seem foolish enough when they come into the hills.

The hills have, however, their own fools, their beautiful women, their liars, their over-sensitive and their easily hurt ones.

Oh, the snobbishness of men! There are prosperous towns and cities in some of the wide valleys, and in the towns and cities men live more easily than their neighbors in the hills. They grow proud and snobbish. Because their fields grow bigger corn, because they live in bigger houses, own automobiles and raise bigger cattle, they feel themselves superior.

Let them try living as the hill men must live, on the same sort of poor, often worn-out, land. Let them try to get what the poor hill men often get out of life. Last year a sculptor from New York came to live for some months in our hills and I took him for several long walks. The sculptor knew something.

We were walking on a mountain road near a mountain town and, as it was Saturday, men, women and children were coming into town for supplies. Even in the broad road they walked in single file, the man followed by his wife, the wife by the children.

"It comes from walking much on mountain trails," I explained to the sculptor.

There were mountain women and girls, some of them quite dressed up, but as is a habit of the country, many were bare-footed. The women carried shoes and stockings in their hands. They were to be put on as the women sat on a creek bank, and after they had washed their feet at the town's edge. Mountain people can't waste shoe leather. It costs too much.

The sculptor kept looking and exclaiming as we passed the women— "See how beautifully they walk." I remember one tall dark woman of thirty. But for the sculptor, I might not have noticed how firmly and beautifully her bare feet met the earth on a mountain road, or how well she carried her slender woman's body.

But I sat down this morning to write the story of the death of an old mountain man named Bill Graves. Bill died, one day last year, at the age of seventy-five. He had three wives during his long life, two of them having died of the hard work and the hard living. There had been a good many children.

He got him a new wife, a young one, when he was sixty-eight. His second wife had died two years earlier, leaving several small children on his hands.

A little mountain family—a man with his wife and daughter—had come through the hills and had put up one night at his house. The daughter might have been eighteen. She was tall and dark-eyed. There often is a curious sadness in these mountain girls, a something born in them. It is like the sadness of a late fall evening when the light is fading and winds blow over the hills.

"I gotta go down this lonesome road."

Bill's new woman's father and mother were drifting through the country. We have a good many such drifters. There is a little family on a mountain farm, and the farm will no longer support it. The man has a bony horse and a wagon. He and his family become drifters, no longer attached to the soil. The man and woman who came to Bill's house were, some of the neighbors said, of the no-account sort. The man was such a fellow as Thomas Lincoln, Abe Lincoln's father. He had drifted out of the same sort of background.

The family stayed for a night with Bill and on the next day, the man and woman, with their broken wagon and the bony horse, went on their way. Bill had talked to the tall daughter during the evening before. She stayed on with him, and the next day they drove to the county seat and got married. She had four children by Bill Graves and then he died.

Bill was one of the tall, lean sort and in early life he had been a lumberjack. It was as a lumberjack, when the hill country was being timbered off, that he made the money to buy his mountain farm.

He was an impressive sort of man. None of his neighbors—at least not the women—were surprised that the young mountain woman stayed with him and became his wife. More and more, as he had grown older, other mountain men of his mountain country had been coming to him with their problems. He was the man in his neighborhood who settled quarrels. He had got himself elected a squire and performed marriage ceremonies. With his tongue in his cheek and pen in hand, he wrote wills and agreements. It was laborious work for Bill. Two of his neighbors had got into a quarrel about a line fence but, although he was a squire, he didn't let them come into his court. He went and looked at the fence. "Put it here," he said. He had a way with men. He made his decisions stick.

Bill Graves had been a hard-drinking man all his life. Every morning when he awoke, he took a tin cupful of raw moon whiskey, and he took several more during the day. Just the same, he never got drunk. He kept his little farm in trim and always was ready to lend a hand to others in the seasons when the farm work in the little valleys and hollows grew heavy.

There was the Widow Littlejohn, who lived on the mountain above his house. Her man died two years ahead of Bill, and in the late fall, after her man died, just when the snow began to fly, Bill drove up to her house with a load of firewood. He had cut the wood on his own land and had hauled it up the mountain side to her place. He hauled six loads, enough to keep her fires going for the winter, stopping his team in the road before her house. He threw the wood over the fence into the yard and, when she came to the door to thank him, he swore at her. He turned his team and drove away, lashing the horses and swearing.

"What the devil'd you mean, letting your man die on you—a woman ought always to die ahead of her man—that's the way to do it," he shouted.

There is some grain, mostly rye, raised in the hill country, but the hill men do not cut it with the modern self-binders. A self-binder would roll down off most of the fields. Men go into the fields with cradles to cut the grain, and when there are several mountain men working in a grain field, it is something to see. There is the long sweep of the cradles, the grain cut by the scythe and caught in the cradle. As the swing is completed, the frame of the cradle catches the bunched grain and it is laid on the ground ready for the women and children to tie into bundles. The grain cutting is something to be remembered. Often there is a group of a half-dozen men swinging across a hillside field, marching forward, the cradles swinging, the women and children following, all the men, women and children of a neighborhood gathered, the shouting and laughing, each man trying to out-march the others.

There is a jug of moon whiskey in a fence corner at the end of the field.

It is the test of the mountaineer's manhood. Can he keep up with the others? Can he lead the others across the field? Can he keep leading them, all through a long hot summer day?

The city man, that sculptor, who came to live in the hills one summer, was walking with me past Bill Graves' place on the afternoon when he died.

Bill's house was on a side road, deep in the hills.

There was the long rye field on a hillside and several mountain men, neighbors of Bill's, had come to help in the harvest. Afterwards, a doctor in town told me about Bill. He said that Bill had suffered with cancer of the stomach for two years. He hadn't let anyone know. Even his wife didn't know. There is a good deal of cancer of the stomach among mountain men. It may be the hog and hominy diet, and I dare say the raw corn whiskey doesn't help. On the day of Bill's death, the sculptor, a small blond man, walked up the road with me, and there on the sloping hillside beside the road was Bill leading a half-dozen of his neighbors across the field. We stopped and looked. I myself am far from a big man, and I'm a town man. What we saw in the field gripped the sculptor. There was a rail fence separating the road from the field, and he went and put his hands on the top rail, and stared.

"Look," he cried. The mountain men were swinging across the field, the sweat pouring from their faces. "Look at the rhythm of it.

"It's a dance," he cried. It was a sweltering hot day. Bill Graves was swearing at the men, taunting them as he led the march across the field and they were laughing at him. He saw us standing in the road and dropping his cradle ran down to us. He must have been full of corn whiskey— had been drinking to keep himself going.

"You! You fellows," he cried to us. "I've been waiting for this.

"You city and town fellows coming in here," he shouted. "I'm going to make you come up here into this field." He stood laughing. "I want to see what you town fellows can do with a cradle."

He had reached the fence and had put his hand on the top rail ready to vault over when something happened. Although Bill had been blustering and swearing, the little sculptor was not alarmed. He also laughed. And then suddenly the laughing died on his lips.

It was late in the afternoon. All day long Bill Graves, now seventy-five, had been leading the others in the grain field. He had kept himself going by drinking quantities of the moon whiskey. The laughing threat he threw at us was the end of him. As he stood by the fence, in the bright late afternoon sunlight, his hand on the top rail, both the sculptor and I saw the quiver that ran through his body. He died as he stood but he died laughing at us.

"I am going to get you," he cried and laughed; and then he turned and called to his young wife who had been at work among the women.

"Come here, Hallie," he called to her and she came, tall and barefooted, down the hillside through the grain stubbles. She was very like that other woman the sculptor and I had seen in the road at the edge of the mountain town. The woman, Hallie, Bill Graves' young girl wife, came down to him as he stood by the fence, his hands behind him gripping the fence rail.

"It's come out all wrong, Hallie," he said, speaking quietly to her.

"A woman should always die before her man, but I was too old when you got me.

"I'm going, I'm going to die on you," he said.

He said the words and slumped to the ground, and all the men, women and children in the field came running toward us. But Hallie, Bill's wife, didn't run.

In the road some twenty yards beyond where I stood with the sculptor from the city, there was a little bridge that crossed a stream. And while Bill's neighbors, who had been helping him in his rye field, were picking him up and carrying what was left of him over the fence and along the road toward his house, the women and children following with frightened faces, the city sculptor and I both turned and looked at Bill's Hallie.

She had jumped lightly over the fence and had walked to the bridge. She sat on the bridge and turned her back to us. She was a young but a proud woman. Afterward the sculptor told me he would never forget her figure as she sat on the low bridge, her feet in the water of a mountain stream.

Although Bill Graves was an old man when he got his Hallie, he had done what a good many younger men never succeeded in doing with their women. He had really got her. She wanted to be alone in the first storm of her grief, and so the city sculptor and I hurried away past the house and around a turn in the road and off into the hills.

———

## A Sentimental Journey

As with many of the stories that strongly attracted him, Anderson wrote two versions of "A Sentimental Journey," both of which were published.[18] The later version is more clearly fictional, with the removal of "E," a reference to Elizabeth Prall, who had separated from Anderson in late 1928, and the addition of a character named David, who becomes the primary narrator. The one reprinted below, however, is the earlier, which is more personal and better focused thematically. The obvious theme is the southern highlander's bond to his native soil. Moreover, this version, depicting the close interactions between the mountain man, Joe, and Anderson and "E," is paradigmatic of the way

Anderson, an outsider, turned strangers into friends in his new surroundings. It also bears the typical Andersonian touch of entering into
the minds of his subjects and evoking their thoughts by means of his
own intuitive imagination.


## A Story

Joe is a thin mountain man of forty with the figure of a boy. He is straight
and tall. I remember the first time I ever saw him. It was a day of the late
fall and I was on a gray horse riding in the hills of our Southwestern
Virginia.

It was a lonely land and I was at that time a newcomer. I was a little
nervous. Romantic tales of mountain men shooting strangers from behind trees or from wooded mountainsides floated through my mind.
Suddenly, out of an old timber road, barely discernible, leading off up
into the hills, Joe emerged.

He was mounted on a beautifully gaited but bony bay horse and while
I admired the horse's gait I feared the rider.

What a fierce-looking man! Stories of men taken for federal agents and
killed by such fellows on lonely roads became suddenly real. His face
was long and lean and he had a huge nose. His thin cheeks had not been
shaved since the last Saturday. He had on, I remember, an old wide-
brimmed black hat, pulled well down over his eyes, and the eyes were
cold and gray. The eyes stared at me. They were as cold as the gray sky
overhead.

Out of the thick golden brown trees, well up the side of the mountain
down which Joe had just come, I saw a thin column of smoke floating up
into the sky. "He has a still up there," I thought. I felt myself in a dangerous position.

Joe rode past me without speaking. My horse stood motionless in the
road. I did not dare take my eyes off the man. "He will shoot me in the
back," I thought. What a silly notion. My hands were trembling. "Well,"
I thought. "Howdy," said the man Joe.

Stopping the bay horse he waited for me and we rode together down
the mountainside. He was curious about me. As to whether he had a still
concealed in the woods I do not now know and I have never asked. No
doubt he had.

And so Joe the mountain man rode with me to my house. It was a small log house "E" and I had built on the bank of a creek. "E" was inside cooking dinner. When we got to the little bridge that crossed the creek I looked at the man who had ridden beside me for half an hour without speaking and he looked at me. "Light," I said, "and come in and eat." We walked across the bridge toward the house. The night was turning cold. Before we entered the house he touched my arm gently with his long bony hand. He made a motion for me to stop and took a bottle from his coat pocket. I took a sip but it was raw new stuff and burned my throat. It seemed to me that Joe took a half pint in one great gulp. "It's new," he said. "He will get drunk," I thought, "he will raise hell in the house." I was afraid for "E" too.

We were sitting in the house by a fireplace and could look through an open door. While we ate "E" was nervous and kept looking at Joe with frightened eyes. There was the open door at her right hand and Joe looked through it and into his hills. Darkness was coming on fast and in the hills above a strong wind blew but it did not come down into our valley. The air above was filled with floating yellow and red leaves. The room was heavy with late fall smells and the smell of moon whiskey. That was Joe's breath.

He was curious about my typewriter and the rows of books on the shelves along the wall, but the fact that we were living in a log house put him at his ease. We were not too grand. Mountain men are as a rule uncommunicative but it turned out that Joe was a talker. He wanted to talk. He said that he had been wanting to come and see us for a long time. Someone had told him we were from distant parts, that we had seen the ocean and foreign lands. He had himself always wanted to go wandering in the big world but had been afraid. The idea of his being frightened of anything seemed absurd. I glanced at "E" and we both smiled. We were feeling easier.

And now Joe began to talk to us of his one attempt to go out of these mountains and into the outside world. It hadn't been successful. He was a hill man and could not escape the hills, had been raised in the hills and had never learned to read or write. He got up and fingered one of my books cautiously and then sat down again. "O Lord," I thought, "the man is lucky." I had just read the book he had touched and after the glowing blurb on the jacket it had been a bitter disappointment to me.

He told us that he had got married when he was sixteen and suggested vaguely that there was a reason. There often is among mountain people. Although he was yet a young man he was the father of fourteen children. Back in the hills somewhere he owned a little strip of land, some twenty acres, on which he raised corn. Most of the corn, I fancied, went into whiskey. A man who has fourteen children and but twenty acres of land has to scratch hard to live. I imagined that the coming of prohibition and the rise in the price of moon had been a big help to him.

All of that, however, came later. On that first evening his being with us had started his mind reaching out into the world. He began talking of the journey he had once taken—that time he had tried to escape from the hills.

It was when he had been married but a short time and had but six children. Suddenly he decided to go out of the hills and into the broad world. Leaving his wife and five of the children at home in his mountain cabin, he set out—taking with him the oldest, a boy of seven.

He said he did it because his corn crop had failed and his two hogs had died. It was an excuse. He really wanted to travel. He had a bony horse and taking the boy on behind he set out over the hills. I gathered he had taken the boy because he was afraid he would be too lonely in the big world without some of his family about. It was late fall and the boy had no shoes.

They went through the hills and down into a plain and came to a coal mining town where there were also factories. It was quite a large town. He got a job in the mines at once and he got good wages. It must have been a good year. Joe had never made so much money before. He told us, as though it were a breath-taking statement, that he made four dollars a day.

It did not cost him much to live. He and the boy slept on the floor in a miner's cabin. The house in which they slept must have belonged to an Italian. Joe spoke of the people as "Tallies."

And there was Joe, the mountain man, in the big world and he was afraid. There were the noises in the house at night. Joe and the boy were accustomed to the silence of the hills. In another room, during the evenings, men gathered and sat talking. They drank and began to sing. Sometimes they fought. They seemed as strange and terrible to Joe and his son as these mountain people had seemed to "E" and myself. At night he came home from the mine, having bought some food at a store, and then he and the boy sat on a bench and ate. There were tears in the boy's eyes. Joe was ashamed. He was only staying in the mining country to make money. His curiosity about the outside world was quite gone. How sweet the distant hills seemed to him now.

On the streets of the mining town crowds of men going along. There was a huge factory with grim-looking walls. What a noise it made. It kept going night and day. The air was filled with black smoke. Freight trains were always switching up and down a siding near the house where Joe and the boy lay on the floor, under the patched quilts they had brought with them from the hills.

And then the winter came. It snowed and froze and then snowed again. In the hills now the snow would be in places ten feet deep. Joe was hungry for its white wonder. He was working in the mines but he said he did not know how to get his money at the week's end. He was shy about asking. You had to go to a certain office where they had your name on a book. Joe said he did not know where it was.

At last he found out. What a lot of money he had. Clutching it in his hand he went to the miner's house at night and got the boy. They had left the horse with a small farmer across the plain at the place where the hills began.

They went there that evening, wading through the deep snow. It was bitter cold. I asked Joe if he had got shoes for the boy and he said no. He said that by the time he got ready to start back into the hills the stores were closed. He figured he had enough money to buy a hog and some corn. He could go back to making whiskey, back to his hills. Both he and the boy were half insane with desire.

He cut up one of the quilts and made a covering for the boy's feet. Sitting in our house as the darkness came he described the journey.

It was an oddly dramatic recital. Joe had the gift. There was really no necessity for his starting off in such a rush. He might have waited until the roads were broken after the great snow.

The only explanation he could give was that he could not wait and the boy was sick with loneliness.

And so, since he had been a boy, Joe had wanted to see the outside world and now, having seen it, he wanted back his hills. He spoke of the happiness of himself and the boy trudging in the darkness in the deep snow.

There was his woman in his cabin some eighty miles away in the hills. What of her? No one in the family could read or write. She might be getting out of wood. It was absurd. Such mountain women can fell trees as well as a man.

It was all sentimentality on Joe's part. He knew that. At midnight he and the boy reached the cabin where they had left the horse and getting on the horse rode all of that night. When they were afraid they would freeze they got off the horse and struggled forward afoot. Joe said it warmed them up.

They kept it up like that all the way home. Occasionally they came to a mountain cabin where there was a fire.

Joe said the trip took three days and three nights and that he lost his way but that he had no desire to sleep. The boy and the horse had, however, to have rest. At one place, while the boy slept on the floor of a mountain house before a fire and the horse ate and rested in a stable, Joe sat up with another mountain man and played cards from after midnight until four in the morning. He said he won two dollars at that.

All the people in the mountain cabins on the way welcomed him and there was but one house where he had trouble. Looking at "E" and myself Joe smiled when he spoke of that night. It was when he had lost his way and had got down out of the hills and into a valley. The people of that house were outsiders. They were not hill people. I fancy they were afraid of Joe, as "E" and I had been afraid, and that being afraid they had wanted to close the door on him and the boy.

When he stopped at the house and called from the road, a man put his head out at a window and told him to go away. The boy was almost frozen. Joe laughed. It was two in the morning.

What he did was to take the boy in his arms and walk to the front door. Then he put his shoulder to the door and pushed it in. There was a little fire in a fireplace in a large front room and he went through the house to the back door and got wood.

The man and his wife, dressed, Joe said, like city folks—that is to say evidently in night clothes, pajamas perhaps—came to the door of a bedroom and looked at him. What he looked like, standing there in the firelight with the old hat pulled down over his face—the long lean face and the cold eyes—the reader may imagine.

He stayed in the house three hours, warming himself and the boy. He went into a stable and fed the horse. The people in the house never showed themselves again. They had taken the one look at Joe and then going quickly back into the bedroom had closed and locked the door.

Joe was curious. He said it was a grand house. I gathered it was much grander than ours, in which he sat talking. The whole inside of the house, he said, was like one big grand piece of furniture. Joe went into the kitchen but would not touch the food he found there. He said he guessed the people of the house were higher-toned than we were. They were, he said, so high and mighty that he would not touch their food. What they were doing with such a house in that country he did not know. In some places, in the valleys among the hills, he said such high-toned people were now coming in.

And, anyway, as Joe said, the people of the grand house evidently did not have any better food than he sometimes had at home. He had been curious and had gone into the kitchen and the pantry to look. I looked at "E." I was glad he had seemed to like our food.

And so Joe and the boy were warmed and the horse was fed and they left the house as they had found it, the two strange people, who might also have heard or read tales of the dangerous character of mountain people, trembling in the room in which they had locked themselves.

They got, Joe said, to their own house late on the next evening and they were almost starved. The snow had grown deeper. After the first heavy snow there had been a rain followed by sleet and then more snow. In some of the mountain passes he and the boy had to go ahead of the horse breaking the way.

They got home at last and Joe did nothing but sleep for two days. He said the boy was all right. He also slept. Joe tried to explain to us that he had taken the desperate trip out of the mining country and back into his own hills in such a hurry because he was afraid his wife, back in her cabin in the hills, would be out of firewood but when he said it he had to smile.

"Pshaw," he said, grinning sheepishly, "there was plenty of wood in the house."

It had, after all, been only the snow-covered hills that had called him back out of the world.

---

# Virginia

By 1929, having lived in Virginia for more than three years, Anderson had developed interests well beyond his home in the southwest. The adopted place he describes in "Virginia" is not the provincial community he had written about in the highlands sketches but rather the state of Virginia, expressed in broad perspectives of geography, history, and social diversity. The major focus is the Civil War, a subject that had fascinated Anderson from his boyhood and that he often talked of writing about. In *A Story Teller's Story* (1924) he had related some of the apocryphal stories spun by his father, a veteran of the war, and a few years before writing this sketch he had discussed with Gertrude Stein a possible collaboration on a book on Grant. Here, however, he talks of the Confederate Generals Lee, Stuart, and Jackson, the "spiritual fathers" who had shaped his early perceptions of Virginia but who were often sentimentalized by modern-day Virginians. Although he never wrote the book about the Civil War, his interest was fed by living in the state where much of it had been fought, and the sketches he wrote about some of the elderly veterans who lived in the Marion area, such as "A Veteran" and "A Stonewall Jackson Man" (both reprinted in chapter 3), are some of his finest.

"Virginia" appeared in *Vanity Fair* 32 (August 1929): 66, 74.

Winchester, Virginia, taken and retaken seventy-two times during the Civil War. I hadn't known that. I got the information out of a motorist guide map. I knew there had been a lot of scrapping up that valley.

I have been in and out of Virginia a good many times in the last four years, living as I am down here. I go in and out by train or by motor.

I am still like a man in a strange house. I keep finding new rooms and hallways. I walk out on little balconies and see the hills, the rivers and the plains. Many people have lived in this house. It is a large, old house. So this is Virginia.

And not only Winchester. There is Manassas, Bull Run, Chancellorsville, Fredericksburg, The Wilderness, Spotsylvania, Cold Harbor, Petersburg, Appomattox, Richmond itself.

The long valleys and the mountains, the Piedmont section of Virginia, Tidewater Virginia, the Southwest.

The Southwest is over beyond the mountain. For a long time it was half forgotten by the older, more stable, more aristocratic Virginia. The people out here, where I am staying, do not really belong to the older, the aristocratic Virginia. The adventurous ones came on out here, on their way west to open up Tennessee and Kentucky, the [George] Rogers Clarks and the Daniel Boones, that sort of fellows. Aristocrats are rarely adventurers. They are aristocrats. The fellows who came out must have been more of my own sort. I am an adventurer too. I do not know what blood runs in me. It may be the blood of kings—or peasants. When I have the courage to do it I try to adventure into places, into thoughts and feelings.

The people of my adopted section of Virginia, the old Virginians who came out into this fine sweet western hill country to live, and were joined out here by solid Germans from Pennsylvania, and incidentally by the Lincolns. The stock that produced Abraham did not like the older colonial Virginians much in an earlier day. They felt themselves neglected, left out in the cold. They still feel that at times. Once they tried to make a state of their own—the State of Franklin, they wanted to call it. It did not come off.

Nancy Hanks' people, they say, came from just over the mountains from where I sit writing. Nancy was no aristocrat. I have seen many Nancy Hanks in this Southwest Virginia hill country—the Blue Ridge, bluegrass country. There are many hard-bodied, easily excited, hard-working hill women here, some of them with a strange haunting loveliness of person shining through their hardness. They are getting them into the factories now. Abraham Lincoln attributed all of his own finer qualities to his mother. There is a special kind of aristocracy in hill people too.

Winchester, Manassas, Chancellorsville, Fredericksburg.

James Madison, George Washington, Thomas Jefferson, Monroe—of the Monroe doctrine.

Stonewall Jackson, Longstreet, Robert E. Lee.

Grant, Meade, Joe Hooker.

J. E. B. Stuart, Hancock, Early.

Sheridan.

No American of any generation could be at all alive and not be excited by these names of men and places. What men have been produced down here in Virginia, what men have come here, have fought here, have left their marks and their memories down here.

Virginia is a state with a past. There was a civilization born down here, made down here. I think Thomas Jefferson came about as near, perhaps a lot nearer than any other one man, even Washington, to making civilization. In a sense he made the old Virginia, set it going, gave it tone and purpose. He made the University of Virginia, and Monticello and the laws and the feel of it. What Jefferson made was what Adams and others of his day, up in New England, were trying to make—that is to say a civilization on which strong individuals could leave their imprint. But Jefferson, it has always seemed to me, had a bigger, a clearer, a more complex conception than the New Englander Adams did, knew more, had felt more, was of greater stature. Adams and Jefferson both failed. Something else came into being, something they would have both fought and instinctively hated—but I will not go into that now.

The Civil War came. It was the great American War. It had to come. There was never any war like it on our American soil and never again will be such another. It came out of the groping of men after something. I am quite sure all of the historians have missed something of the inner meaning of the story. It is perhaps brash of me to say that but I feel it. It may just be that America had promised men too much, that it always promised men too much.

There is a growing feeling among some men that America is too large, that it is too physically vast, that the whole notion of a unified America is an impossible dream.

A war full of drama, of one kind of civilization, one culture, fighting another. I myself was born and grew to manhood in the Middlewest. I think the Middlewest and Virginia fought out, between them, the Civil War, the great war.

New England made it and the far South and South Carolina made it, and Virginia and the Middlewest fought it. Neither wanted it. They did not understand it, or each other.

The abolitionists seemed to want it and the fire-eating southerners from down in the cotton country seemed to want it.

The Virginians were not southerners, never were. They were Virginians. There was a kind of integrity, a sense of wholeness growing up inside the state.

And incidentally the middlewesterners were not abolitionists. They were middlewesterners.

There was an empire building in the Middlewest before the Civil War. There is one building there now. The Middlewest fought for the Mississippi River. It fought for its place in the sun. The Middlewest was, and is, the Imperial German Empire of this American Europe.

But Virginia was not England, nor France, nor Italy. It was Virginia.

And why did Virginia fight? It had to be dragged in, but once in, how it did fight. All the rest of the South quit, was licked, long before it quit.

It never did quit, was never licked. Virginia was starved out of the Civil War. Battles never did it. Virginia won the battles.

When Virginia, with Robert E. Lee at its head, had to quit at Appomattox, having no more food, having no more powder and shot, most of the rest of the South had already leaked out of the struggle. Lee was surrounded largely by Virginians that day. It was Virginia that marched out, laid down its guns, and went home horseback on the horses Grant let it keep. The rest of the South was already far on its way home by that time.

How can I help wondering now how much of the old Virginia is left here? I have an odd feeling about it.

I myself came into Virginia from the South. I alighted in the southwest corner of the state and felt at home here.

Other Virginians, from the Tidewater and from the Piedmont, kept coming down. I dined with some of them, talked with others.

They were politicians out of old Virginia, come down here to get votes; university men, newspaper editors.

It made no difference to me that some of them were politicians. I remembered that Thomas Jefferson was himself a master politician.

I sought something in them—out of my own middlewestern boyhood and middlewestern impression—and [am] still seeking it. With me it was like this.

I am a man who had spent his boyhood in a small Ohio town, just such a town as I am now living in, here in Southwestern Virginia.

We lived there in a little yellow house in a side street.

My father was what he was. I have written a lot about him in some of my books, too much perhaps. He was a southerner so-called—from the hills of North Carolina. I suspect he was a mountain man. He used to get off a saying I have heard many times since, that North Carolina was, in the old days, a valley of humility between two mountains of pride. The mountains of pride were South Carolina and Virginia, he said.

He had been a soldier on the northern side, and evening after evening, when I was a small boy, other soldiers came to sit with him.

They were all talkers, story tellers. There was a little green lawn before our house. They lounged and sat there, some with their backs against the front wall of the house.

The point is that they sat there and talked, always of the war, always of Virginia and of the Virginians.

J. E. B. Stuart, Robert E. Lee.

Other names, names of men, battles, places.

The Shenandoah Valley. The Wilderness. The Crater. Cold Harbor. The Rappahannock. The North Anna. The Potomac.

They made a living stream of talk, centered about Virginia. It stirred me, stayed with me.

I read books, every book I could lay my hands on. Even as a boy I said, "Some day I may write my own history of the Civil War."

I have never in any way attempted it yet. "It is my job," I used to say to myself. "I am the man for it."

It seemed to me then that I could feel the call of the thing in my blood. Once I spoke to a neighbor of the project when I was a small boy. We were walking along a street. He was an Irishman, a store-keeper of the town. He also had been a soldier. He patted me on the head.

"You are both southern and northern," he said. "I respect the women of both the North and the South."

Why he threw that last in I don't know. I am quite sure my father, had I consulted him, would have felt me capable of any gigantic project, being his son.

I think I had the notion, vaguely then, that if I ever wrote my book, if I ever got leisure and money and stability enough to work on it steadily, digest the matter, visit places—perhaps for years—I would center my story about Virginia.

I would try to sense the cultural struggle that must have gone on between New England and the Middlewest.

Then I would try to catch the difference between Virginia and the rest of the South.

You can see the drama of the Middlewest and of Virginia, fighting it out, about something in which they were not either one directly concerned.

Fighting in the midst of misunderstanding, admiration too.

Oh, the admiration of my own middlewestern—may I call them my spiritual fathers—for Robert E. Lee, J. E. B. Stuart, Stonewall Jackson. It was not sentimentality in them. They were not slobbering on Lee and Jackson, as is so much the fashion now.

My father was a Jeffersonian. He was deeply that. His talk and the talk of his friends egged me on.

It comes back to me, sweeps over me again, every time I go out of my Southwest Virginia and into the old Virginia.

My heart hungers for an understanding I haven't got yet.

It may be Virginia has lost what I seek. It may have gone quite modern. I go into the older Virginia now, in my car, traveling from town to town, on trains, seeing the Valley of Virginia, seeing Piedmont.

Seeing the physical University of Virginia, seeing the Monticello, seeing statues of Lee, hearing talk of Lee, of Jackson, of J. E. B. Stuart.

I do this actually seeing these men sometimes. I sleep and dream. Robert E. Lee comes into my room. Jackson comes, Longstreet, Grant, Sheridan.

These men come into my bedroom in dreams sometimes and talk of the war, of what got them into it, how they felt, what they think they meant by it.

They come in there, into my bedroom, talking, I know their voices.

Do I know their minds? Do I know yet what the American Civil War, the great war, was about?

Why do I not write my own Civil War? Is it because I am too lazy, that I haven't money and leisure enough?

Or is it because I do not understand enough? Have I really come to Virginia seeking that understanding?

Will I ever attempt to write my book, and if I do write it, will I call it in the end *The Civil War*—or will I call it simply *Virginia*?

Every year I stay here it seems to me I am a little nearer the thing, although it may well turn out that I may never put my pen to the paper.

# 3 A Country Editor

The first year in Virginia did not produce the security or tranquillity Anderson had anticipated. He later claimed that the weekly draw of one hundred dollars, sent by his publisher, Horace Liveright, had an unsettling effect on his creativity. Even though Liveright was flexible in his expectations, Anderson felt both an obligation and a loss of freedom. He was also experiencing an initial awkwardness as a property owner. The winter of 1926–27, which he spent in Paris, was a miserable experience filled with illness and depression.

In the late summer of 1927 he learned that the two weekly newspapers in nearby Marion, Virginia, were for sale. He decided to purchase them almost immediately, arranging for financing through a wealthy friend. His operating plans had to be formulated with equal haste. *The Marion Democrat* was Democratic, *The Smyth County News* Republican. Realizing that his readership was strongly partisan, he would have to avoid favoritism. Moreover, he had no experience publishing newspapers and scarcely more writing for them. What he did possess were keen instincts, a flair for affability, cleverness, and of course a facility with his pen. The week before his first issue appeared (the *Democrat* of November 1, 1927), Anderson addressed a Kiwanis meeting where local teachers and Marion College professors were special guests. Anticipating his journalistic debut, he spoke in flattering terms about the "Mountain Empire" and its people. A *News* reporter noted that he "charmed his hearers with his happy expressions, and by the time he was finished they all felt that he was an old time friend and that they were all mighty glad that they knew him."

One of the greatest attractions of his job, Anderson found, was the opportunity to talk with the people who came into the shop—at least those who interested him. One of his employees, Joe Stephenson, in a 1991 interview remarked that Anderson "loved old people. You take a farmer with dirt on his shoes and overalls, he'd sit down and talk to him for an hour and enjoy it. But you let a salesman come in there, he'd say, 'The boys'll take care of you.'"

Anderson spoke in his newspapers with a light, familiar voice. While this might not have been unexpected in feature articles, or even in certain editorial statements, he carried it over to news stories as well. Though he could, and did, write "straight" reportage on occasion, as a rule he assigned such weighty matters as politics to other writers. For his own "news" items he frequently adopted a mildly satiric posture, from which he could comment ironically rather than literally. Among his most popular innovations were the satiric masks through which he often spoke. "Buck Fever" was by far the most popular.

The papers were admittedly an experiment, but one that proved highly successful. At the end of his first year Anderson collected his columns and published them in a volume titled *Hello Towns!* (1929). Also, once his success was assured, he wrote repeatedly of his experiences as a small-town journalist and of the responsibilities and rewards inherent in the role. A traveller by nature, and always restless, he roamed through much of the South during the early 1930s observing the effects of the depression and becoming involved with labor issues. Many of these experiences he recounted to his newspaper readers. At the end of 1931 he ceded ownership of the papers to his son Robert Lane Anderson; however, he did not sever his connection completely. His occasional articles continued to appear, and his journalistic role expanded as he travelled through the South and published his interpretations in various national magazines.

# How I Ran a Small-Town Newspaper

Several months after he had purchased the two Marion newspapers, Anderson reflected on what had prompted his decision. He recalled that at the time he had been "associating altogether too much with one Sherwood Anderson. I never grew so tired of a man in my life." His release from this preoccupation was due primarily to a chance meeting with Denny Culbert in the grandstand at the Smyth County fair in late August 1927. When Culbert told him that the two Marion newspapers were for sale, he immediately decided to look into purchasing them. "There was no doubt in Sherwood's mind," Elizabeth Anderson recalled. "It was his destiny. On the spot he told [the owner Arthur] Cox that he would buy the papers and then set about to raise money to pay for them."

Although "How I Ran A Small-Town Newspaper" was apparently never published, it contains a more detailed statement on how he regarded the role of the newspapers in the life of the community than most of his published accounts.[1] It also details how he went about shaping the content of those papers. The statement that "There was this imagined life going on in our town and based on the real life of the town" succinctly expresses the unique blending of straight journalism and artistic innovation that he sought. He also observes that he saw his own role as combining enjoyment and responsibility. Judged by the standards of traditional American journalism, his experimental approach seems somewhat eccentric; however, its success was immediate and long lasting.


The man in the grandstand suggested the idea to me. It was during the time of the county fair over in our county seat town, and the horse races were on. He came up to where I sat alone in the grandstand. He had spotted me. He wanted to know how I liked living in that country. "Are you going to write a book about us?" he asked and I assured him that I had nothing of the sort in mind. He told me that he had once written a book. "I tried my hand at it," he said. He laughed, I thought a little bitterly. "Boy, they panned me," he said.
[ . . . ]

We began to warm to each other. It was this man who suggested the idea of my becoming a newspaper publisher. I now think that a secret yearning for a long time had been going on in me. I was to find out later that it was a pretty widespread yearning, attacking all sorts of men. The man in the grandstand had it. We got around to the subject by way of the horse races going on down on the half-mile track. I had written some horse race stories that he had read. "I always wondered how much a fellow like you lied when he wrote his stories," he said. He spoke as a brother author and as he had brought up a matter that had always been a puzzle to me, it led to a long and rather intimate conversation. Some of my stories had been written in the first person. Did this or that actually happen to me? I didn't know, had never known. We spoke at length of that and then I began to tell him something that had been bothering me. I had come to live in that country, had bought a small farm, and built a house there. I had always been, in feeling at least, a small-town man. I liked small-town life.

But for years I had lived in cities, had been compelled to. I had already written several novels, books of verses, books of short stories, but my books had not sold much. It was true I had got a certain recognition, was mentioned as being what was called "one of the moderns" . . . whatever that meant . . . but had not gathered in many shekels. I had been compelled to stay in cities, work there, had for years been making my living as an advertising writer.

I hadn't wanted to, had wanted all the time to return to small-town life. I had come there to that country, had got a little money ahead, hoped to stay there, make my friends among the men of the town. There is a certain intimacy about small-town life that can be both rather fine and at times a little terrible. I knew all that but I wanted it.

There was, however, a difficulty. I tried to explain it to the man in the grandstand. Someone had told the people of the town that I was an author. City newspapers came there and occasionally my name was mentioned. The man in the grandstand had begun our conversation by asking if I was going to write about the people of that community and there were plenty of others with the same idea in their heads. The truth was that people were a little afraid of me. An author was something special, and just a little queer. You couldn't quite trust him. If you got at all intimate with him, the first thing you knew there you would be, stuck into a book. It was a thing that sent the shivers down your back. "I'll keep out of that fellow's way," you said to yourself. "I'll sure give him a wide berth."

There was that feeling in the air of my adopted town. It was the town to which I drove almost every day from my farm. I was really a farmer. I was a small-town man. I wanted to hang about with lawyers and doctors, sit sometimes in the backs of stores, go sit in garages, talk to men just as another like themselves, no difference. We writers aren't looking for material for stories. We have too much material. There never was a story teller worth his salt who didn't know too many stories. Knowing stories and being able to tell them are two quite different matters. It is true that a man is always trying to catch the tone of the life going on about him. There is something he wants of people. People are to the writer what nature is to the painter.

But he doesn't want to give them away, tell on them, tell their secrets. He wants only the tone of life in many people, the feel of it. It is sometimes pretty hard to explain what he wants.

There was, however, a want I could explain, living as I had decided I would live in that community. I tried to tell the man in the grandstand. His being a fellow author would I thought be a help. It was a mountain country with many broad and rich valleys. The towns up and down the broadest and richest of the valleys were I thought very alive, very American towns. "I would like something to do here that would make me more a part of the community," I said. I explained my situation. I had put most of the money I had made by my writing into a farm and a house. I was tired of flitting about. "What about it?" I asked. "What can I do that will make me less the author, less suspected by people?"

It was then he put into my head the idea of becoming a country newspaper man. There were two papers, both run from the same office in town, one, he said, a Democratic, the other a Republican paper, that he thought could be bought. He had himself thought of buying the newspapers, of becoming a newspaper man, but his experience as author had frightened him off. He explained that, although we were in the South, we were in a mountain section of the South and that there was, had always been ever since the Civil War, almost as many Republicans as Democrats in that particular county but that if I went and bought the two papers of the county, became the publisher of both, the editor of both, it would not be necessary for me to align myself with either party. An arrangement, he said, had been made. The man who owned and edited the papers stayed out of politics. He went to the county chairman of each of the two strong parties. "I will let you appoint a man to be political editor," he said to him. He did not pay such a man any money. There were always men, often rising young political figures, who were glad to do it. He put his name on the masthead as political editor, let him say what he pleased. If the two political editors of the two papers wanted to fight . . . good . . . he let them fight.

I became a country newspaper publisher. I went immediately from the fairground where I had met the author to the newspaper office. I was excited and a little frightened. The office of the papers was just off the main street of the town and faced the county jail and there were churches all about. There was the county courthouse, a quite dignified looking stone building, facing the main street, and back of that the jail with a vacant lot . . . filled at that time with the town's road-building machinery . . . between the jail and the low brick building containing the newspaper plant and clustered about these the Lutheran, the Presbyterian and the Baptist churches.

I went that day to the door of the newspaper office, had my hand on the knob of the door and then turned away. "Eeny, meeny, miny, mo," I said to myself. "Shall I or shall I not?" I had been on several occasions to the newspaper office to buy paper for my scribbling. The man in there who owned and edited the paper would know me. I hadn't a notion in the world what such a property was worth. The man would probably stick me. "In such a matter, involving no doubt more money than you have so that you will have to go about borrowing money, you should employ an agent," I told myself. However, I could see no reason why I should not go and ask. I remember that I went along a street practicing what I should say.

"Mister, do you want to sell your plant, your papers? How much do you want?" It all sounded a little silly to me. It was, I thought, a good deal like going to ask the consent of the father of some girl you wanted to marry. I had that feeling but presently I did go into the office and did ask my questions and when the man answered, naming a price . . . I hadn't then or haven't now any notion of whether or not he stung me . . . I suddenly found myself saying that I would take him up.

So there I was. I had my papers. I had become suddenly, all in one short afternoon, something I had never been before. To be sure there were arrangements to be made, money borrowed, notes and other things to be signed, promises made to pay what I didn't rightly know whether I could pay or not, but presently there I was, sitting on my throne, an editor at last, a man in a great tradition. The figures of old Ben Franklin, Dana, Bennett, Horace Greeley, Colonel Watterson,[2] seemed to be walking before me up and down the makeup stones and the type cases of my dark little shop. I was to become a molder of public opinion, a figure in the social scheme of the community. Having done the thing, made the plunge, I was at once doubtful and a good deal frightened. What would the people of the town think of me as editor? On that first day . . . I thanked Heaven that I had taken charge on Friday . . . my two papers were both weeklies, one issuing on Tuesday and the other on Thursday . . . I would have time in any event to get my breath. On that first day a woman came in.

She was a very wise looking woman. She had grey hair and might have been sixty. She had shrewd and, I thought, rather kindly eyes. She sat down beside my desk. "So you are going to be our new editor?" she said. "I want to know," she said, "what you think you are going to do to us." She had me puzzled and a good deal frightened, but when she began to talk I felt a little better.

"We are here a community," she said, "and you are, a good deal, a stranger to us." She pointed out that, although I had bought the local papers, I had not, by that act, at all bought for myself a place in the community life. She had herself, she said, lived in that one community all of her life. She had been born there, had lived her life there and, as it was with her, so it was with many others.

"You have come," she said, "to live among us. You have bought a farm here, have built you a house. We have seen you walking in our streets." She said that she had read some of my books and when I tried to explain to her, as I had tried to explain to my brother author in the grandstand, what I thought the real reason back of my eagerness to become a small-town editor, she smiled and shook her head. I thought that she also had decided that I was merely up to getting material for stories, using the people of the town for that purpose.

"We'll wait and see," she said.

She disturbed me, set me to thinking. "Well, old boy, you have got yourself into it now," I said to myself. Obviously this business of running these small town and county weeklies wasn't such a simple thing after all. I was forced to realize that, after all, I was a good deal of a stranger in that community. On that first day in my newspaper office and after the woman who had come in to check up on me had left, I sat for a long time looking out a window.

There were, I now remember, people coming and going. There was a man, a farmer, who came in to renew his subscription. He went past me to old Gil [Stephenson], who was my makeup man. Gil always had a big chew of tobacco in his mouth. He kept a box filled with sawdust on the floor by the print shop stove. In the summer Gil kept the door of the stove open and spat into it. He had himself once owned one of the papers I had just bought, had once been an editor. Now, having run to the open stove door to unload, Gil and a farmer were whispering together at the back of the shop. "Gil will be telling him about me," I said to myself. Gil was joined by his son, my linotype machine man, and presently the job printer had joined them. My imagination had got to working. They would be whispering about me.

And so . . . "What kind of an editor have we here?"

"An author, eh? A story writer, eh?"

"What is he up to, Gil?"

Gil would be saying he didn't know. He was an independent old man, that Gil. I doubt that, all the time we were together, working together, he ever had much faith in me. There was, I am sure, always lurking at the back of his mind, the suspicion that had been in the mind of that other author and in the woman who had just left the shop, that I was there only to use him and the people of the town, to study and observe him, in the end to make up stories about him.

"All right," I said to myself, on that first day in my new position. "I'll write out a declaration," I said to myself. I went to work, wrote and wrote, the pages piling up on my desk. I must have written thousands of words that day, trying to explain myself and my purpose, but in the end I threw it all away. "If I am any good at this job, they will in the end find it out, and if I am not, well then, I'm not," I told myself and walked out of the shop.

It was late in the afternoon of a summer day and I went for a walk, a long walk, through many streets of the town and into the hills from which I could survey the town. I was a little like a general who is surveying a field where he expects to be compelled to fight a battle. With us writers and professional story tellers it is like this. We go about looking at people, we overhear conversations. We don't pretend, even to ourselves, to be factual reporters of life. Certain figures of men and women we see and sometimes even know rather well appeal to our imaginations. We begin playing with these figures. The larger part of the writer's work is not done at his typewriter but as he walks about. Our imaginations begin to play with these figures. With some of us, when the fancy lights thus upon the figure of another human, we try to cover up. We make the tall one short, the fat one lean. To our male figure we perhaps add a mustache or a scar on the cheek and we put glasses on the noses of our females or change the color of their hair. All of this we do, partially at least I am sure, to protect our victims and partly for self protection. A man doesn't want a beating or a lawsuit on his hands. Have you not noted, printed at the front of many books, the declaration that all the characters in the book are purely fictitious? That is for protection and, anyway, it is true in part. It is the publisher and the author taking to the bushes. They are, as we say down in our mountain country, where we do yet occasionally make a little illegal liquor and occasionally get caught up with, "taking to the laurel." "Where's Jim?" we ask and someone answers, "He's in the laurel."

And what has all of this to do with being a country weekly newspaper editor? It has a good deal to do with it. I'll try to explain.

I have tried to make clear here my own position, what I felt myself up against in the job I had taken on. I have told how, on my first day as a small-town editor, I went for a walk. "Look here, man," I said to myself, "you are going to be up against something here." I decided at once that the writer's way of work wouldn't answer. The people of the town and the farmers who took my papers weren't after all imagined people. I would have to live with them, be with them day after day. I would have to work out a new technique.

Now I think it is pretty plain that a man who has been for years a story teller, making up stories about people, can't overnight change his whole nature. That day, as I was walking about, I thought of something. Years before, when I had lived for a time in New Orleans, I had been about a good deal with the writer William Faulkner and we used to walk about sometimes making up stories about the city. It happened that we both lived in the neighborhood of the cathedral in the French Quarter, and in the little park before the cathedral there was a statue of old Andrew Jackson, conqueror of the British in the famous battle of New Orleans.

Our imaginations alighted upon the figure of old Andy. We imagined descendants of his still living in the old city. As the famous battle had been fought in the swamps south of the city, we created a web-footed race and used to toss them back and forth, making up stories of things happening to these web-footed men and women, descendants of old Andy and his soldiers still living. We even picked some of them out among passers-by in the streets as we walked about, creating little tales of their adventures for our own amusement.

As the newspapers I ran in the American town were but small week-lies, I knew that I would myself have to do most of the writing for them. I was a comparative stranger in the community. As already suggested, I felt myself more or less suspected. I couldn't afford to hire local reporters to work for me. "All right," I said to myself, "I'll invent some."

I went to work on that idea. It may be that the comic strips in our daily newspapers also gave me an idea. I invented the figure of a young moun-tain man who owned a store in a place called Coon Hollow and had a partner in his business. The firm name was Fever and Ague, and the young man who came down to work for me was named Buck Fever.

Buck, as I conceived him, was a young man of eighteen. He was, like most mountain men, a tall lean one, and, like most mountain men also, he was shrewd. He had a girl up there, in the mountain hollow, to whom he wished to be true, but he was ambitious, and to him coming to live in our town and to work for me, being from the first my star reporter, was a kind of going into the big time.

So there was Buck, running about the town, picking up the news, mak-ing his comments. It is quite true that the mountain people, north and south of the rather rich county where my papers were located, were often so-called illiterate people, that is to say a good many of them had great difficulty in reading or writing, but that did not mean that they were fools. If a man wanted to test the caliber of their minds, he had but to go and try trading horses with one of them, and my Buck, as I thought of him and as he presently became in the minds and in the imaginations of the readers of my papers, was, I'm sure, a pretty good sample of a high-grade mountain boy.

And there was something else I at once found out. Buck could say things about people, make cracks at them, have fun at people's expense that, had I been writing under my own name, would have at once got me into trouble. I had but one rule for him but on that I laid down the law. "Buck," I said to him, "go as far as you like. If you write about Burley Ellis, calling him 'The Commodore' and speaking of his car, in which he cruises about the country going to country dances, as his 'flag ship,' if you think that our jailer over there at the jail is in appearance like your notion of an old nobleman so that you want to write of him always as 'Sir Oliver Hopkins,' if you choose to rename that section of town down be-low the tracks as 'The Third Ward,' it's O.K. with me, but do not write what will rob any man of his self-respect." I put that up to Buck, made him toe the line. By keeping it in mind, neither Buck nor I ever got into too much trouble.

There was Buck as my star reporter and, I've an idea, the favorite among my inventions, but there were others. There was a Mrs. Homing Pigeon, a rather cultivated, refined lady who took an interest in public affairs, and there was also Colonel Star Dust. The Colonel worked in one of our local banks but he was not first of all interested in financial affairs. He was absorbed in the scientific side of life and in particular in the heavens.

So there was this troupe I had working for me, these people created for that purpose and writing for my papers. On the whole I think I had the most trouble with Buck. He kept wanting a raise. It was a good thing for me that the Newspaper Guild hadn't yet got started because I was determined not to give him a raise. I had my reasons. Buck had become a distinct character in the town life, much as some of the better known characters of the comic strips in the city dailies have become something like friends to many city dwellers. Buck was like that to the people of our town except that his adventures in life took place right in the streets of our town. I think that made him close to our readers.

As for his wages, his quarrel with me, his boss, was based on a secret desire to get himself married and I was against it. Some of the young girls, of the high school age, in town had begun writing Buck mash notes. They had entered into the game. They called him on the phone but whoever was in the shop when the phone rang always said the same thing. "Why, Buck has just stepped out," we said. The printers working in the shop were all in on the game and, in the matter of his wage, I kept maintaining that if he got a raise he'd be likely to go off and make a foolish marriage. There was that gal he had left in Coon Hollow. I wanted him to be true to her. I didn't want his character blasted by some flirtatious town gal. I never did pay Buck more than a meager six dollars a week, maintaining that I didn't want him to get the big head.

There was this imagined life going on in our town and based on the real life of the town. It was rather fun. I think we all enjoyed it and I think also that it was pretty healthy. And we did get some things done. It wasn't all play.

Ours was rather a proud little town, with clean streets and, on the whole, very comfortable houses, and the one black spot on the town life was our county jail. I think the same thing is true of many American county seat towns. This was during the time of prohibition, and a good many pretty nice kids were from time to time thrown into jail.

Some such a young fellow had been to a dance and he had something on the hip. He had taken a bit too much of it. It was rather the fashion to do so at that time.

Or there was a young mountain lad picked up at the still, up in the hills, in the laurel. He was doing what his father, his grandfather and his great-grandfather had always done. He couldn't get the idea out of his head that to make his scant crop of corn, grown in some little hillside field, into liquor was wrong. It was such an easy way to transport the corn and you get more money for your crop. He thought the law against it was an interference with his natural rights. "I raised the corn, didn't I?" he said. "It was my own corn." I had known such young mountain men, working in that way to get money to go to college.

These lads were also thrown into our rather nasty unsanitary hole of a county jail. Buck went after the jail, Mrs. Homing Pigeon had her word to say, and I even put in my own oar occasionally, and, in the end, we got a new clean jail, but I do not mean to say that we, Buck, Mrs. Homing Pigeon or myself, deserved all the credit for cleaning up the town's pest hole. Others certainly worked on it. We did, I think, make the town conscious of it.

And then there was that vacant lot, just back of our courthouse and facing our shop. It was owned by the town and it was an eyesore. The town road machinery was parked in the lot and there were always the piles of tar barrels, and Buck, Mrs. Homing Pigeon and I had a meeting and decided this eyesore would have to be made over into a little town park.

But we didn't say so, not us. We didn't ask the town to do it. We just imagined the little park into existence.

We began to write of it. We kept it up week after week. We just assumed that the park was already there. We spoke of sitting on the benches in the park on hot summer evenings, of tired farm women who had come into town resting there, of children playing in the park. We spoke of flower-bordered paths and of roses blooming and of the flowering bushes and presently it worked. We got our park. We had fixed the charming little park in the imagined life of the people of the town and, after a time, the fact that it had not yet been built became unbearable to them.

I have been trying here to point out what I think our small-town week-lies should be. It is, I think, absurd for such papers to try to handle na-tional or international news. The old-time country newspaper editor writing long preachy editorials to his people is out. What is wanted is more interest taken in the life lived in our town. In our own papers we did not attempt to compete with the city dailies and in fact often advised our readers that if they were after state or national news they should take a daily or one of the national magazines. I have a notion that nowadays we of the towns have too much the inclination toward what I think of as "big thinking" when what we really want and need is more color, more interest taken in just our own daily lives. They are often drab enough but it is a fact that others, besides so-called artists, have imaginations and the imagination can certainly be used. It is too little used.

## On Being a Country Editor

Early on in his role as country editor Anderson had decided that news-papers serving a small town and rural community should restrict them-selves to local affairs. "On Being A Country Editor" is filled with anec-dotal examples of his own role in putting that principle into practice. It shows the ease with which he interacted with people in Marion—the sheriff, judges, the Civil War veteran who drops by for a lengthy chat, the individuals whose personal items he accepts for publication. It also conveys his appreciation of the slow pace of life in Marion and the luxury of taking deadlines lightly. Another characteristic touch is the prose snapshot of everyday people, such as the bag lady he sees in the alley behind his print shop. She is delineated in much greater detail than such "important" Marionites as the lawyers and businessmen, who receive only a passing mention. He expresses empathy for the boy on the witness stand who has been primed to give fabricated testimony. Overall, the tone of the piece reveals Anderson's satisfaction with his new role, which allows him to bring to bear some of his most effective artistic strengths.

"On Being a Country Editor" was first published in *Vanity Fair* 29 (February 1928): 70, 92; and reprinted in *Hello Towns!* as "Notes for Newspaper Readers," 30–36.

There is a little alleyway back of the shop. From the window where I sit writing I can, by turning my head slightly, see into the courthouse yard and to the post office door.

The post office is the town gathering place. The morning mail from the east comes in just after eight o'clock. Men begin to gather at about that hour. Back of the glass front of the post office the clerks are at work distributing the mail.

I see the prominent men of the town gathered. There is the judge, three or four lawyers, the merchants, the bankers. This is a Virginia town. These people have not moved about much. Not many new people have come in. As yet, I feel a little strange here.

There is a poor, bedraggled woman in the alleyway. She has two small children with her. The children look half starved. They are picking up bits of coal and wood and putting them in a basket. Presently she and her children will go home and build a fire. They will huddle about it. The morning is cold.

Thoughts drifting in a man's mind. Mountains rise up out of this valley in all directions. The valley is broad and rich. Ever since I have been in this valley, I have been reading every book I could find about the life here. Everyone knows that Virginia is one of our oldest states. In the early days, when all eastern and central Virginia had already been settled for a long time, this country remained untouched.

There was the country east of the mountains. The whites had that. Then came the Blue Ridge range. Beyond that another range, the tail end of the Appalachians, trailing down across Virginia and into North Carolina.

A rich country of little upland valleys. There was a great salt lick at Roanoke and another near us, at Saltville. Game was abundant. In all of this country, blue grass grows naturally. It is wonderful for fattening stock. During the spring, summer and fall months, thousands of fat cattle and sheep are driven down through our main street to the railroad yards.

Before the white men got over the mountains and into these valleys, all of this country was the happy hunting ground of the Indians. None of the tribes lived here, but the Shawnees, the Chickasaws, the Mingos, even the Indians from Ohio and New York state came here to hunt.

Then the white hunters came, Daniel Boone and the others. They went back over the mountains telling great tales. Settlers came. Each settler picked out his own little valley and built his cabin.

Great land companies were formed to exploit the country. George

Washington got in on that. The English governor owed him something for his services during the French and Indian War. George knew how to take care of himself in a financial way. The early settlers in the little valleys had to fight the Indians for their lives on the one hand, and fight it out with the great speculative land company for the very soil under their feet.

An independent people, full of personality. The town has not yet had the problem of assimilating foreign-born citizens.

Everyone knows everyone else. Their fathers were known and their grandfathers. A newcomer like myself—I have been in this country only three years—sees the change going on here that has gone on all over America.

Presently there will be more factories. Labor is plentiful and can yet be bought at a low price. That, in the end, will bring the factories.

The drama of a small town always unrolling before the eyes. Now a crier comes out and calls from the courthouse steps. Court is about to go into session.

It is a case involving mountain people. I go over there. Courts have always frightened me a little. Formerly, when I lived in Chicago, I knew a good many newspaper men. They went freely into the courts, even into the judge's chamber. They spoke freely to the judge. "Hello, Jim," they said.

And there was the sheriff. I have always been afraid of sheriffs. It may be that every writer is instinctively afraid of being arrested. I was arrested once. That was up in Ohio. A sheriff picked me up as a diamond thief. He took me off to a police court. Two or three men in uniform gathered about and began hurling questions at me. I stood trembling. What a queer feeling of guilt.

Now, I go into our courtroom freely. The sheriff and the judge smile at me. Behold, I am a power in the land. I own a newspaper. I even go into the sheriff's office. He and I have a cigarette together.

In the courtroom outside country people are gathered. They are afraid in the presence of the law, as I was once afraid. A court official is telling me about his daughter, who has got a prize in school. I know what he wants. He is proud of his daughter. He wants that put in the paper. It will go in.

In the courtroom I can go into the sacred precincts inside the bar. How brave I am. These days I feel as I did when I was a boy and got a job tending race horses. What did I care about wages? I could consort shoulder to shoulder with the great, with horsemen.

I walked beside drivers of race horses, touched their elbows.

The witness on the witness stand is lying. He is a small boy. His father and his uncle have had a fight. One has hauled the other into court. The fight took place on a country road, just as evening was coming on. The men threw rocks at each other.

The boy has been told a story he must repeat in court. What a ridiculous story. He is swearing that his father stood just so, beside the road. The uncle came along the road, swearing. He threw rocks at the boy's father. The father stood like a statue beside the road. He did not throw any rocks until he had been hit twice. What an amazingly gentle, patient mountain man. Now the lawyers are asking the boy searching questions. He is confused. The color leaves his face. His hands grip the chair in which he sits. I know how the boy feels. He feels as I used to feel when I went into court—before I became an editor and, therefore, brave.

Frightened country people gathered in the courtroom. Presently their turn will come. What a terrible thing is the law.

I am glad I am not a lawyer. I am a newspaper man.

A brother newspaper man has come in. He runs another weekly newspaper in a neighboring town. I have become part of a vast brotherhood. We talk of the cost of getting out a newspaper; how to make the merchants advertise more than they do. Advertising is the breath of our nostrils.

The newspaper man has gone out. After all, running a country weekly is not running a newspaper. In our hearts, we country editors know that. We are not after news. If anyone wants news, let them take a daily. We are after the small events of small-town people's lives.

The country newspaper is the drug store; it is the space back of the stove in the hardware store; it is the farmhouse kitchen.

There was a man on a grey horse went along a mountain road one day last week. Farmer Cooper was in a distant field and could not make out the rider of the grey horse. He has been bothered ever since. "Ma, who do you suppose it was?" Now he has his weekly copy of our paper. He is sitting in the kitchen, reading.

Aha, there it is. "Ed Barrow, from up Sugar Ridge way, rode his grey horse into town on Wednesday of last week. He reports a fine bunch of steers to sell."

An old colonel with a gray beard comes into the office and takes a chair near my own. His hands tremble. In the Civil War he was a reb. Once there was a raid of Union troops down into this country. There was a battle over near Saltville, just across Walker's Mountain from where we are sitting now.

The old man describes the battle in which he took part as a young soldier. It was getting toward the end of the war. The colonel was but a boy then. All of the men of this section had gone off to join Lee before Richmond. Grant was pounding away at Lee during those days. It was near the end of things.

And a battle here—in this quiet place. Old men and boys rushing to the Stars and Bars. Who knows, my own father may have been along on that raiding party. They were trying to get up to the Norfolk and Western Railroad, to tear it up. Stealing chickens on the way, too.

Old men and boys rushing through the hills, the colonel among them. He describes the battle in the hills, the driving off of the Yanks. It takes an hour to tell. It is a good story. Well, no hurry. We country editors have no deadline. If we do not get to press today, we will go to press tomorrow. After the colonel leaves, leaning heavily on his cane, a heavy-faced woman with a determined jaw comes in.

She wants a piece put in the paper. She had two sons. One of them was killed last year in a railroad accident. With several other boys he was in a Ford. There was moon whiskey in the Ford. The driver was reckless. He drove before an on-coming train at a grade crossing and two boys were killed.

The boy's mother has written a piece about the boy. She says he was a good boy and feared God. "I hope," she says in the piece, "that what has happened to Harry will be a warning to his brother, Zeb." Evidently Zeb is a bit out of hand, too.

"Will you print it?" she asks. Surely, we will.

She is followed by a shy, fair maiden in a blue dress.

The maiden also has something to put in the paper. She hands it to me and goes out. I look at the paper. "Miss Ruby Small of Carrollville was in town Tuesday to get her teeth fixed."

Well, well, Ruby, are you having trouble with your teeth, and you so young, too.

There is no question, the dentists of this town should do more advertising in our paper.

Night. Your country editor walks about his town. He belongs to the great brotherhood of the ink pots. He does not have to rush like the city newspaper man, nor does he need to be high toned and literary, like your magazine editor.

Your country editor is thinking up schemes. He is trying to think how to make the merchants of his town advertise more. He thinks of that for a time, and then thinks of his town.

More and more he is growing familiar with it. The threads of its life run through his fingers. He knows, O, what does he not know?

And the people of the town, knowing what he knows, a little afraid, keep passing and looking at him. He is just a little outside their lives. He is something special. He writes. That alone sets him apart.

---

## God and the Machine Age

Nowhere is Anderson's journalistic method more obvious than in his reporting of local news. In "God and the Machine Age," which appeared in the *Smyth County News* on June 27, 1929, he treats a fairly routine event with several touches not found in traditional news stories. The reportorial voice is far from objective as it relates the events of a court case of conflicting noises—a private citizen's radio versus a religious sect's zealous effusions. Rather, it freely comments, often wryly and ironically, on the more ridiculous aspects of the case. The result is an account that reads more like a fictional vignette, or a slightly sardonic anecdote, than an item of news. Writing in this vein does not profess to be objective reportage, and in this story the "Holy Rollers" take a fair drubbing. However, the humor tends to lighten the narrator's bias, and the overall effect is more comic than censorious.

There was a trial at Chilhowie[3] on Wednesday the 26th that was certainly full of significance. Here is the story. At Chilhowie there lives a man named Charlie Hankla. Charlie, as we get the story, is a hardworking honest man who hauls coal. As everyone knows, Chilhowie is an up and coming town. Houses are not so easy to get there. They do not have many empty ones.

So Mr. Hankla, in looking for a place to house himself and family, found an empty store room. He rented half of it and fixed it up nicely. He is a strictly modern man and so he equipped it with electricity.

Then a church organization called "The Holiness Church"—sometimes "The Holy Rollers," came along and rented the other half for their meetings. An agreement was made with Hankla. They were not to hold their meetings later than nine-thirty at night.

Now, it seems that the Holiness people are on particularly intimate terms with God. They do not do things of their own volition. God tells them what to do and they do it. Sometimes he tells them to pray, sometimes to jump up and down on the floor, sometimes to pound on partitions. They did all these things in their new meeting place and they did them as late sometimes as ten-thirty at night.

It was a bit rough on Hankla so he, being a modern, got in a radio and turned it on. He got the baseball scores and occasionally a bit of jazz. He says his children couldn't sleep anyway so he thought he would entertain himself and the kids.

Then the Holiness people had him arrested on the charge of disturbing public worship. He was tried before Mayor Beattie at Chilhowie, our own Mr. Funk going down to represent the majesty of the state and Mr. Burt Dickinson,[4] an ardent fellow radio fan, to represent Mr. Hankla.

There was a big crowd present, mostly Holiness people, and Mayor Beattie's office in Chilhowie isn't large. Mr. Funk being not to say skinny but at least somewhat lath-like and his Honor rather small, they got in all right, but our Mr. Dickinson is a man of size. To get him in to represent his client, they had to move out about six of the holy ones.

They protested at this and protested loudly, in fact these people are some protesters. When things do not go their way, they are in the habit of calling God down to straighten them out.

For example there were two trees growing in a yard nearby and they got God to come and strike one of them with lightning. This, they said, was a warning to Hankla. In the neighborhood there lives a carpenter who was not in their good graces, he having complained of the noise they made, so they began to pray God to have a house fall on him or a fellow workman drop a hammer on his head. At least the carpenter so testified.

He said they got him too. He fell off a ladder and nearly broke his neck.

Question—"Did he push you off the ladder or jerk it out from under you?"

Carpenter's answer—"I don't know. I fell all right."

Question—"Are you going to quit the carpenter business?"

Answer—"I can't. I got a family to support."

The Holiness people testified that the noise they made was a matter of God's directions. He, they said, always told them what to do and they did it. Mayor Beattie decided that the charge against Mr. Hankla, that of disturbing public worship, would not stick, he, as well as Attorney Dickinson and Boggs and Rice of Marion, having a perfect right to entertain himself with the radio, this being a modern machine age, and that the Holiness people would have to pay the cost of the proceedings.

Mr. Hankla was nice about this but the holy ones were not so nice. Hankla said that, if these people would quiet down at nine-thirty, as per agreement, he would forgo the joys of the radio, but the Holiness crowd were noisier than ever. They did pay the costs, finally, but they did it under strong protest. Some of them moved out into the street, still protesting.

It happened that someone had parked a new Ford in the street nearby, and a child of one of the holy ones, who had on hob-nail shoes, got up and danced on the new and shining fenders.

Of course, the Ford owner protested and this started a new row.

It is hard to tell what will happen to Mr. Ford now. Ford sales may fall off. Anyway, they all went home and the carpenter and Mr. Hankla also went, as did our Mr. Dickinson and our Mr. Funk.

The outlook is, however, discouraging. Who can tell what God will direct these people to do next? It looks bad for that other tree in the yard down there and for the peace of one Chilhowie neighborhood. We suspect that the Black Cat of Chilhowie[5] has got crossed up with these people. He, or she, has not been heard from for a long time now.

---

## Negro Singing: Hampton Quartette Entertains Large Crowd

Of the various references to music in Anderson's writings, the form most frequently mentioned is African-American singing. He had a particular preference for this music in its most primitive, untrained form—for instance, the kind sung by the chorus of servants on a southern plantation in "The South" (see Chapter 1). He also made mention in the newspapers of Warren Johnson, a black singer who would come into the print shop and perform. Dubbing him "the print shop nightingale" and "the brown Dude of Church Street," Anderson would "wave his hands like an orchestra leader" as Johnson sang (*Marion Democrat,* May 27, 1930).

Anderson's fondness for the purer forms of this music perhaps explains his rather lukewarm comments on a concert by the well-trained Hampton Quartette. "In the arts you have to lose all before you begin to gain anything," he concludes. In other words, training dulls the edge of the true primitive, the "so-called ignorant" singer.

This article appeared in the *Marion Democrat* on March 20, 1928.

It is something inherent in the Negro race. It comes to the surface in singing and in dancing. The Hampton Quartette sang here last night. It was fine song singing, having the peculiar quality of song singing, a thing different than any other kind of music making, but I have heard infinitely better Negro singing.

Who can doubt that the Negro race has something the white race has lost. I mean an unconscious giving of himself to the song by the singer. The average white lady singer, for example, who gets up before an audience, is conscious of her clothes, of her physical beauty, if she has any, of a thousand things other than the song she is singing.

Surely education is all right but education, in the white man's sense, does something to the black and the brown man.

I remember a hot night on the Mississippi at Baton Rouge. Negroes were carrying bags of evil smelling fertilizer up a steep gang plank and singing a song called "The las sack."

Another night, years ago, up the Mobile River. The boat tied up on the river bank. Lonely forests all about. The song that time was a work song of some sort. "O, my babe. The banjo dog." A queer medley of words, meaning nothing. I sat in a dark part of the boat with the pilot. It was hot. The song of the workers suddenly caught something lost when the Negro came out of his native Africa.

These were real black boys. Not a man could read or write. Suddenly the song seemed a real part of the lonely forests, of the river, the night. To describe its quality is impossible to me.

Organizations like the Hampton singers are at their worst when they think they are at their best. They are good, surely. But when you have heard Negro singing, as I have, in lonely places in the far South—Negroes on lumber rafts in the turpentine forest or on the lower Mississippi.

There is a quality to Negro singing going out fast. Music is the most primitive of all the arts. The Negro, in coming into the more cultivated arts, the singing and creation of classic and semi-classic music, and the other arts that are sophisticated, has a long trail ahead. In spite of his native voice quality, a thing also that will go from the educated Negro, the white man will beat him a thousand miles at all of the sophisticated arts.

The Hampton singers still sing well. They do not sing beautifully as do some of the Negroes of the fields and rivers who have not tried yet to swing into the white man's world. I can soon forget the admittedly fine singing of the trained Negro singers. I will never forget some of the Negro singing I have heard from the lips of so-called ignorant Negro workers.

In the arts you have to lose all before you begin to gain anything. The arts are like religion in that.

---

## Buck Fever Says *and* Buck Fever Says: The Three Hens

Buck Fever, the popular fictional reporter, was one of the principal reasons why Anderson's experiment in creative journalism was quick to catch on with readers of the *Marion Democrat* and *Smyth County News*. Buck made his initial appearance in Anderson's third issue of the *News* and thereafter appeared regularly in both papers for more than two years. As a fictional mask for Anderson, Buck's persona was always familiar but never completely transparent. True, he was a kind of everyman of the community; however, the particulars of his characterization were solid enough to afford Anderson freedom of movement in the background.

The first of the following selections contains details of Buck's family; his home (the fictional Coon Hollow); the low wages Anderson pays him; and his wry observations on locals he sees on "The Rialto," Marion's Main Street. Such details were commonplace in the "Buck Fever

Says" columns. The second, subtitled "The Three Hens," is more polished. Although some of the familiar details of the first are woven in, the piece is in fact a well-formed narrative in which an ordinary civil case of chicken stealing is transformed into a whimsical beast fable. Although the narrator is unquestionably Buck Fever, the gentle humor of Anderson, focusing on the rooster rather than on the human complainant, is easily discernible.

## Buck Fever Says (March 15, 1928)

Paw has been after me, ever since I came down here to work on the papers, to get his picture in. He says, "You get your name in and Spring and Maw get theirs; what's the matter with me?"

He was kicking only the other night. "Well," he says, "I see George Cook in the paper and J. L. C. Anderson and Bob and John Buchanan and Col. Tate and all the rest. Are they any better than I am?"

So anyway here he is. Meet H. A. Fever of the firm of Fever and Ague, Coon Hollow, Virginia. Now, I hope Paw will be satisfied.

If you see any improvement in this paper, don't give the boss or me all the credit, nor half. I claim that we have got the best lot of correspondents of any weekly paper I ever see. When there is anything nice or exciting happening in this whole country if we don't hear about it it isn't our correspondents' fault. A good one at Chilhowie, Saltville—live notes all the time from Groseclose, Konnarock, St. Clair, Sugar Grove, Teas, Attoway, Nebo, Broadford and all over the county. I heard the boss say the other day that the only place from which we are not getting enough good notes is from Seven Mile Ford. Wake up down there or the boss may send me to Seven Mile Ford to stir things up.

These warm early spring days are sure bringing the boys out onto the Rialto. Saw the boss, George Cook and Andy Funk, all sporting canes down Main Street the other day.

Gee some Dems are Dems O.K. Saw a letter the boss got from a Dem down east. He says he hopes the arm with which the boss writes for our Rep paper will get a stroke.

There has been a lot of fishermen out but if anyone has got a string yet we haven't seen it. Coon Hollow is the place to get horneys if you want to know it.

At that I'm glad I don't get much wages and don't own some of the swell cars I see at the auto show. I got temptations enough as it is.

I'm trying to be a good boy, O.K., all right, but spring is spring.


## Buck Fever Says: The Three Hens (July 5, 1928)

Here is how it is. Mrs. Handy moved down—or up—or over from Troutdale to the St. Clair country. She had several hens. Mrs. Handy has had, as she herself says, heaps and heaps of trouble. Life has been in short a troublous voyage for her. I neglected to say that she has also a rooster to attend her hens—being I fancy a fair-minded woman.

What are hens without a rooster, or for that matter what is a rooster without his hens?

Three of Mrs. Handy's hens were stolen. This was at night. In the morning Mrs. Handy got up and listened for the glad morning cry of her rooster. He was sad and silent. His hens were gone. A sad morning it was for him. Well do I know how he felt—or if I don't know I guess my Paw does. I have heard him lots of times, when he had been scrapping with Maw. "I wish I was a rooster," he said.

Mrs. Handy claimed, or at least she heard, that some boys had stolen her hens. For plain and fancy "he said" and "she said," the St. Clair District is the best in the world. You can just about hear anything you want down there and a lot you don't want to hear.

Mrs. Handy went to see the parents of the boys. They claim they said to her, "No our boys did not steal your hens but you are a woman who has had her troubles. We will just give you three hens. But you must not start any trouble." But Mrs. Handy did start trouble. The boys were arrested and tried in Justice Dickinson's Juvenile Court, the whole countryside coming in for the trial. One of the boys was convicted and sent to the reform farm, the other was let go.

"But what about our three hens?" the parents said to Mrs. Handy and to Justice Dickinson. "Do we get them back?"

Mrs. Handy shook her head. Justice Dickinson shook his head. "I don't see how that could be," he said

And there was something else to this matter. We don't know whether or not it should be mentioned in a family journal but here goes. Truth will out. Mrs. Handy's rooster had really become attached to the three strange hens in the yard. Never had he crowed more cheerfully. Joyfully did he greet each coming day, etc., etc

And then up comes the parents and relatives of the boys and gets the hens—as one might say, "off" Mrs. Handy.

There is a moral question involved. Were the hens given Mrs. Handy on the understanding that she would keep quiet about the whole matter? One of the hens was about to become a mother. That complicates matters too. There is always a complicated situation.

The St. Clair District is shaken to its roots. Who do those hens belong to? Where is the right and wrong of this matter? If the hens belong to those who have recently got them off Mrs. Handy, should they be separated from the rooster? Can families and family life be ruthlessly broken up in this way?

It is a serious question. Three other hens might be found for Mrs. Handy but what about the rooster? Does anyone know that a rooster will take up family life with just any hen?

Mrs. Handy's rooster is said to be sad. He is to droop and waste away. Something ought to be done. But where is the right and wrong of this matter?

(Written for this paper by Buck Fever. All poultry paper rights reserved.)

---

## Baptist Foot-Washing Off: Brother Admits Vote for Al

In relating the outlandish story of cancelling an important religious ritual because one of the faithful had voted for democrat Al Smith in the recent presidential election, Anderson in effect reverses the techniques employed above in his account of the Holy Rollers and the man with the radio. Here sidelong comments are kept to a minimum; little humor is injected. Rather, by relating the events of the story more or less objectively, Anderson allows the facts to speak for themselves. This selection illustrates Anderson's fondness for humorous stories that he knew his readers would like. On another occasion, for example, the papers reported the arrest of a man for striking a match to the contents of a barrel of illicit liquor and causing a fire to spread down the gutters of Marion's Main Street ("Burning Liquor Starts Fire on Old Rialto," *Smyth County News,* June 18, 1931).

"Baptist Foot-Washing Off" appeared in the *Marion Democrat* on December 4, 1928.


Ashland, Ky.—The famous annual public foot-washing and sacrament bestowal, so great an attraction in the mountains of Eastern Kentucky, will not be held by the Baptists this year.

It had been called to meet at Glo, Lawrence County, and hundreds heeded the summons, according to word from there today, but because one official of the church where the sessions were to be held, admitted he had voted for Al Smith, such a disturbance arose that the ceremonies were cancelled.

All arrangements had been made for the most successful of all public foot-washings, which have been a notable religious feature of a division of the Baptist Church in the mountains many years, being based on the Biblical story of Jesus Christ bathing the feet of disciples. The element practicing this idea hold it brings the selected few who perform the duty to a higher degree of religious favor and to the extreme of humility.

During the preliminary exercises, the recent election was under discussion. Congratulations were extended that Hoover had been elected whereupon it came out that one of the church officials had voted for Gov. Smith. Aghast at this, apparently, members of the brotherhood were in action immediately. The "offending brother" was questioned, according to the story reaching here, and not only admitted he had voted for the Democratic nominee, but expressed his emphatic satisfaction over his course. The argument got so hot that the entire proceedings, foot-washing, sacrament, benediction and all were called off, unceremoniously, leaving a considerable number of unwashed feet.

No religious ceremony in Kentucky is quite like this foot-washing. It is made a gathering place of livestock traders from miles around. Women of the neighborhood in which the meeting is to be held cook the best food they know how and all who come are welcome to partake. The stockmen ply their trade all around the place where the ceremonies are held, during recesses, but when the meeting is called to order all "business" is stopped at once and deepest religious decorum begins.

Sometimes the foot-washing and other exercises go on for days. When all is over, the mountaineers load their families in horse or ox wagons and travel home.

---

## A Veteran *and* A Stonewall Jackson Man

Though their number was rapidly dwindling, there were still veterans of the Civil War living near Marion when Anderson bought the newspapers (the final reunion of Confederate soldiers would take place in Richmond in 1932). Having been reared on his father's stories of the Civil War, and being himself an avid reader on the subject,[6] Anderson was fascinated by these elderly gentlemen and their reminiscences and wrote sketches about several of them.[7] The approaches in the following two examples differ somewhat from each other. The first is a kind of interview with a former Union soldier named W. W. Roberts, whose "eye is clear and so is his brain" despite his eighty-eight years. Anderson draws him out with questions, which he answers directly and often revealingly.

The second sketch treats George Sells, a Confederate veteran who had recently died. Therefore, much of his story is told in paraphrase. It is further molded by Anderson's commentary, by occasional fragments of reconstructed conversation, and by his own memories of the man.

"A Veteran" appeared in the *Marion Democrat* on June 5, 1928, and was reprinted in *Hello Towns!*, 225–27. "A Stonewall Jackson Man," initially published in the *Marion Democrat* on September 11, 1934, was included in *No Swank* (1934), a collection of prose portraits of individuals whose genuineness and lack of pretension Anderson admired.

### A Veteran

A fine old man of eighty-eight, Mr. W. W. Roberts of Roberts' Cove. Have you ever met him?

Age has bent his back a trifle but he is much alive and you never saw brighter old eyes or talked with a man who had a clearer mind.

He came into the print shop and sat down on the bench by the door. For forty years he had taken our paper. He had a right to respect here.

And so we talked of the Civil War and the part he took in it.

"Were there many Union sympathizers in here?"

"Not so many of us. All of us from Roberts' Cove went in on that side. There were four of us.

"And two killed."

"From where did you enlist?"

"From Cincinnati. I went out there.

"I was in the fighting right in this town, in Marion."

"Were you now?"

"I was. We were in Knoxville and were hemmed in there. We thought we were gone that time.

"Then, you know, Grant came in there with Sherman and they licked the Confederates that time. They came and got us out too.

"We came up here in the winter of sixty-four. We had a skirmish outside Marion and then we came on through. There was some fighting in the streets here. Our captain rode up to a man. He had a sabre in his hand. 'Surrender,' he said. The man shot our captain and one of our boys shot him.

"We went on up to Wytheville and destroyed the lead mines up there.

"When we were coming back, the Confederate general, Breckinridge,[8] got after us.

"We met, just outside of Marion, to the east and had a skirmish there but we were too strong for Breckenridge's crowd. There was a lot of shooting but not many hurt.

"Then we went on over to Saltville and broke that up. We broke up all the salt kettles.

"General Breckenridge and his men went off up Staley's Creek. They went on back out east to join Lee, I guess. We broke a lot of railroads up east of here.

"Some of the Union troops went back over the mountains toward Ohio. It got bitter cold and a lot of them froze their feet so that they had to be cut off.

"We went back west again and then south. We were down there when Lee surrendered."

Mr. Roberts of Roberts' Cove, Grayson County, near the Smyth County line, was among the troops that pursued and captured Jefferson Davis but was not in at the capture. He came back in here.

He says that when he came back a Marion woman stopped him on the streets once. "You look like one of the Union men who took my saddle," she said. "I didn't take it," Mr. Roberts said and laughed. "I always managed to have a good horse and a good saddle. I was a cavalryman in the war.

"I never took her saddle," he said again.

"But was there much unfriendliness when you came back in here to live? Was Grayson County strong on the Union side?" "No," he said. "They sent out five companies to fight for the Confederacy.

"I came back and went to the old farm, have been there ever since, the Roberts farm in Roberts' Cove.

"I believed what I believed and so did those on the Confederate side. We never had any slaves on our farm, in Roberts' Cove.

"Some of the worst ones to be bitter were people who had nothing to do with the war. They didn't fight. They stayed at home and talked.

"Those that fought weren't bitter when it was over. I was neighbors, same as I always was."

"Were you wounded in the war?"

"Some. Not much. I [don't?] like to talk of it.

"We used to talk during the war, boys from both sides when they had a chance.

"Once, on picket line, when a messenger from the Confederates had come in they blindfolded him and left his escort on the picket line with us. One of them was from down this way. I asked him about a girl I knew. She was all right, he said. I said I was going to sneak down in here and have a look at her. 'I wish you would,' he said. 'That's a good warm overcoat, you got on. I'd like to have it myself,' he said.

"He never got it though," Mr. Roberts said and laughed.

Mr. Roberts, of Roberts' Cove, Grayson, went out. He is eighty-eight now. A fine old man. There is a merry twinkle in his old eyes. His eye is clear and so is his brain.


## A Stonewall Jackson Man

On August tenth of this year (1934) there died, at the home of John Woods of Grayson County, Virginia, a fine old commoner, George W. Sells. He was almost ninety-three years old and except for a short interval, had lived all of his life in the one mountain community. The interval was full of rich meaning for him.

Mr. Sells left Grayson County, Virginia, when he was a young man to go into the Confederate army and to become a Stonewall Jackson man and he was with Jackson in the swift marches, the plunging attacks and the determined stands that made Jackson what Lee called "his right arm."

They didn't begin to get Lee until Jackson was gone, shot by accident by one of his own men in the same battle . . . the bloody battle of Chancellorsville . . . in which battle the mountain man George Sells was also desperately wounded.

The bullet that got George went through his upper arm as he was raising the arm to fire. The ball went on into his shoulder making a great hole, and lodged there, stayed there until he died.

In the last five years of his life the old man, a thin tough-fibered old fellow, rode often past my Virginia house. He stopped many times to talk by a bridge or under a tree beside the road and we talked always of the Civil War.

"And did you go by the Furnace Road and then by the Brock Road to get to Hooker's flank?"

"Yes. In the night."

In every battle there must be a moment. Grant knew and Lee knew. "Wait until they think you are licked and then turn upon them." Grant at Shiloh and Lee at Chancellorsville. Joe Hooker, the Northern general, sending messages to Washington. "Lee is licked," etc. It is exciting to talk to a man who has taken part in such a moment.

It was a turning point in the war, when Lee began to thrust desperately into the North, the thrust that ended at Gettysburg, and in Washington Lincoln was desperate. He had tried McClellan and then Burnside, who got his at Fredericksburg.[9]

And then came Joe Hooker, called "Fighting Joe." Joe was a good deal the braggart. He talked too much and too big. He had even gone about talking of a dictatorship . . . "What this country needs is a dictator."

Nevertheless Lincoln put him in there to stop Lee and at Chancellorsville Hooker thought he had done it. "You give us victories and I'll take care of the dictatorships," Lincoln had said to Hooker.

And Hooker thought he had done it until Stonewall Jackson made his march.

Another quick march, in the late day, in the night, by little country roads . . . George Sells, the Grayson County Virginia boy, marching with the others at the heels of Stonewall Jackson's horse. O thou grim Presbyterian!

Through the woods, past little old Virginia houses, much like

Southern mountaineers' houses. "There goes Stonewall Jackson and his men. Look out, Hooker."

There was Howard,[10] trying to feel his way around Lee's flank when Jackson and his men came roaring down at them.

(Me, to George Sells, on a country road.)

"And did you give 'em the Rebel yell?"

"We did that."

"And would you give me a sample of it now? I'm a Yank, you know."

He did. He sat on his horse and I was standing beside the horse in a country road. He stood up in his stirrups and there was a wild yell, half scream. The cry itself seemed like a living thing, flying over the hills, under the trees, and I shivered, hearing it. It may have been some old Yank tribal fear in me, hearing the yell on a rainy day in the Virginia hills.

So there was George Sells coming down, "out of the wilderness," with the Stonewall Jackson men, they giving that yell, Howard's forces crumbling up before the attack, another northern disaster . . . goodbye, fighting Joe Hooker, thou windy one . . . make way for Meade now and presently for Grant . . . another Westerner, like Hooker, but no braggart.

"Old Joe Hooker
Won't you come out of the wilderness.
Out of the wilderness,
Out of the wilderness."

Jackson's men roaring down on Howard and, at the same moment, Lee was himself on the move.

They got George Sells. He went down, lay writhing on the ground, blood spurting from his wounds.

"How long did you lie there?"

He said it must have been many hours. They didn't get to him, to cart him in to the field hospital, until the next day. They dropped him there. He said doctors kept going past him. "Look here," he cried, "I want some attention here."

Now and then a doctor would stop for a moment, look down at him, take a look at his wounds. "I'd take your arm off, man, but it's no use. You'll be dead in an hour. There are men here who have a chance for life."

"Dead, eh?"

George Sells chuckled telling me of it. The doctors were like Joe Hooker. They were too cock-sure. "I told 'em: 'I'll live past all of ye,' and I have. They told me that and they're all dead now and I'm here and I've got my arm.

"I got my Yankee bullet too. It's flat there, against the bone of my shoulder." The old man chuckled the last time he told me about it. He gave me, at my request, the Rebel yell again.

Mr. George Sells was a sturdy American commoner, a farmer. He worked hard all of his life on the land. He acquired land, a strip of woods here, a valley bottom piece there. He asked favors of no man. He was a man worth knowing. He was a good neighbor. He died, at ninety-three, August tenth, nineteen hundred and thirty-four at the home of John Woods, in Grayson County, Virginia.

---

## In the Rich Valley

For all the artistic innovations that Anderson introduced into the columns of his newspapers, there were times when he spoke straight from the heart in forthright terms. "In the Rich Valley" is one such example. Although he enjoyed ribbing certain of its residents in the newspapers for their fierce community pride,[11] in this article Anderson speaks of a day-long visit to the valley, in April 1928, with unabashed pleasure. After discoursing about the land, livestock, scenery, people, and food, he ends his paean with the simple statement, "A day of impressions too vivid to put down, of a sturdy generous people, a rich sweet land." It summarizes his impressions of the region as effectively as any he ever made. Some of his happiest experiences in the South were times such as these, spent in the out-of-doors amidst the spectacular scenery of the Virginia mountains.

Your correspondent had, in the car, going to the show of fine export cattle, just come through the winter feeding period, Jack Sheffey, Sam Kent, Bascom Copenhaver[12] and a young man named Tuckwiller from the state agricultural department of West Virginia, a young man who sure did seem to know his beef cattle but with whose name everyone had trouble all day.

The occasion of this trip was that Bob Richardson got up the idea last fall that he and the Clark brothers would get up a little winter feeding contest among the men feeding out their beef cattle for the winter. The idea was to see what fellow brought the cattle through the winter in the best shape and at the least cost.

It was one of those ideas that just catch on and spread out, like throwing a little stone in a big pool.

And then county agent [Paul E.] Bird took it up and put back of it his peculiar kind of smiling, insistent energy that would make a balky horse into a runaway.

The result was perhaps twenty men in cars from Marion, men from Tennessee, West Virginia, Chilhowie, Seven Mile Ford, the Rye Valley, and V.P.I.

All standing together in the feed lots, looking at fine export cattle in three feed lots belonging to Richardson and Clark and one fine bunch belonging to T. W. Buchanan.

And one grand feed served by the Presbyterian women at the residence of Mrs. Joe Roberts near Broadford, a feast that had all of the real Smyth County touch, than which, well, you know. O, ham, that really am.

We have eaten our way through the Methodist, the Episcopalian, the Baptist, and the Presbyterian, and all of our own religious notions have simply got in a muddle now.

And the Smyth County women. We'll end by being a Mormon yet.

But this was a cattle day. We went over Lyon's Gap, a newly re-vamped smooth road, a magnificent country. The day cold and a bit raw. From the top of Lyon's Gap one of the finest views in America. All that rich Chilhowie, Seven Mile Ford valley behind, old White Top[13] with its notch.

In front the Rich Valley spreading out, warm and rich. Clouds climbing up to the sky, looking like higher mountains in the distance. We went through Possum Hollow, another sweet land, with a clear falling stream.

Then the cattle yards. Squire Ed Clark's place first. We saw some grand steers there. Squire Ed a man who knows his business, a genial man making everyone feel at home.

We looked at his cattle and then he and Buck and Charlie Clark led the way down to another big Clark Richardson place.

On the way down, those in our car got to listening to Sam Kent tell rabbit stories; seems in his early days at Broadford Sam used to catch rabbits around there between his thumb and forefinger as they jumped out of gate posts and hollow trees, and then he would snap his finger. One snap of the finger and the rabbit was skinned. One more and it was fried, etc. We all got so fascinated that we landed at the old Captain Taylor place instead of the place we were headed for.

So Sam was muzzled and we started again. They took us all across a wide clear river on a hayrack, your correspondent thinking of bass fishing and making summer plans.

Then some more grand cattle on a beautiful farm and on to that dinner at the Joe Roberts place. Mr. Case of V.P.I.[14] made a talk. Mr. Richardson of Tenn., Roy Bell of Tenn., a big feeder over there, Mr. Patterson of Roanoke.

Then to the Tom Buchanan place. Saw there as fine a looking roan steer as I ever saw in my life. A fine old house on a hill at this historic place.

Afterwards we went down to the Fulton place where W. F. Keezee is master of ceremonies. More grand steers.

A day of impressions too vivid to be put down, of a sturdy generous people, a rich sweet land. Charlie, Ed and Buck Clark and Mr. Buchanan real cattle men. Some good straight cattle talks.

We were to have gone over to the Rich Valley High School, a thing your correspondent much wanted to do, but we got switched off.

A grand country. I am going back there again and again.

---

## Marion to Roanoke

Though lacking in the unqualified enthusiasm expressed in the Rich Valley sketch, "Marion to Roanoke," written almost a year later, is nevertheless typical of Anderson's travel writings. Decidedly impressionistic, they often contain vivid images of color ("tawny yellow fields," "a purple and grey river") and form (the two lovers walking in the rain, the suckling lambs). Because he was by nature restless and loathed idleness, and was always attuned to sources of fresh material (jotting down notes on any available scrap of paper), travel satisfied an inherent hunger. His journeys through the southeastern United States were particularly rewarding in this respect. True, he finds the smoke stacks of Pulaski, Virginia, a blight on the landscape and Salem "a sad looking town," but his impressions of the natural landscape more than compensate. In the final image he is shivering from having left the windows of the car open in order not to miss anything, but pleased "that fate has sent [him] to live in so gracious a country."

Apparently the travel articles were popular with the readers of Anderson's newspapers, as he ran a large number of them, even after his son took over the management. At a time when travel was not so commonplace as today, local readers probably enjoyed his evocations of places they might never see. Even when he wrote of familiar settings, he offered fresh perspectives. This article appeared in the *Marion Democrat* on February 12, 1929.

It is no doubt a notable drive. This writer has never driven through a more delectable land. For the procession of choice landscapes along the way, for color and land contour, there is not, I believe, a finer three or four hours' drive to be found in the country—at least not that I have seen.

About Marion and all through Smyth County the hills have a soft sensual quality. I drove to Roanoke recently on a cold grey January Sunday. There was that peculiar hushed still Sunday feeling everyone knows. It could be felt on the road, in the towns, about farm houses and almost in the fields and woods. Everyone was indoors. Sunday dinners were on. You know how they eat in Smyth County.

I left Marion at noon and what few people I met on the road were in their Sunday best. As I got over toward Roanoke more cars appeared. The Sunday dinners were over. People were out for an afternoon's drive. Near Christiansburg, on a side road, a lover walked with his lady in the cold drizzle of rain. He had an umbrella in his hand but had forgotten to put it up. I didn't particularly blame him after I looked at his lady.

In one field the spring lambing had begun. There had been four lambs born, all black. I wondered if black lambs were more forward-looking than white ones. "I must ask Paul Bird about that," I thought. All four lambs were busily nursing.

I have been told, by Mr. Burt Dickinson (who next to Mr. Henry Staley is no doubt our best classicist) [15] that in Smyth County the hills have a particular soft roundness because our country is so old. (Deep Sea Club please take note of this.) [16] It came up out of the sea earlier than most places in America. The land has had time to soften its outlines. As I have often said, it will become, some day, a painter's land.

Just this side the Reed Creek Bridge, and just beyond, as you go east, on top the two hills, the mountains in the foreground break away and you have a view of distant hills and mountains. It is breath-taking. I know of no better place on this drive to stop the car and fill yourself with the beauty of our country. Grey and tawny hills in these winter months. I thought of the view from the top of Iron Mountain, [17] at the crossing of Smyth and Grayson Counties, where you look away into North Carolina.

O, the soft beauty of our Virginia landscapes. There are no such hills anywhere I have been—and where in America have I not been? When painters come into our land and begin to paint here I hope they will be good painters and not the sloppy sentimental kind that spoil everything they touch.

Wytheville, with its wide main street, is an enticing town. There is always a peculiar air of leisureliness that comes from the sense of space. I dare say that the citizens there are as alert as in any of our towns.

Christiansburg, in Montgomery County, is another lovely place but Pulaski is pretty bad. It seems rather a shame that all through traffic must go some seven or eight miles out of the way to pass through this town. The hills there are also not so inviting. They are more sharp and rugged. I suppose it is politics that takes us all around that long detour to get us east or west.

Pulaski itself given over to the factories. They protrude everywhere. The town a little makes the flesh quiver after the beauty of Smyth, Wythe, and Montgomery Counties. It is like being in some industrial suburb of Chicago. Gaunt, half-ruined mills are everywhere. The very ground is black.

Beyond Pulaski again the lovely soft hills. I like the red brick and the comfortable-looking white frame houses they build here in this section of Virginia. Usually they stand well back from the road with green and, in the winter, tawny yellow fields between them and the highway. White farm houses built clinging to the sides of hills are particularly nice. It was a painter who first called my attention to this. It would be hard, however, to find, in all America, a more charming country home than that of Oscar K. Harris, just east of Marion, that stands right out on the highway.

At one place on the drive to Roanoke you plunge abruptly down a winding hill and find yourself following a purple and grey river in a long horseshoe bend. It is a marvelous place.

Many breath-taking places during this drive. Hills and fields and houses and then more lovely hills.

At last Salem. It does not take long to get through Salem. It is a sad looking town.

The factories and mills have not spoiled Roanoke yet. It is a hard town to spoil. A beautifully situated town, the Roanoke River, the hills, the pleasant valley in which the town stands. From your hotel bedroom window, provided you arrive before dark of a winter evening, as I did, and are fortunate enough to get a room far up and looking away to the west, as I did—and there is a smoky rain falling over the hills in the distance and the city streets.

Providing all these things happen to you, as they did to me, you will stand a moment by the window looking out and shake a bit with cold because you left the car door slides open to miss nothing, and you will be glad, as I was, that fate has sent you to live in so gracious a country.

---

## Let's Go Somewhere *and* A Traveler's Notes: The Shenandoah Valley

> In this open "letter" to Charles Bockler, a young painter whose work he admired, and in his "Traveler's Notes" on the Shenandoah Valley, Anderson introduces themes that are amplified elsewhere in his work. Maintaining that in order to see the real South one had to travel deep, to places such as New Orleans and Mobile, he invites Bockler to venture forth with him to these settings. He also contrasts this "real" South with large cities of the North and the Midwest, asserting that the cities stifle the creative spirit, whereas the unspoiled South enriches it. Anderson later added to this letter "An Automobile Trip," a journal of an actual trip from Marion to Florida in February 1929 with his friend Burt Dickinson, which he originally published separately in the Marion papers.[18]

The entries, while uneven, come to life in his descriptions of the landscape, impressions of migrating Americans, and the vignettes of human encounters.

The combined texts are from a manuscript apparently intended to be a part of his memoirs.

Anderson's account of a trip through the Shenandoah Valley of Virginia is similarly impressionistic. He expresses an abhorrence of the billboards he sees along the road. To him they are desecrations of the historical valley he had envisioned as a boy when Civil War veterans would tell gripping stories of the military campaigns that had been waged there. The Natural Bridge functions as a symbol of natural grandeur against the crass commercialization that dominates the modern age.

"A Traveler's Notes: The Shenandoah Valley" was published in the *Marion Democrat* on April 30, 1929.

# Let's Go Somewhere

Dear Charles:

It is a terribly serious lot of questions you have asked me. "Is the South to be industrialized?" "Am I trying to escape industrialism by living in the South?" "What am I up to down here?"

You must be careful, Charles. If you are not more careful you will be speaking to me of "the psychology of escape."

Only a few weeks ago I dined with a lady who spoke of "spiral evolution." My head snapped back. Do you know they even talk that way in the South sometimes nowadays. Young, intellectual Negroes do it. Perhaps I am trying to escape the age of words. I have a dreadful fear of being psychoanalyzed by a psychoanalyst. On some nights I dream of these birds. One has got me cornered on West 8th Street in New York. I squirm and squirm but cannot escape. I tore a bed sheet to pieces trying to get away from one.

She was a female psychoanalyst, too. You understand this was in a dream.

The South! Your letter has stirred me, of course. Why, man, Virginia is not of the South, nor is North Carolina, Tennessee, Kentucky, Missouri, Oklahoma. If you want that you've got to go far down.

I do not know about Florida, have never been there yet but am going soon. Once, in Paris, on a cold bleak day Fred Frieseke,[19] the painter, showed me some things he had done once when he was far down somewhere on the Florida coast. He, that is to say Frieseke, had been doing a lot of paintings of young girls and women, as full of innocence as a picnic is full of bread. I wonder why innocence tires me so. After ten minutes of it my bones ached.

So Fred Frieseke got out these other things. They wouldn't sell, he said. He knew that when he did them, so he had done them for the pure fun of it. There was one, I remember sharply, of a stretch of sand road. The sea was somewhere in the distance and there was an old Negro man struggling up along the road. A sense of the vastness of seas and yellow sand stretching, and this old black man in the midst of it—going God knows where. Something felt, put down, a painter's job well done for once anyway.

So you want the South too, Charles. You want the warm sun, cockroaches on the wall and in cracks, birds floating in a hot still blue sky, that amazing, never-to-be-forgotten song of insect life under your feet. At any rate I understand your mood. Chicago, New York, Cleveland, Detroit, all of these cities are like clenched fists. New Orleans and Mobile are like open hands.[20] They will never industrialize these cities quite. Life is too languid.

The sun shines down there, the rains are warm.

Mobile is a city few people know about. It is a sweet city. The land up above is all red and three strong rivers come racing down and pour into the bay.

The rivers wash the red earth down into the bay. I have seen the bay of Mobile like blood. I tried to make a painting of it so, but I can't paint much. You, who are a painter, know that.

There is a fountain filled with blood
Drawn from Immanuel's veins.[21]

I dare say Palm Beach and the other big swell places, down along the Florida coast, are all right but a writer or a painter, who is any good, as you and I are, can't get together the money for them. Some day a very rich man or woman will invite me down there and I'll go too. I want to see how much money they spend, how bored they are, what fine clothes the women wear. No one loves fine clothes on a woman more than I do, when I don't have to pay for them.

Of course industrial America is going to spread out everywhere. In the long run there will be factories in every town. How they are going to use all the goods they make I don't know, but folks can use a lot. Waste is an art, too. I should be a frugal man myself because I so love to go my own way, not be under too many obligations—but you should see the things with which I am cluttered.

The factories and things and more things. All the bare bones of life quite gone. Things get all mixed up. Women now can spend more money, being two-thirds naked, than their mothers were able to spend covering up everything from the eyebrows to the toes. It's a talent.

But, my dear friend, you ask me if I want to escape the industrial age. Why not? I belong to the artist class, as do you. Thank God, it is a small class. James wrote me last week.

He said he had got all het up on the industrial age, working men, etc., etc., and had gone Bolshevik.

Then he said he got to thinking—suppose, he thought, I had to listen to Max Eastman reading poems to street car conductors on strike, or Floyd Dell discussing love at a radical forum.[22] You know, women's place in the industrial scheme, something like that.

The thought threw him, he said, into something near convulsions. He got what he called "crowd fear" and fell right out of the Bolshevik class.

"I've come home," he said. "Let's go walk in a city and swear at tall buildings." He said he wanted to swear and laugh and love the world. We'll probably go some place together soon.

The South and the warm sun.

Memories.

If you want to see and feel something beautiful in this world go some time to New Orleans. Well, evening is coming on—say in early March or April. Go into the old city, to the Pontalba Building.[23] There are two of them. Take the one that faces down river. Go to the top story and get out through a window into the balcony. They call it a gallery down there.

Very well, be there, Charles, as the evening falls, and the light begins to fall—grey and golden and red and purple and blue. A man who can paint still-lifes, as you can sometimes.

Who can feel the wonder and glory in an old empty bottle, a basket of apples, a kitchen knife and a loaf of bread—a man like you can stand up there and see the tops of ships in our great American river, and see the buildings men loved when they built them, and Chartres street, and the very essence of the South, and be glad and go to bed afterwards and sleep praising his gods.

Tears in the eyes, for once anyway, because inanimate things can be so lovely.

Wharton and I were once in a little shaky cabin far down Mobile Bay.[24] We used to build bonfires there on the beach, outside the house—not because it was cold—it was hot all right—but because we both liked the sun and the flicker of the reflection of the dancing flames—come through the windows—on the walls.

The walls were of old grey wood, unpainted. We had little enough furniture, I'll tell you that.

There wasn't an antique piece within a thousand miles that we knew about.

And so the cockroaches used to come out—as big as my thumb—and walk across the grey wall. It was the South all right. The cockroaches liked the light too. We had them named.

"There goes Clara," said Wharton, and sure enough it was Clara. What a charming slender brown cockroach she was. Such legs. Such eyes. She made a little dry shuffling noise—her feet on the grey wall lit by the dancing flames. So there was Clara, and Tom and Joe came out and pursued her.

Then Isabelle came plumper than Clara, and Clarence and Jake and Martha and Cicero. They loved to dance and run in the firelight and Wharton and I sat in the darkness and saw our share of love and life.

There were cockroaches in the kitchen too. We used to leave the dishes unwashed and the cockroaches did most of our housekeeping. They ate all the bread crumbs off the floor. We hardly had to sweep at all.

Why, I like Ohio, Charles. I was born and was a boy there. When I travel from New York to Chicago, as I do sometimes, my heart always gives a little jump when I cross the state line.

I love it and I have written about it and I have paid my debt. I was twenty years in its factory towns and in the cities of the North.

I have love for Chicago too, where I lived, and its winds and the reach of the lake shore.

And men there—not artists specially, but advertising men, scribblers, as I was once, and distracted salesmen selling carpet sweepers and newspaper reporters and insurance agents.

And New York, with its clean sea winds and its smart women. That is a town.

O, I love the women of the northern cities, with their style and their graceful figures, like beautiful automobiles. I love to see them walk and ride in their expensive cars and wear their lovely gowns—if I only don't have to buy them.

But, Charles, I have, through my mother, a touch of the Wop in me.[25] It is in my eyes and in my hair and in my tummy. It works in me like yeast.

I like some dirt the sun has made pure, and some leisure and warm places and men.

I like the South—you had better come, Charles.

I like the little lumber camps down in Louisiana—the bayou country—Weeks Hall's place on the Teche[26]—and the low wet country over toward Florida; and Georgia, with its red hills, when the peach trees bloom.

And Negroes and sweat and sun.

And mules in the sandy roads.

The roads at evening when all the Negro boys and girls get out in the big road and walk and sing and talk and make love.

Soft voices untouched yet by our intense neurotic age. No neuroticism in the skies, in the trees.

They kept telling me I am trying to escape, that I am running away. It may be true. I saw a boy once step on a rattlesnake and shall never forget his white, frightened face nor how he ran. He was trying to escape too. He had, I should say, an escape psychology, spiral evolution—there was a kind of spiral movement to him—and the Lord knows what else.

That I was not born of the South was not my fault, Charles. I did not manage that. I am only writing you because I am thinking of something.

If you want to go somewhere, Charles, bring your paint brushes and come on. We'll head south—the sun over our shoulders.

Come on, Charles, let's go somewhere south.


*An Automobile Trip*

Dear Charles,

From my own town in Virginia to the town of Bristol . . . forty-five miles, early on Sunday morning, in the month of February. The start at six o'clock. You couldn't or wouldn't come so I got a man named Burt. The road was clear. We, that is to say Burt and I, were in Bristol at seven-thirty. At Bristol we turned south through Elizabethton, Tennessee, and then to Cranberry, Spruce Pine, where Burt once worked in a lumber camp when he was a boy, through a mountainous country in Asheville, where we had lunch.

In the afternoon a leisurely drive along the edge of the Great Smoky Mountains and finally over them through a high pass in Waynesville, Sylvia, Dillsboro, Bryson, Andres and to Murphy, where we spent the night.

The day cool and clear with the sun occasionally coming out.

Some of the views from the Smoky Mountains were magnificent.

At the hotel, at Murphy, a big wood fire was burning in the hotel office. Already we are in the real South. There were more Negroes about and the rooms in the hotels were not so clean and modern as in the North.

There are, however, the high ceilings, characteristic of the South, and everywhere a sense of spaciousness.

This place is at the edge of the real South, the South of pine trees, cotton, still hot nights, cruel white men, kindly fine white men. It is a place of contrasts—always a little strange—the intensity hidden away under the outward hot listlessness.

The proprietor of the hotel at Murphy knew men from our Virginia county. He was a cordial man.

After dining, he, Burt, myself and a traveling salesman sat down to talk.

We talked of the Stone Mountain Memorial, near Atlanta. Our host brought out a stone he had bought as a souvenir with a paper picture of the proposed carving of the mountain pasted on the side of the stone.

He said they stuck him for twenty-five cents. He went and put it on the mantle over the fireplace in the hotel lobby.

There had been, it seemed, a violent discussion. Jeff Davis, Lee and Stonewall Jackson were to be the chief figures of the carving. Which should go first across the face of the mountain?

It was settled Lee would be in the middle, in the foreground. That was all right. But someone had to tail the procession. Should it be Stonewall Jackson or Jeff Davis? A violent discussion arose over that point. The committee fell out with Borglum, the sculptor.[27] Millions of money was raised but a lot was spent on banquets, on speeches and on traveling.

After the quarrel they cut off all Borglum had sculpted. That cost a lot.

The proprietor of the hotel speaking—"If Jeff Davis had looked down in time and had kept his mouth shut, we southerners might have got paid for our Negroes."

He seemed to think Jeff Davis was the one to tail the procession. Burt thought so too. Being a Virginian he thought Lee and Stonewall Jackson should head the procession across the face of Stone Mountain.

As it turned out we never did see Stone Mountain, although we had planned to go there—we saved ourselves twenty-five cents—for a souvenir.

[ . . . ]

We are in the pecan belt. Where they raise anything down here they sell it too. Everyone offers you pecans—the waitresses in the restaurants, the hotel clerks, the policemen. They hold a little package or a paper sack behind their backs and approach smiling. I think it is someone from my home state, Ohio, and perhaps it is. As I once lived in Ohio, in fact was born there, I prepare for a special Ohio handshake. I get high-pressure pecan salesmanship instead.

"But I am thinking of pecans now," I said to one rather good looking maid. "I have already eaten so many I dream of them."

"But is not all of life a dream?" she asked. I bought another package.

[ . . . ]

We have passed through the great coastal plain of south Georgia and into Florida. After the hills the climate changes abruptly. Truck loads of oranges are coming up from the south and farmers are preparing the fields—plowing and planting. The smell of the new ground and the oranges in the trucks is pleasant above the all-pervading smell of gasoline.

Everyone is in business. They run gas stations, restaurants, keep roomers, conduct tourist camps.

Ohio camps, Indiana camps, Michigan camps. In an Ohio camp, with perhaps twenty cottages, we saw no one but a Negro asleep on a bench.

Michigan seemed to prevail on the road. At times we thought Michigan must just have moved down here, on four wheels. Some of the cars had little but the four wheels.

[ . . . ]

We are in Florida and have come upon orange groves. How charming they are. The trees are heavy with the golden fruit. The trees stand in yellow sand. The sky is blue overhead.

The trunks of most of the trees down here are grey, with many delicate shades of color where they stand in groups. The live oak trees are putting out their new leaves. What a living scarlet. It is lively against the grey of tree trunks and the Spanish moss.

The Spanish moss is mostly on the live oaks, of which there are magnificent ones in the older towns, but it has also invaded the groves of pecan trees and now grows on telegraph and telephone wires.

I am told it gets its food out of the air and needs no roots. We are raising a race of Americans like that.

What a strange quiet sleepy land this must have been before the northern boomers came in. The towns were buried there in the deep pine forests. No one came in and men seldom went out.

It is not an uncommon thing now to travel ten miles over a magnificently smooth road without seeing a house. A ragged Negro or a lean rancher walks in the road. Lean flea- and tick-bitten cattle hunt the sparse grass. Overhead great white clouds float, accentuating the pale blue of the sky.

Sand and more sand.

We went to a place called "The Silver Springs"—near Ocala. It is a small lake, the source of the Silver River. For a dollar they take you out in a glass bottom boat. There were fourteen in our boat. There was Burt and myself and all about us Iowa, Illinois, Michigan and Bucyrus, Ohio. We might just as well have been in Detroit.

But when we looked down—what a strange world down below. There was a waving forest of growth. There are, in the small lake, at least a dozen springs, some of them, says the Negro rowing the boat, eighty feet deep. A small forest of growth, the bottom of the lake and the springs as clearly seen as this page. Great fish lazily swimming, huge turtles with spotted blue legs and necks half hidden in the waving grass.

We were silenced—with admiration for the wonderful sight and with admiration also for the man or woman who had got his, or her, paws on the property and who must be raking in—during the season from tourists like us—as high as a thousand dollars a day.

[ . . . ]

On the trip down we did not stop in the large towns. I like the little southern towns of from two to five thousand. The hotels are not so clean as those of the North. The food is, however, good and the Negro men and boys who take care of you are something special.

They fly grinning at your slightest request. They are after your dimes, nickels and quarters but how cheerfully they go about it.

And, as everyone knows, dimes, nickels and quarters mean much. Colored girls like flashy clothes, flashy jewelry. These colored boys have problems not unlike our own. They must keep their women satisfied, if they can. My heart goes out in sympathy to them. "Here is twenty-five cents. Go get your girl a bauble. Earn a moment of happiness for yourself."

I asked a Negro man, in a hotel in Georgia, if it were not so with him and into his eyes came a peculiar look I always enjoy seeing in the eyes of another man.

There is a moment. Every man recognizes it. There has been something, a kind of wall, between two men. What matters that they are black and white, that one man is an author and the other a middle-aged hotel bell hop with a black skin, wooly hair and very white teeth.

For each man has the same problem—women—how to hold them when you want to hold them—how to unhold them when you want to unhold.

A man wants peace in this world.

[ . . . ]

We catch here in Florida a fish called the "sheephead" and it does indeed have an expression on its face not unlike that of the sheep. As with the sheep the sheephead's face comes to a point, containing the nose and mouth. It is the kind of face, innocent, unformed by thought, that, for some reason, gives you a sense of great weariness—that is to say if you look steadily at it. Some women and not a few men, as well as sheep and fishes, have such faces.

This fish, the sheephead, wears a prison uniform. Large bands of white and black go about its large flat body. We take them here from a pound to five pounds in weight and they are said to be good in the pan and on the table.

I have not eaten any of them yet although I catch a good many.

There is a long pier going out into a bay from the land and at the outer end of the dock steamers land. A railroad siding goes out there. To catch the sheephead it is necessary to have small crawfish or sand crabs but these are only to be caught in the morning when the tide is out.

At that hour I am at my desk at work and so I repair to a little stretch of sand where the pier leaves the shore.

A one-eyed Negro, very black, comes to me there. He has attached himself to me and has made with me a very good bargain. In the first place, for twenty-five cents, he supplies me with the bait needed for the afternoon of fishing and then, in addition, he takes all the fish.

So then we start, joining some five or six other Negroes who fish on the pier. The sheephead live largely upon the barnacles that cling to the piling on which the pier is built. The Negro has a long pole with a blade at the end with which he scrapes barnacles off one of the piles. The fish come to feed and then we drop our hooks.

## A Traveler's Notes: The Shenandoah Valley

The spring is a hard time to get through at best. In our country nature is a bit too lovely, too exciting. The year's passion is on. It affects everyone.

Now I am on the road alone in a car. Tough looking young men hail me at the edge of each town. I do not stop. I do not want incidental companionship. Just the same I feel lonely. Human beings must ever be lonely in the spring. Last week I wrote a story about spring loneliness. I gave it the title "Ashamed."[28]

The story was of two men made ashamed by the loveliness of earth in the springtime. They were common men made suddenly sensitive, suddenly come to the realization that when all the earth was lovely they did not feel themselves so.

One of the men felt the same way about his wife. He came home in the evening along a mountain road and had dinner with her. He could not stay in the house so went to walk alone and found another man. Each wanted to tell the other what he felt but could not find words to express it.

They were both dumb and ashamed in the presence of trees putting on leaves, a river flowing through a valley, the smell of new growth at night.

There is a great feeling of guilt connected with not picking up another man on the road, even when he looks a tough one. Why should I own this car while he has no car? This is something I cannot understand. I have money in my pocket. Where did it come from?

What right do I have to anything all men can't have? On all sides of me are men who have been more honest, who have been better citizens, who have worked harder and suffered more.

I cannot understand why things fall out for me as they do. I am a lucky man. I take what I can get.

I am in the Valley of Virginia and what a noble valley it is. My mind leaps back to my childhood. Now men have come in the evenings to sit on the front porch of the little yellow house on a back street in an Ohio town and talk to my father.

That was in the days of saloons. Some of the men have been drinking. There is the peculiar pungent smell of alcohol in the air. It is combined with the spring smells.

A great beech tree reaches with its long arms out over the porch, the house, and the little front yard.

Men are talking of other spring mornings in the Valley of Virginia, of Manassas, Winchester, Lexington, Bull Run. Once the attention of the entire world was centered on this Valley and on the Virginia country down about Richmond.

Men were struggling bitterly here. Death and carnage were on all sides. It was the North against the South. There was never any bitterness in the voices of the Yankee soldiers who came in the evenings to our house to tell over and over the tales of the war in the Valley. They admired the fighting qualities of their foes.

There were little incidental tales told. There was a man alone on a dark road at night. It might have been the very country road I have just passed in my car. The man had been out foraging and up came a group of cavalrymen. It was dark and he did not know whether they were friends or foes, so plunged across the road and got into a field. The men shouted at him and two or three shots were fired. He may have run across that field there, past that old barn and into the woods I see yonder. In the tale he told when I was a boy he got lost and wandered about all night, not knowing whether he was within his own lines or within the enemy's lines. I do not remember all the details of his night of adventure, but do remember how, as a small boy, he made me feel the darkness and terror of the night.

Nearly all old soldiers are good story-tellers. They must have learned the art at night in the camps or when, with two or three companions, they were out on picket duty or on a foraging expedition.

Now, if there were another war, the men would all be equipped with radio sets. At night cheap singers in city burlesque houses would bawl at them about some blue vaudeville Heaven.

The Valley opens out gloriously on both sides of the road. How many times it has been described. The rolling fields, the orchards, the fine old houses standing on hills among the trees. I remember the descriptions given by the Northern men come home from the war. They, however, said nothing about the sign boards.

There are fine houses to be seen and fine cattle and, as I ride up the Valley mountains, are always in sight to the right and to the left.

The yanks were down here once and must have come again. A friend in New York told me recently that the yankees were all becoming southerners and the southerners were all becoming yanks. The whole Valley now is plastered with sign boards and every other old Virginia house is a Tourist's Rest.

Cave shouts at Cave along the road and Tourist's Rest shouts at Tourist's Rest. How many caves to be gone down into and how much money to be made getting tourists down under the ground.

I am not ready to go down under the ground yet. I ignore the sign boards.

There is a persistent merchant at Roanoke. He has put up signs every mile, telling how far away you are from him. Now you are forty-two miles from his store, forty-three, forty-four, forty-five, forty-six, fifty miles from his store, fifty-one, fifty-two, fifty-three. Well, what the hell of it? Are we to be made glad, getting so far away from his store?

I went to the Natural Bridge. I could not resist that, although I did stay out of the caves. The bridge is lovely beyond words, the nearest thing to the cathedrals of the old world I have seen on this side of the water.

There is something Gothic in nature as it expresses itself here. The Natural Bridge is really majestic and vast, the great stone arch of it seeming to spring up from earth as men in the age of faith once made the great stone arches of the cathedrals go up to God. The Natural Bridge left me dumb and deeply moved.

In an age of faith men would have gone to that place to worship. But what modern preacher would dare preach a sermon down there in the deep valley under that strange and lovely arch?

---

## At the Derby

Having worked around racetracks as a boy, Sherwood Anderson never lost his fondness for horses and horse racing. This is well known from the early short stories "I'm a Fool," "The Man Who Became a Woman,"

and "I Want to Know Why." In his view horses embodied a pure innocence and keen instincts. When these powerful, primitive creatures ran
at their best they embodied a kind of mystical perfection of which few
human beings are capable. These points resonate in Anderson's account
of the running of the Kentucky Derby of 1929. It is, he suggests, something of an elitist spectacle, where police attempt to turn away college
students who lack the price of admission. It is also an exclusive social
occasion when wealthy people from the North and Midwest rent the
houses of Louisville families and install their own servants in order to
entertain their friends. Contrasted to such pretense are "these lovely
delicate creatures, so swift and so courageous." These criticisms aside,
Anderson's account of the race itself is vividly told, even though we
know beforehand that the "small trim little creature" named Clyde Van
Dusen, his jockey sitting quietly in the saddle, will win.

"At the Derby" appeared in the *Marion Democrat* on May 28, 1929.[29]

It is the great horse race of the year and horsemen are there from all
America. Year by year the racetrack at Louisville, known as Churchill
Downs, has grown. New grandstands have been added. Now they extend
nearly the whole length of the home stretch of the mile track and around
the first bend. Around the whole enclosure there is a wire fence, some
ten feet high and with strands of barbed wire across the top, but this does
not prevent boys and girls from crawling over. All day they are on the
alert. They are boys from the city and hundreds of young men from col-
leges of the Middlewest who have come to the races in Fords or have
hitch-hiked their way. They gather outside the fence while the police
stand inside. "You kids can't break in here today." "We can't, eh? We will
show you presently."

Every day they do break in, thousands of them. This year they did it
by a concerted rush at one of the gates.

There were police standing there and the boys and young men stood
outside. They began throwing mud-balls. The mud-balls came thicker
and thicker. Suddenly the rush came. Thousands went pouring in and
lost themselves in the crowd. The crowds cheered. The police looked
helpless.

It was raining this year when the great Derby was run.[30] Almost every
year it rains.

There were seven races during the afternoon and the Derby was to be the fifth race. The distance is one and one-fourth miles. There were twenty-one horses entered in the race.

They are the best of all three-year-old race horses, raised on hundreds of the big stock farms in the blue grass regions of Kentucky and in Virginia and other states where running horses are bred and raised.

This is a rich man's sport. It costs money to maintain a stable of running horses. These horses are so finely bred, they are such delicate creatures that great care must be taken. They are the sons and grandsons of other famous horses of the past. Certain sires are noted for producing sons who have tremendous speed for a short distance while others produce sons that have staying qualities. The great thing is to get both qualities in the same horse.

The horse that has both qualities becomes a famous horse, a Sir Barton, an Exterminator, a Reigh Count, an Old Rosebud. Formerly the Derby race, that has been run every year now for fifty-five years, was at the distance of a mile and a half but in recent years it has been cut to one and one-quarter mile.

A horse, to take part in this race, must be entered when he is born. An entrance fee of $25.00 must be paid at that time. Big breeders sometimes enter as many as a dozen colts. The colts begin racing as two-year-olds. If a colt seems to have both speed and staying power, ability to run the distance at speed, he is selected as the entry of some rich owner. Then an additional fee of five hundred dollars must be paid to start the horse.

To this is added fifty thousand by the Kentucky Jockey Club, owners of the track at Churchill Downs.

This year there were 159 horses entered for the race, all of whom, except twenty-one, were withdrawn before the race started.

And now the sports, the gamblers, the rich men and women have come for the race. They have come in special trains, by cars, they have tramped and beat their way there. Hotels are crowded and private homes are thrown open. During the Derby week many Louisville people rent their entire house to some rich man from New York, Boston or Chicago. He takes over the house and installs his own servants. All during Derby week he will entertain his friends at the house.

Wine flows, there is dancing and merriment. The Derby race has become a great pagan festival.

At the center of it the race horses, these lovely delicate creatures, so swift so courageous.

Many of those who come are horse lovers while others come either to gamble on the horses or to see and be a part of the great crowd.

Now the big daily newspapers all over America have been talking horse for weeks. Special writers have been employed. Every horse in the race, his chances, his record as a two-year-old is discussed and rediscussed. There is a special racetrack language.

"Put two megs bang on the beezer of Blue Larkspur. It is a shame to take the kale. Believe me I know where the wise dough is planted, etc., etc."

There are those who have come to see the beautiful creatures run and those who have come to gamble. The betting sheds are crowded now. Men and women are walking about with their hands full of money. Seats in the grandstand are at a premium. Men have paid two or three hundred dollars for a box, containing some half dozen seats, high up and overlooking the track.

The boxes are open to the weather and when it rains, as it did this year, they are a dead loss.

Thousands of people jammed into the enclosure before the stands, more thousands in the center enclosure, thousands caught in the jam in the betting sheds who will never see the race they have travelled so far to see.

And here they come, the horses, walking daintily in the deep mud. The jocks are little men with drawn tough little faces. They are dressed in gay colors.

The favorite this year was Blue Larkspur, owned by Bradley,[31] a famous breeder and racer of thoroughbreds, who has already won two Derbies. He has two horses in the race, Blue Larkspur and Bay Beauty.

And there is Clyde Van Dusen, a small trim little creature, who is to be the winner, Naishapur, from the far West, Karl Eitel, from Chicago, Voltear, Calf Roper, Windy City and many others.

They are now parading before the grandstand. The crowd pushes and squirms. Last minute bets are being made. The track is deep in water. It begins to rain again.

The horses go to the head of the stretch where the starting gate is placed. They will stand behind a tape that will suddenly spring up and send them away. They are prancing now. What intense nervous creatures. They fly at the tape, break it, so that it must be repaired time and again, they rear and kick, wanting to run, run, run.

The jocks are swearing at each other, and the starter and his assistants are swearing at the jocks. In such a press of horse it is a tremendous advantage to get off in front, to "beat the barrier," in race track parlance.

Every horse is trying to do that, every jock trying.

At last, after long minutes of intense waiting, they are for a moment all lined up and the barrier springs.

How tremendously they start, with what amazing quickness. They run desperately down the long stretch, each jock plying his whip and shouting. The horse that reaches first that lower turn can cut over now and take the inside place. He will cut the distance he has to run, he will get better footing there.

Clyde Van Dusen wins that first rush. He won the race by it. On the inside track and in front he throws mud and water into the faces of all the other horses and jocks.

He runs easily, beautifully, with a long swinging stride. His jockey sits quietly, looking back from time to time. When another horse threatens to overtake him the jockey touches the flying horse with his whip.

Can he keep that stride up, will he tire? It is a long run in such going. He does keep the lead. At the last, coming out of the mass of horses behind, Naishapur, from the far West, rushes forward but cannot quite do it. Clyde Van Dusen springs over the finishing line ahead. He has won some fifty thousand dollars for his owner and for himself the honor of seeing his name go into the records as one of the winners of the most famous American race.

---

## Adrift in Georgia: Savannah; A Traveler's Notes: Macon, Georgia; *and* Piney Woods

Late winter and early spring were favorite travel times for Anderson. Beginning in 1929 and for several years thereafter he set out for destinations farther south, recording his observations along the way in sketches that he would dispatch to Marion for publication in the newspapers. The following three selections deal with travels in Georgia.

The first, published in the *Marion Democrat* on February 4, 1930, is based on a short visit to Savannah. As a reader of history, Anderson often sought out destinations with a storied past, which of course explains part of his fascination for Savannah. However, he expresses an even greater interest in the fanciful impressions it inspires—the predominance of red in the land, the river, the sunset; the sudden disappearance of the sun; night arriving as a nude woman running through the streets.

The other two sketches derive from a trip in March 1931 and convey somewhat different moods. In speaking of the agricultural economy in Georgia, Anderson sounds more like an investigative reporter than an artist. The successful entrepreneur with no taste and down-trodden farmers living in poverty and ignorance were themes that Anderson voiced frequently during the depression years. Two weeks later, he writes of an even more characteristic incident when he gives a ride to a young Irish hitchhiker. Always an avid listener, Anderson finds that the man is a gifted raconteur who makes him "see pictures." He reminds Anderson of Maurice Long, an Irish friend who had planned to accompany him on the trip. After driving though the Piney Woods country Anderson heads for Mobile Bay and a visit with the family of Wharton Esherick, mentioned in "Let's Go Somewhere." "Traveler's Notes: Macon, Georgia" and "Piney Woods" appeared in the *Marion Democrat* on March 17 and 24, 1931, respectively.

## Adrift in Georgia: Savannah

Savannah—an old city, beside a red river, with old houses, not unlike those in the old French quarter of New Orleans. The streets are filled with Negroes. Ocean-going ships come up the red Savannah River to the docks lying below but facing the city.

The city is built about little squares, heavily wooded and with benches under the trees. There is everywhere a feeling of leisure. No one seems in a hurry. Many wealthy people from the North have come here, have bought old houses and live here through the winter months.

The city is some sixteen miles up-river from the sea and at the river's mouth are many islands. They build big country houses on the islands.

I did not go down river to any of the great houses owned by the northern rich men. None of them asked me to.

This is the land for your sunsets. Even when it has been raining all day down here the sky has a way of clearing in the late afternoon—as though to say—"Hello, Yank. Stand by. We will put on the daily show now."

It is sure a gorgeous show. There is the red land, the red Savannah River and the flaming red sky. Once I tried to paint such a sunset and when I had finished my canvas a friend looked at it. It was, beyond a doubt, a pool of blood. My friend shook his head. The secret of all modern art is to do something that no one understands. I had him there.

"It's pretty sad," he said, "who got murdered here?"

"Art," I said.

Negro boys are on the Savannah River in their row boats. They take people across the river for five cents a ride. A half dozen boats rush eagerly to meet each passenger. The Negro boys, from rowing all day against the stiff current, have become strong of arm and body. Strong men are graceful. Some of them sing as they row the passengers across the river.

Your river bank in your late afternoon—anywhere, any river—is your grand place for your idlers. I sit on the end of a pile, see the red water of the river, see a majestic ship coming slowly upstream, see the sun going down in a sea of blood.

I hear Negroes singing. I see gulls flying. "This is the place for me," I say to myself, "this suits me."

I have become like an old Negro man, walking on the big road. I talk aloud to myself. I burn cigarettes and throw the ends into the river.

The gulls are circling and diving, the water in the red river is running swiftly, Negro boys are rowing their boats and singing, a fat wench with a basket on her head comes down a flight of stone steps to the river's edge.

I should be at work. I should be writing smart magazine articles. I should be earning money.

"However," I tell myself, "if I do not patronize swell hotels, if I eat fish stews in riverside restaurants, I'll bet I can survive without working for a long time yet.

"Money will come in. Don't worry, boy. Take it easy. My own books—there are seventeen of them sailing the seas now—every now and then some poor fish will buy one.

"People in towns and cities, all over America and all over Europe, will go into book stores. They will buy books and every now and then one of them will buy a book of mine.

"Books are like ships, sailing the ports of the world. They sail into a port here and one there. They pick up little cargoes of nice, round shining nickels and dimes."

I sit thus on the end of a pile on the shore of the red Savannah River and think of myself as the master of a whole fleet of ships.

The sun sets quickly, with a strange, abrupt quickness. This is a characteristic of the sun when he goes south. There is no evening twilight. There is broad daylight, this gaudy show—the evening sun going down—and then, suddenly night.

I saw a night coming as I stood on one of the little public squares in Savannah. I was reading the stately sentences carved on the monument erected to Oglethorpe, who founded the state of Georgia.[32]

Did you know that George II gave to Oglethorpe and his pals in that adventure all the land lying between the Savannah River and a river to the south called the Altamaha, and "westward to the South Seas?" He did.

"A gaudy stretch of country, surely," I said to myself as I stood reading the words of the charter, carved in the stone.

I turned westward, facing the setting sun, thinking now of the South Seas, thinking of all that stretch of land and sea lying between me and the South Seas, thinking of Alabama and Texas, of the deserts of the movie-makers in Hollywood, of the calm and wide Pacific with whales besporting themselves, of the Hawaiian Islands and girls dancing on the beaches.

"Onward! Onward!" I cried. "On to Hawaii!"

King George gave it all away. He didn't care. "Take it," he said.

As I stood thus, wishing, as a man will wish sometimes, with large loose simplicity, that I could be King George II, giving to my friends islands and continents, rivers, forest and deserts, saying to this one, "Here, Jimmy Jones, take this hundred thousand square miles of land, plow it, plant it to crops, keep yourself warm"; and to that one, "Here, Charlie, have a Pacific Ocean, put some of these islands into your pockets—you may need them—they may come in handy."

I say as I was thinking all this, standing in the city of Savannah and reading over the old Georgia state charter, and as night came on, I saw, or imagined I saw, a woman running through the street.

Before her was the day and back of her the brown night. She was nude, a slender thing. She ran bare-footed on the stones of the city street and—at first—I could not see her clearly. She passed and I myself stood in darkness. I could not read the words on Oglethorpe's monument now.

It was the figure of night, the southern night, coming and passing. Of course, it couldn't have been a white woman, being Night.

It wasn't a black woman either. It was a brown, a high-brown, so I walked off singing a little song I know:

"It takes a long, slim, high-brown gal,
To make a preacher lay his Bible down,"

I sang.

There isn't any question but that, being in the South, being a loafer here, seeing red rivers and red lands, starts something down inside me singing again.

## A Traveler's Notes: Macon, Georgia

The peach trees are just coming into blossom in Georgia now. Macon and Fort Valley, near here, are in the very heart of the peach country. Some of the larger orchards contain thirty or forty acres. Formerly, until a few years ago, they held a spring festival at the blossom time, the festival being held at Fort Valley. There was a queen selected and the merchants all made floats, such as we had on the Fourth of July at Marion, some two or three years ago. I remember we did not select a queen. There was, however, a king. Marvin Anderson [33] (the famous Tex) enacted that role.

Last year some of the peach growers made a good deal of money while most of them failed. There was a late frost that caught most of the orchards. A few escaped and these cleaned up. One of the reasons for giving up the blossom festival was that people came for it from all parts of the United States. There was a lot of money made in peaches for a time. Too many went into it. More and more hundreds of acres went into peaches. I guess they thought they had better quit bragging about what a great peach country it was. Soon they were raising so many peaches they could not sell them.

There is a man at Columbus, Georgia, near here, named Tom [Huston]. He is a kind of peanut king. You will see his peanuts in a glass jar on the counters of drug stores at Marion. This Tom is known all over this

Georgia country. He is a southern go-getter. They have them down here too. Last year I went to visit his peanut factory. There was a great light room with thousands of bushels of peanuts rolling through it, being made into all kinds of peanut candies, peanut brittle etc. Also they were putting up the little papers of peanuts sold in the stores.

Later I was in the country, spending the day at a lake. This Tom, the go-getter, had built himself a summer home out there. I went into it. I guess he will never read this. It was atrocious. It gave you the jim-jams. There are a lot of men who know about making money but mighty few of them know much about spending it. The two gifts rarely go together. I have seen more than one man who could make his million O.K. but when he came to the job of building himself a place to live in he seemed to go fantod. Ostentation, showiness, rarely go with real comfort and elegance.

But this Tom is ingenious. Now he has invented, or has got hold of, a scheme for freezing peaches. He takes the fresh peaches and freezes them, all put up in little jars. It is said that if you eat them a year later they taste as fresh as though they had just come off the tree. When Tom opened his factory he got all the society girls from this part of the country to go work in his factory for a few days. They all got their pictures in the papers, one said to me. The peach farmer by doing that and Tom, of course, got a lot of free publicity. I don't think any of them held onto their jobs after they got their pictures in the papers. A lot of these society girls are like Dorothy Dix.[34] "Gee, I sure like my publicity," she once said to me. The peach farmers here are all looking to Tom to save the peach situation. If he can freeze onto the surplus and freeze it up they figure they'll be O.K. I guess maybe he'll do it all right.

The soil down here is almost blood red. Farming conditions in Georgia, however, are nothing to brag of. A man here told me the other day that there were several hundred thousand farmers in the state whose income was less than eighty dollars a year. There are some eighty million acres of waste land in this state. I am not sure I have my figures just right but they are big. What is a few million acres of waste land between friends? Most of this land is worn-out cotton land. Sometimes when I hear southerners talking of the glorious pre–Civil War days in the South it makes me pretty sick. These old slave owners never did any country they were in any good. Talk about love of country. They wore it out and moved on. That's what they did.

Most of the country is still worked, when it is worked at all, on the ten acres and a mule plan. Sometimes the Negro or the poor white owns the mule but more often he does not. These people live in poor little shacks out on the hot Georgia plains. There is a whole race of white men in the South, the poor whites, who have not advanced an inch in a hundred years. They are one of the real problems of the South. This is the cheap white labor the factories are moving down here to exploit. Naturally these people are ignorant. Most of them cannot read or write. They live at as low a level I suppose as white men ever did in this world. They could not get anywhere in slavery days and they haven't got much of anywhere since. They are like the priest-ridden peasantry of Europe, in that they are pretty well ridden by low-grade Protestant preachers down here, I'm told. These are the people now being crowded into the cotton mill towns. Don't blame the cotton mill men too much. I notice we all seem to be pretty hot in getting the best of the other fellow when we have the chance. At least when these people get into town they learn to read and write. They may begin to get somewhere one of these days.

I have been spending days riding on side roads among these low hills. Now and then I stop to gossip with one of these men or with a Negro farmer. Mr. J. C. Campbell or Mr. Emmett Thomas[35] should be with me here, or any man who likes to loaf and talk to all kinds of people in all kinds of positions in life. Andy Funk would like this too. One thing about spending a vacation like this, rather than going to Florida, is that you don't get in with a lot of high-livers and spend a lot of money. The trouble with spending a lot of money is that you have to go to work and earn some more.

It is rather glorious here now. Southern people have a way of taking care of you. There is an alive intelligent newspaper crowd here at Macon. The Macon *Telegraph* is one of the outstanding dailies of the South. There are men on the *Telegraph* staff who will ride with you most any afternoon. (I trust their boss doesn't see this.)[36]

Still their boss isn't any better. He's an Anderson and I never saw one of that tribe that was so hot on working.

We go and sit on a hill. There the peach orchards are spread out before us. They are just coming into full bloom. Often the hills [are] blood red. The yellow and red road runs away into pine forests. The whole country becomes sometimes a sweep of color. It is something that would drive a painter daffy. If I were a painter it seems to me I never could leave this country.

## Piney Woods

You get into the piney woods as you drive south from Macon, Ga. I drove from Macon to Pensacola, going directly south into Florida and then west. A friend at Macon had told me of a short cut and I tried to take it and got lost. I got into little back country roads but did not care. I liked it. It had rained enough to lay the dust. I passed out of the land of blossoming peach orchards and into the cotton land. The country, from being red and yellow, became grey and Spanish moss hung on the trees.

In the back country you are not afraid to pick up people on the road. On the great highways there are always men wanting to ride. You have heard of so many men held up and robbed, perhaps beaten, that you ignore them. Every time you do it, you feel guilty. The tough-looking young man you just passed up may be but a man out of work. You are uncomfortable as you hurry past him.

You have got an automobile and he has not. It is always so with possessions. There is always someone needing what you have got. Your imagination gets to work. That fellow you passed, refusing to pick him up, may be trying to get home to a sick wife and children.

O damn. You almost decide to go back and pick him up.

On the back road you pick them all up. There was an Irishman talked to me of his coming to this country as a boy. That day I had the flu. I was dopey with it. I warned him. "I'm not afraid of it," he said. Maurice Long[37] of Washington had promised to go with me down there but I had stopped him when the flu came on. I was afraid I would give him my disease.

Besides, I had the blues. It is a dirty trick to ask a friend to go anywhere with you when the black dog is on your back.

The Irishman I picked up had Maurice's flair for story telling. Most Irishmen have it. He began telling me of his father's potato fields in Ireland. His people were Irish peasants and used to come in from work on the field. There were seven big strong sons.

The mother brought a steaming dish of potatoes to the table, potatoes in their jackets. "It was all we had to eat, with perhaps a bit of meat of a Sunday but we were all strong men and good at a fight," the Irishman said. He rode a long way with me, talking and telling stories. He made me see pictures. I hope he did not get my flu.

I was getting down into the piney woods. I had lived in that country before. Once I spent a winter down there, painting and writing. I wrote a part of the novel *Poor White* down there.

Along the gulf, from far west of New Orleans to Mobile and beyond, there are everywhere deep indentations from the gulf, but over to the east, beyond Mobile, the ground rises sharply. It is there you get into the piney woods, the turpentine forests. There must be millions of acres.

It is a clean sweet land. The pine trees grow straight up with no low branches and there is no undergrowth. Below on the ground there is a soft greyish-brown carpet of pine needles. There are no fences.

The trees have all been wounded so that the sap may flow and there is a small tin pan attached to each tree. Little roads lead back, sometimes for miles, into the forests. They are the roads followed by the sap gatherers. In such a clean wood, with the roof of branches overhead, sounds carry far. At one place there were some men at work somewhere, a long way off. They must have been Negro sap gatherers. They were singing and I could hear their voices running under the trees. I stopped my car and sat for a long time listening to the sweet sounds. No people sing like Negroes at work. The song makes you glad you are alive.

The sunlight flickers down through the trees. Everywhere there is a good piney smell. I sat in my car, deep in the woods, reading a book. What did I care when I got anywhere? A man with a pack on his back walked through the woods near me without seeing me. He never did see me. He was talking to himself. Perhaps he had just come from his home, from some cabin in the piney woods, and had been quarreling with his wife. So husbands and wives quarrel in the piney woods too. He must have imagined her walking with him. "No, I won't," he growled. "I want you to shut up. I'll see you in hell." He passed. He never saw me.

Having recovered from the flu but still depressed, I went to the house of a painter I know, down on Mobile Bay.[38] The painter was in the North but his wife and children were there, in their winter home. We all went for an afternoon down on the lower end of the bay and the children and I played on the beach. The painter's wife had been ill but had begun to grow strong again. I slept on the porch of the house with the two children and at daylight felt a stirring in my bed. The two children had come and got into bed with me. There was a mockingbird singing in a nearby live oak. One of the kids put his hand to my face. "Gee, I wish you were Wharton," he said, meaning his dad, the painter who was somewhere in the North.

# 4 Southern Labor

During 1928, Anderson's first full year as owner-editor of the Marion weeklies and the period of his most intense involvement in them, his marriage to Elizabeth Prall was deteriorating. In December she left to visit her family in California; the two never saw each other again. Sometime during 1928 the Andersons had met Eleanor Copenhaver, daughter of a prominent Marion family and a representative of the national YWCA, whose primary assignment was working with women in the South. Following Elizabeth's departure, Anderson's friendship with the Copenhavers deepened, and Eleanor began to enlist his interest in her work. In early April she invited him to a meeting of striking rayon workers in Elizabethton, Tennessee. His account of this meeting, published a few days later, makes note of "the woman I had driven to Elizabethton."

This marked the beginning of a new dimension in Anderson's interests and work. His explorations into southern labor would eventually take him to other sites in Virginia, such as Danville and Abingdon, and still farther afield to North Carolina, Georgia, and West Virginia. His accounts of these expeditions would follow the familiar pattern of treating the larger issues in terms of selected individual lives and incidents that revealed their effects. For example, his novel *Beyond Desire* (1932) would deal with labor conflicts in a North Carolina mill town.

The region during this period was rapidly becoming the embodiment of Henry Grady's prophetic vision of a "New South" expressed some forty years before. In this exhortation, Grady had encouraged northern labor interests to put former sectional differences behind them and to locate their industries in the South. There they would be welcomed by a skilled work force, unlimited land, and a supportive social infrastructure.

Though southern industrialization had proceeded with a seemingly inexorable momentum, many in the South thought its effects deleterious and sought to stem the tide by advocating a return to traditional agrarian values. But Anderson's overriding concern was for the common worker. He was also a proponent of unionization, which he saw as labor's best hope for decent working conditions. The issue dominated this period of the South's industrial history, and Anderson was uncharacteristically outspoken in advocating it.

The extent of Anderson's involvement in southern mills and factories in the 1930s can be determined in part from such sources as *Perhaps Women* (1931), *Puzzled America* (1935), and *Sherwood Anderson's Memoirs* (1942); however, he wrote extensively on other forms of labor as well.

---

## Elizabethton, Tennessee

The situation in Elizabethton, a new mill town in eastern Tennessee near the Virginia border, was classic in the South of the 1920s and 1930s. A textile plant was employing large numbers of women from the hill country who worked for low wages under stringent working conditions. When they struck, management dug in its heels. Anderson's sympathies were of course on the side of the workers; however, his means of expressing them reflect the artist far more than the laborite. He approaches the workers' plight from the standpoint of the inherent dignity he recognizes in the women, citing their firm, straight bodies, their natural grace. In contrast, he pictures the cheaply built buildings in the town and its new "monument" with the cement already falling off. Here and throughout his work, it is the human measure by which he assesses a situation. Institutions—the church, government, big business, societies in general—were strong but corrupt and uncaring for the individual. It was as true in Elizabethton as it had been in Winesburg.

"Elizabethton, Tennessee" was published first in *The Nation*[1] and reprinted in *Puzzled America.*

To Elizabethton, Tennessee, where there had been a recent flareup of labor trouble among the employees of a huge rayon plant. This is the town so often written up as "the wonder city," "Elizabethton the beautiful," etc. To me it seemed neither very beautiful nor very ugly.

But surely the town is in a lovely place. I had with me a woman engaged with an organization that works for the betterment of the condition of mill women and as we drove down through the beautiful valley toward the town she told me many interesting and sometimes terrible things about the condition of working girls in Southern mill towns.

To me the town, when we got into it, seemed not unlike hundreds of Iowa, Illinois, and Ohio county-seat towns. Earlier there was a period of better building in America. New England felt its influence as did parts of Pennsylvania and all of the South. For some reason these earlier buildings, of stone, brick, and heavy timbers, had more beautiful outlines than the buildings of a later period.

Then followed a period of box construction. Someone discovered the scroll-saw. Cheap buildings with cheap do-dads on them.

Here is a town that, when I was there, was not more than five years old.[2] Already the buildings had that half-decrepit, worn-out look that makes so many American towns such disheartening places. There is a sense of cheapness, hurry, no care for the buildings in which men and women are to live and work. "The premature aging of buildings in America," said my friend Van Wyck Brooks, "is the saddest thing in America."

We went to the hotel to dine and I went into the washroom. Such places—intimate, personal places—mark a town. The hotel, but a few years old, already had that shoddy, weary air characteristic of cheap, careless construction.

There were a few tiny fragments of cheap soap. The wash-bowls were dirty. Such things are important. They tell a story. "We are not in this place to live. We are here to make money."

We drove out to the two great rayon plants in the evening, just as the employees were leaving. This was mountain white labor. About three-fourths of all the laborers employed were girls.

They were shockingly young. I saw many girls that could not have been beyond twelve or thirteen. In these towns, I am told, children have two ages, the real age and the "mill age." It is easy to escape responsibility. "If she lies about her age," etc.

Of course she lies. These are the poorest of poor people, from the hills, the mountain gullies. They went with weary steps along the road. Many of the young girls were already developing goiters, that sure sign of overwork and nervous debility. They had thin legs and stooped shoulders.

The mills themselves had that combination of the terrible with the magnificent that is so disconcerting. Anyone working in these places must feel the power of the mills and there is a sense in which all power is beautiful—and also, to be sure, ugly. Oh, the beauty and wonder of the modern intricate machine! It is said that many of the girls and women in these places are half in love with the machines at which they work.

There is always the old question—to make men rise in nobility to the nobility of the machines.

It is obvious there had not been much nobility in Elizabethton. The girls there were underpaid, they were not organized, they had no power.

A strike flared up, starting, I was told, as a kind of spontaneous movement among the girls. It might have been met easily at first. The employers were brutally casual about it.

The girls began to organize and the American Federation of Labor sent an organizer. His name was Hoffman,[3] a fat man, of the characteristic sledge-hammer, labor-organizer type. A group of men of the town—they had not all been identified yet—went to his hotel at night and escorted him out of town at the point of a gun.

Another bit of characteristic stupidity. He came right back. Such a man would know well the publicity value of such a crude performance on the part of the local business men. It was all nuts for him. Obviously it is true that labor as well as industry and capital has the right to organize. If you own a factory you do not have to employ organized labor if you can get out of doing so. But you cannot stop labor organizing. You cannot throw a man out of town because he comes there to help labor organize. Modern, more intelligent and shrewd industrialists have learned there is a better way to handle such matters. They give labor what it wants. Tack the price on for the buyers at the other end. They throw the burden on over to the consuming public. The middle-class do not know how to organize and apparently the farmers will not organize. And the industrialists are slowly finding out that cheap, underpaid labor is in the end no good.

So here were these girls organizing and the movement grew like wildfire. The men came in. All Elizabethton was apparently being organized. Later, as almost always happens, it all fell to pieces.

There is one thing about being a writer. You can go anywhere. Had I not written a book called *Poor White*? It was the industrial history of a town very like Elizabethton. And I had written *Winesburg, Ohio,* stories of the private lives of poor people in small towns.

I myself came from the working class. When I was a young man I worked in factories. These working people were close to me, although I was no longer a working-class man. I had my own class. I kept looking and wondering. Occasionally I tried to put down in words what I saw and felt.

And here is a peculiar thing. I am thinking now of working women. I take it that all women want beauty of person. Why not? How often I go to dine, for example, at one of the hotels in my own town. There are the guests coming in. We, in my town, are on the Lee Highway. Many women come here. They are rich women, going south to Florida, or returning to the North from Florida. They are dining at the hotel.

How few of them have any grace of person, any grace of body. I look from these women to the working women, the waitresses. How much nicer they seem.

It is true everywhere I have been. In the great fashionable hotels a man does sometimes see beautiful young girls but the older people among them are usually quite miserable looking. I mean they are usually smug, self-satisfied about nothing, without character. Hard work, trouble in life does, it seems, after all beautify, to one with an eye at all trained to see beauty.

A moment ago I spoke of my own position in life. I am accepted by working people everywhere as one of themselves and am proud of that fact. The other evening in Elizabethton there was a secret union meeting being held. I went up into a rather dirty hallway, crowded with girls. "Perhaps this Mr. Hoffman has read some of my books," I thought, "he may let me in here." There was no doubt about the woman I had driven to Elizabethton. They would let her in. And so I sat in a window-sill and along came this man Hoffman, the labor organizer. "Hello, Sherwood Anderson," he said. "Do you want in here?"

"Yes, of course. I want in everywhere. To go in is my aim in life. I want into fashionable hotels and clubs, I want into banks, into people's houses, into labor meetings, into courthouses. I want to see all I can of how people live their lives. That is my business in life—to find out what I can—to go in."

I did not say all this. "Sure," I said.

And so I was escorted into a room packed with girls, with women, boys, and men.

It was a business meeting of this new trades organization, a certain local of the Textile Workers of America.

There were girls everywhere. What a different looking crowd from the one I saw but two hours ago, coming from the factories.

There was life in this crowd. On the evening I was there some fifty new members were sworn into the organization. They came forward in groups, awkward young girls, awkward boys, men and women with prematurely old faces, not tired now, full of life. As each member was sworn in, applause shook the room. A woman was outside who had no money to join. "I'll pay for her," cried a working man, coming forward out of the crowd. He put his hand into his overall pocket and slapped the money down on a table.

More and more men and women were crowding up the narrow hallway outside. They wanted to join. The crowd laughed, jokes were shouted about the room. "Why, there's Red. Hello, Red. Are you in?"

"You bet I am in."

There is a report that the company is going to fire all those who join. "Well, then we will go back to the hills. I lived on birdeye beans before there was any rayon plant and I can live on birdeye beans again."

At least there was joy in this room. Men and women, for the time at least, walked with new joy in their bodies. The men became more dignified, more manly in their bearing, the women more beautiful.

And many of these mountain girls are lovely little creatures. They have, at least when excited, straight hard little bodies, delicately featured faces. I sat beside a child that couldn't have been over thirteen—no matter what her "mill age"—and as I looked at her I thought how proud I would be to have been her father.

I felt that way about all of the people in the room. Those working men I could accept as brothers, those girls as sisters. They were and are closer to me, as are men everywhere who work in fields, in factories, and shops, than any other class of men or women will ever be.

And who loves luxury more than myself?

It is very puzzling. I came away from Elizabethton puzzled. How will it all come out?

"At least," I thought, "these working men and women have got, out of this business of organizing, of standing thus, even for the moment, shoulder to shoulder, a new dignity. They have got a realization of each other. They have got for the moment a kind of religion of brotherhood and that is something."

It is a great deal more than any wage increase they may win from their struggle.

They had built a monument in Elizabethton. It was at the head of the main street. I fancy they felt that the town should have a monument. Almost all towns have. Perhaps also there was nothing in particular to build a monument about. Apparently they just built one anyway. I walked around it several times but could find no inscription on it. It was built of brick with a thin outer coating of cement. Already it was falling to pieces. How I would have liked to see one of those delicately featured, hard-bodied, little mountain girls, done in stone by some real artist, standing up there on the main street of that town.

---

## O Ye Poets

For all his concern with the human standard, Anderson did not see modern machines as inherently evil. To the contrary, he was fascinated with them and the feats they could perform. In such sketches as "Machine Song"[4] he even maintained that they took on a kind of mystical life of their own. His major concern lay in the issue of accommodation: how can machines be made to serve and respect human needs, rather than dominate them? Or, conversely, can human workers adapt to the superhuman challenge represented by the machine? He implied time and again that mechanization had proceeded at a much more rapid pace than the human ability to respond. Until the proper balance could be achieved, machines would be the masters and people the slaves. But as a progressive thinker, he did not regard the situation as hopeless. "O Ye Poets" is, rather, a modernist's challenge to devise a new language capable of giving expression to the miraculous spectacle of mechanization.

"O Ye Poets" and "Night" (which follows), both previously unpublished, are part of a series of "Industrial Notes" that Anderson apparently intended to publish as a unit. The factory tours he describes occurred in February 1930 in Greenville, South Carolina.⁵

Eighteen hundred looms in a room. I kept thinking of race tracks. At first I did not know why.

It was because of the mill superintendent. He was a tall man with stooped shoulders. One shoulder hunched up. His pants hung on him in a peculiar way. He had impersonal gray eyes.

He did not want to fool with me. I could see him sizing me up. He had no doubt been given instructions. "Give this man your attention." He did not want to do it.

"I have only thirty minutes. I have to see some men."

"Very well, turn me loose in there. I'll get what I want."

We started. This is a very fine mill. It is a large one. They make fine cloth.

They weave silk and rayon. They weave fine cotton. South Carolina and Georgia cannot raise cotton fine enough, with long enough fibre, for this mill. Their cotton comes from New Mexico. It is grown on new land.

I know now why I am thinking of race tracks. In the very heart of the mill, in the spinning room, the long batteries ("sides" they call them) of spinners going away into the distances—side after side—the spindles flying, movement everywhere—not here the crazy dance of the looms but something flying swiftly, swiftly just the same—

There is a clear track down between the sides. It is like the home stretch of a race track.

There is a little mill girl coming along, between the long motor-driven sides.

Think of her as walking rather rapidly, with apparent unconcern, amid two thousand flying spindles. She is watching for broken threads.

She is a slight little thing. She has put rouge on her lips. Like all mill girls, her hands are very much alive.

The mill superintendent looks exactly like a man I once knew. He is dead now. He was a famous man whose name was Pop Geers.⁶ He was the best trotting and pacing horse driver that ever lived.

The same impersonal expression of the eyes—the same walk. Pop Geers's pants hung on him just like that. You were always thinking they were going to fall off.

I used to see Pop at the tracks in the evenings. He seldom left the tracks to go up and sport about town in the evening, as other drivers did. He sat on an old chair or an upturned box. It was always quiet there.

He was a quiet man when he was not driving a race and in a race he remained quiet until the vital moment came.

Then he became all alive. A kind of fire seemed to run through him. It was transmitted to the flying horse.

More speed. More speed.

As though reading my thoughts, the mill superintendent said, "At night I go home. I have my supper. I sit in a chair and take off my shoes. You see, I'm on my feet all day. I turn the radio on."

"Well?"

"I just sit there."

I hadn't asked him what he did in the evening.

This is the fastest, the cleanest, the most efficient mill I have been in. The floor is clean, the walls, the machinery, the ceilings.

The room seems as large as the whole fairground with its race track, where Pop Geers drove fast horses through waiting breathless crowds to the wire.

The ceilings and walls of the spinning room in this mill are white. There are fifty-six thousand flying spindles in this one room. Each spindle goes thousands of revolutions a minute. Let's say four thousand. If a man is going to push off into this ocean of modern American industry, he might as well get used to figures. Four times fifty-six is two hundred and twenty-four. Let's say two hundred and twenty-four million revolutions a minute in this room.

What the hell is a millionaire?

Let's go on a figure jag.

The cotton brought into this mill from New Mexico, the long staple New Mexico cotton, is cleaned and tossed and pitched and dampened and dried.

It is picked up and put down.

It is shaken. It is blown through pipes.

Presently it emerges in a flat sheet.

Two such sheets are rolled into one, then four, then eight.

It is drawn out into yarn. The yarn from four spindles is twisted into one strand of yarn.

As that is done, it is stretched out, elongated.

It is done time after time, four into one, eight into one, sixteen into one.

It is called "doubling."

Now look. These are mountain white people working in this room. In the mountains they have always made moon whiskey. In the old days, before prohibition, when they made moon they ran it through the still. Then they ran it through again. They called that "doubling."

Sometimes they did it three or four times, to make the moon pure, to get the poisons out.

They don't do it since prohibition. Who gives a damn for poison now?

Do you know what they do in this mill?

They "double" the cotton one million, nine hundred and sixty-nine thousand, nine hundred and twenty times.

What's the use worrying about being a millionaire? Millions are as common as dirt in here.

Millions of bolls of cotton in fields, millions of particles of dirt in the air, in cotton mills, millions of spindles flying, millions of miles of yarn being spun, millions of dollars raked in, a million wheels revolving, belts flying, motors humming.

When you push off into modern industry you push off into a sea, a Pacific Ocean of millions.

The walls and ceilings of the great room are white. The floor is yellow, a dark yellow. There are some beams in the ceiling not painted. They are yellow, a dark yellow.

They have painted some of the flying wheels blue, some green, some red.

There are baths of color being given yarn in this mill. Here in this town there is a dye works. Millions of balls of yarn and thread go there to be impregnated with colors.

They come back red, blue, green, yellow.

There are a thousand shades.

There are delicate pastel colors.

Great bins are filled with colored yarn and thread.

The silk and rayon comes in many colors. It shines. It glistens. There are machines here, handling cotton, silk, rayon, all at [high] speed—flying color here.

Do you know what quilling is? Have you seen the girls "drawing in," harnessing looms?

Have you seen the man "tying in?" The man I saw was a cripple. He had lost a leg somewhere. He had soft brown eyes.

He combed the glistening hair of the loom. He brushed it. He made each shining hair lie in its place.

He tied it in, hair by hair, perfectly, each of the thousands of tiny strands in its place, not one wrong. He put a thousand strands, each in its place, in three minutes. I saw this wonder. I saw him tie the strands in.

Let us not speak of the old craftsmanship being gone. I have said that. I lied.

Who made these machines in this room?

Go into the clattering roaring loom room. If I keep writing I shall worry the mill men to death. A thousand people will be wanting to go into the mills.

Look at that loom. Watch its movements. Catch the dance of it. Note the infinite multiplication of parts, each moving, each doing its work.

Perfectly. Delicately.

The roaring sound in this room, the deafening clatter, is made up of a hundred thousand little sounds, each in its place.

Man has done all this. His brain conceived it. His fingers made all of these parts. His fingers fitted them into place.

There are warpers. There are silk winders. There is glistening rayon in hanks. There are machines I do not yet know the names of.

There is color everywhere. There is movement.

Who says craftsmanship is dead?

I said it?

I lied.

There is a thing in all this modern industry no one takes into account. The mill owner says to me, "These people, on the farm, worked longer hours than they do here.

"A man follows a plow and a mule from dawn until dark. It is brutally heavy labor.

"He gets little enough pay for it.

"You watch these girls and young men in our mills. They do not work hard. They walk quietly up and down.

"You watch them. Are they working hard?

"To mend, now and then, a broken thread. Is that hard work?"

What is not taken into account is speed. The more efficient your mill the faster it moves.

Do they think I'm a fool? I spent two hours in a room with eighteen hundred looms flying. At the end of that time I stumbled out of there so exhausted I could hardly walk.

Suppose I grant you that I am more sensitive than these people. I note color, movement, everything in this room.

I see the beauty of the machinery, its terrible swift movement.

Emotions pass through me, emotions these people do not feel.

But look at me. I am a strong man, in the flush of my manhood.

I do not stay in here ten hours. (In mills in Georgia little mill girls stay twelve hours.)

It is not for nothing they want young kids.

All people, if they are to stay in modern industry, have to acquire more speed. Kids acquire it more quickly.

It cuts them down though, wears them out. They grow dull.

The only salvation is to grow dull.

The mill owners, modern industrialists everywhere, are not facing facts.

There are nerve facts to be considered too.


A mill owner says to me sharply—"Do you pretend that you know more of my people than I, who have lived with them all my life?"

"Yes. I would know more of your clerk, in the outer office there, in ten minutes than you would know in a whole lifetime spent sitting in a room with her."

Have you ever seen a beam warper work? Once Pop Geers drove three fast horses almost at top speed, for a mile, setting a new race record. He said afterward that he would never do it again in this life.

A beam warper doesn't mind. It drives sixteen, thirty-two, sixty-four, any number of flying spools, with absolute accuracy. When they are working rayon or silk or colored cotton you should see that sight.

There is something Greek here. At the moment the modern textile mill, as you stand at the heart of it, seeing these complex machines, the movement, the play of color, the intricate dance and drive of all these complex high-powered machines—at the moment the whole place becomes a place of Greek gods and goddesses.

Who drives the horses of the sun
Shall lord it but a day.[7]

A beam warper, I declare it in the name of the old gods, a beam warper, working with glistening and colored cotton, silk or rayon and with all the spools flying, is as beautiful a thing as man ever made.

A beam warper. A hot air slasher. A waste cord breaker.

A tyer in. A warper in.
A hank clock and gearing.
A tape slasher. A size kettle.
A flying twister, a ring twister, a birkenhead creel.
Come on, ye poets. Where are you?
Do you want language? Get ye into the mills.

The mill superintendent who went through the mill with me was just Pop Geers. He had the same eyes, the same impersonal air.

He was like all of the others. He spoke with contempt of those who say mill workers are slaves, that they are overworked.

He was in the mill with me three hours.

We came out and I looked at him. He was like me. He was tired.

He would have denied it but you may depend upon it—all the nerves of his body were tired.

---

# Night

Anderson left unpublished a three-part manuscript titled "Guns—Women—Night" that deals with the interplay of people and machines as seen from three different points of view. The third section is the best developed and continues the theme of accommodation between worker and machine. Unlike the strike setting of "Elizabethton, Tennessee," the factory in this sketch is pictured during a regular night shift. There are no villains or heroes. Anderson has kind words for the plant manager, to whom he introduces himself as "an artist in a machine age" wanting to draw near to working machines and to see their effects on people. Their exchange is open, nonaccusatory; there is even a touch of humor when the lights go out. Anderson ends by remarking on the ability of young women workers to cope under these conditions. The observation recalls the central theme of *Perhaps Women*—that the best hope for modern men, confused and weakened by the machine age, lies in the strength of modern women.

I had gone into the mill at night. It was a big textile mill. All had been arranged.

There were thoughts of that sort in my head that night when I stumbled with muddy shoes through a mill village to a mill.

I had been seeing many beautiful machines in many mills. I had been thinking of the men who had created these machines, who still create them.

I remember stopping in the road that night, looking toward the mill, hearing its roar.

Not entirely unconscious of the night and the stars over-head.

Thinking the men who create new machines constantly, new variations, elaborations and refinements of the machines, must be really creative men.

Thinking of the women at the machines in the mill.

There had come to me several times the odd notion that modern working women, in mills I had visited, were half in love with the machines they tended.

"Perhaps," I thought that night, "they but reach through the machine and toward the creative imaginative man in whose brain it was born."

Thinking thus, I came to the mill gate where, by appointment, the mill superintendent was to meet me at a certain time.

He was a tall, heavily built, blond young northern man.

(Although southern owners of mills object terribly to the coming of northern labor organizers into the South, they do not object to the coming of capable mill superintendents, capable northern mill managers.)

The young superintendent who took me into his mill that night was a very capable one. Like all such men he was curious about my coming.

"What are you up to? What do you want?"

It is a little difficult to explain.

"I am an artist in a machine age. I want to draw near the machine at work.

"I want to see what it does to people.

"I want to see what it does to me."

"Are you trying to make trouble between us and our employees?"

"That is not my purpose.

"You must understand that naturally successful men, men who own mills, millionaires and the like, are less interesting to men like myself than unsuccessful, defeated men."

Usually on such occasions there are no such direct questions asked or direct answers given.

The particular mill superintendent I was with that night was a modern machine man. He was not much aware of workmen and workwomen as people. The whole mill was to him one vast machine. He felt it that way. From the point of view of modern industry he was a tremendously capable, up-to-date mill man. I liked him.

That particular mill did things for its employees. They built clubs and conducted schools. They had men and women recreation supervisors. During the walk through the mill he told me, quite frankly, he thought it was all nonsense.

It was a kind of fad with mill owners.

To square themselves with themselves perhaps.

"But why need I square myself with myself? I have a job, running this mill. I'll show you how I run it."

I liked him. If I had to work in a mill I should like to work for him. I told him that. He had it coming to him. He was a good one all right.

We were in the great loom room. It was one of the largest I was ever in. There were twenty-six hundred looms going in that one vast room.

There was speed, speed, speed.

There was a room of modern power.

My nerves are becoming somewhat attuned.

I can stand it better than I could at first.

I will not try to describe again here the sustained roar, the play of colors. No one who has not been in a modern mill will understand it anyway.

It shakes you. It turns you inside out. It plays with you.

The looms dance with the crazy modern dance of modern industry.

You have to be trained to it to be able to talk in such a place. People who work in there learn to strike with their voices a certain key that will carry through and above the uproar. There are trained modern industrial men who can go into such a room and point out to you distant machines that are not running to the fullest capacity. They tell by the sound as a trained man tells you what strings are slack in a piano.

The mill superintendent led me upstairs to a little elevated platform and left me there.

Blue lights were playing over the room.

The mill at night is something different than the mill during the day.

It is somewhat crazier, more vital.

Everyone feels it.

The women, working in the mills at night, go a little crazy, everyone says.

There is a sea of moving color, touched always by the strange blue night lights.

The roar and clatter goes on and on.

There are machines under the ceiling that throw a fine mist down over the machines.

That is to dampen the cotton a bit, make it more flexible, more workable.

The blue lights play in the mist too.

The room is vast. At night it becomes more vast.

That mill superintendent had done something I had never seen before. In order to help the operators to see in what loom a thread had broken (the looms automatically stop when a thread breaks) he had placed atop each loom a slender steel wire.

On the top of each of these upright wires a colored card had been placed.

The colored cards also danced crazily in that room that night.

It all went on and on, the dance of the looms, the roar of sound, the play of colors. The play of the lights in the mist went on and on.

And then something happened.

Nothing serious.

The lights went out. Something, some little temporary thing, had happened to the lighting system in the mill.

We were plunged in darkness.

I stood on the elevated platform. There was the same sustained roar.

But now there was no light in the mill. It was night in there as it was outside.

The whole thing was intensely dramatic. Perhaps my nerves were a little upset. I leaned over a rail on that little raised platform, looking down. I had been having thoughts about men and working women earlier that night.

And then, out of the darkness down there, a voice came up. It was a clear feminine voice.

"Kiss me, dear, quick," it said.

"Kiss me, hold me tight, quick, before the lights come on again," the voice said.[8]

And then the lights came on. There were the men and women, the workmen and the workwomen down there under the looms.

They had been standing still while the lights were out. Now they moved again, going from machine to machine, mending broken threads.

That was all. The superintendent had come and got me and led me out of the mill.

I walked past many workmen and workwomen. The women all smiled. Some of them laughed.

They had all heard what I had heard while the lights were out.

Was it just a woman, some young workwoman, laughing at the mill and at all the men who had created the mill?

I have seen more than one modern working woman entirely capable of that.

---

## Moderating the Ransom-Barr Debate

The discussion of industrialization in the South reached a crescendo in 1930. This was the year that John Crowe Ransom and eleven other southern Agrarians issued their manifesto, *I'll Take My Stand*. It was also the year that Stringfellow Barr, editor of the *Virginia Quarterly Review*, published in the pages of that journal an article titled "Shall Slavery Come South?" that challenged Ransom's conviction that the region should remain rural and agrarian, thereby retaining the finest qualities of its past. But Barr argued that industrialism was already here. The best use of southern resources would assure that workers be treated fairly and that industry be properly controlled. This did not satisfy the Agrarians, who associated industrialism with Communism and who wanted nothing short of an agricultural economy for the South. The dialogue soon became more than a war of words on paper. On November 14, 1930, the Richmond *Times-Dispatch* sponsored a debate between Ransom and Barr at the Richmond City Auditorium; the topic was "Industrialism vs. Agrarianism." Sherwood Anderson was chosen to moderate.

Anderson often claimed that he disliked public speaking. However, when an opportunity came he rose to the occasion, and frequently boasted of stealing the show.[9] The full typescript of the debate's introductory speech by Anderson suggests just such a virtuoso attempt, as the text runs to fifteen pages. The following text omits several digressions and offers passages having the closest bearing on the topic.

[ . . . ]

There are a lot of things about this meeting and this debate. Personally, I am not much worried about these two men . . . Barr and Ransom. I think they are really up to about the same thing. They have different slants but the same impulse. That is about it. This debate is being held in Richmond, Virginia, the former capital of the southern confederacy and that is good too. Now I want you here in this audience to take a look at me. I'm not so young. I'm a post–Civil War man, not a post–World War man. I'm not a son of Virginia. If there is any connection between a man like me and the state of Virginia, it will not bear going into too closely. If I am in any sense at all a son of Virginia, I am an illegitimate son.

And I am here, a middlewesterner, as I have suggested, whose father fought on the northern side during the Civil War and I am introducing these two men who are both interested in combatting the effects of the northern victory in that war.

The South fought that war and lost it, but do not be confused by that fact. The North fought and lost it too. They got something they never knew they were fighting for or they wouldn't have fought. They got industrialism. Do not be confused about that. There are a lot of northern men not so sure nowadays that the results of the Civil War in America were exactly the glad joyous things we have all, North and South, been told they were.

This debate here concerns, as I understand it, primarily the South, what attitude the South shall take toward this strange perplexing new life, into which we are all nowadays plunged because of the machine.

We are, as everyone knows, in a time of depression. Well, the depression is not altogether a financial matter. It is deeper than that. This is, I think, not only in the South but throughout all America a time when thoughtful or sensitive people are beginning to question, as perhaps it has never been questioned before, the tone and effect on all of us of our American life.

We are to hear debated here the question as to whether it is better for the South to definitely attempt to set its face against industrialism and attempt to recreate the old southern life, an agrarian life, or whether it shall embrace industrialism and try to make of it something better . . . more fitted to the need of southern people.

I am myself, as I have said, not a southerner. I was born in the industrial North, under the shadow of the very kind of factories that are now invading the South and so profoundly affecting southern life. At present I live in the South and I can truly say that since I have been a grown man there has always been in me something that has called me south.

And it is not because of the climate or the soil down here. It is not because of your southern aristocracy. I don't believe in that in one way but there is a way in which I do believe. I am, I hope, not the kind of man, as commonly found in the North . . . a professional southerner. In so far as you born southerners become pretentious in your southernness, thinking that your own cotton-raising fathers were better than my own corn- and steer-raising middlewestern fathers, I am against you, but in so far as you hold up the ideal of an aristocracy as meaning a desire for gentleness, for sympathy, for tenderness toward life, I'm for you.

What I like about the South is that I think that you do hold onto something like this.

I have been coming south since I was a young man. I am a writer and almost every book I have ever written has been written in the South. There is yet (who with any knowledge of American life can doubt it?) a difference in the tone of life in the North and in the South.

It is because of industrialism, these factories sweeping across the country, invading cities, invading towns. They have changed things.

But I am not going to cut into the field of these speakers here tonight. What I am trying to say to you is that in the North, in my day, life has been too much the life of the closed fist. There does still remain in the South something that suggests the life of the open hand.

Well, I like the life of the open hand. I think it is the only decent life. I think success has been overdone in America. I think bigness has been overdone. Personally, I would like to think of myself as not primarily a northerner or a southerner but as an American who is fed up with bigness, with the grand manner. I would like to be, for a change, a little worm, let us say, in the fair apple of progress. I'm fed up on progress, represented only by money, too.

I like also the idea of the southern men, Mr. Stringfellow Barr of the University of Virginia and Mr. John Crowe Ransom of Vanderbilt University, coming here to debate a question like this. Why, as to what we shall do with the machine, with industrialism, it is overwhelmingly the biggest question men and women are now facing.

Not so long ago, in my own lifetime at least, and at least in the North, no man would have dared question industrialism. It has a lot to answer for. It has killed or is killing, many of us believe, some of the finest and most basic of man's impulses.

There is a tendency, who can doubt it, for modern industrialized man to lose sense of earth, sun, stars, fellow men and even his own hands. The machine, so blithely accepted by most of us, is doing all sorts of obscure and hateful things to men. Why, the very automobile in which I drove here to this meeting from my home in Virginia's Southwest does something to me every time I drive it.

And there is something else. You will find everywhere in America nowadays thoughtful men who believe that industrialism, unchecked, must lead straight into communism. They do not want communism. They believe that individualism should have yet another chance. Communism and industrialism are really brothers; in both of them there is implicit the same patronism, the same determined regimentation of life, the same determinism to crush individualism.

For one thing there has been released into our hands by industrialism all of this new power. Now power and in particular this sort of vicarious power, unearned, uncreated by man, is dangerous to us. That we accept it so blithely shows a kind of stupidity in us and, in as much as we accept the vicarious power released into the world by the machine as our own power and become proud and vain because of it, we are fools.

Real power is something very different. I mean imaginative power, creative power, power of the hands and of the head. It is a long slow job coming at that kind of power, and the effort to get it commonly makes a man more humble, not more arrogant and proud as does the power we are getting nowadays so cheaply from the machine.

But I think we are all beginning to understand this. We understand that every man and woman now living is in danger. What is endangered is our real manhood and womanhood.

Both of these men who are to speak here tonight, Mr. Stringfellow Barr and Mr. John Crowe Ransom, have as clear a vision of the danger of which I speak as any two men in America could have. They have different ideas as to how to meet the situation. I will therefore turn the meeting over to them and do what I came here to do, that is to say, sit and listen.

## Danville, Virginia

On his way back to Marion from the Ransom-Barr debate, Anderson stopped over in Danville, Virginia, a textile town on the Virginia– North Carolina line, where Dan River mill workers were striking for the right to organize. The depression in America was now entering its second year. Anderson, having observed economic conditions in other sections of the country, felt drawn to the people; however, in several places in the following text he expresses frustration over his or anyone else's ability to effect an instantaneous cure. However, he did speak to the strikers on November 15. The following day the Richmond *Times-Dispatch* reported that he told them: "There is something we have in common and that is that we are all Virginians and Virginia has a tradition for freedom and rights that makes me ashamed to know that there are men in Virginia who are not willing to grant you your rights and to deal with you fairly." He ended by saying, "I hope to God you will win."

Anderson returned to Danville in mid-January 1931. On January 13 he made a long emotional speech.[10] Two days later, thirty-one hundred of the four thousand striking workers went back to work. The strike effectively ended in a stalemate, management's agreement to rehire being a tacit acknowledgment that the union had won a point. Though it was not the victory Anderson or the workers had sought, he hoped that his words had added "a bit more dignity to the defeat in the minds of the people defeated."[11]

"Danville, Virginia" was published in the *New Republic* 65: (January 21, 1931): 266–68.

At Danville, Virginia, I got a picture of the futility of what might be called goodness. There was a Mr. [H. R.] Fitzgerald there, who is at the head of the Dan River Cotton Mills. There were two mills on strike there, the

Dan River and the Riverside. Mr. Fitzgerald was the controlling man at the mills and of the town. No one doubts much that he was a good man with good intentions.

The cotton mills have been there a long time. The modern industrial town of Danville has really been made by them, but Danville is itself an old town. It was once, for a brief passing moment, the capital of the southern Confederacy. Mr. Davis, with his Cabinet, fled to Danville when Grant took Richmond. There must still have been some hope, a feverish kind of uncertain hope. "We may win yet. Something may happen," the men there must have been saying to themselves, whistling in the dark to keep up courage, like the strikers, when I was there.

I went down to Danville from Richmond, driving down in the rain, and at Richmond I had told several men where I was going. They all said the same thing. "Why do these men strike now? There are many men out of work everywhere. It will be too easy to whip them now."

We went puddling through the rain and drove down past one of the mills. There were pickets scattered about. They had built up temporary shelters. One group had got an old piece of canvas such as farmers use to cover haystacks, and had propped it up on sticks. Two men and a girl were huddled in under there and as we passed slowly the girl put out her head. We waved our hands and she grinned, a girlish grin. "Hello," we called and "Hot stuff," she replied. There was that American thing. These youngsters. They get you by the throat. I wasn't in the late war myself, but I get a picture, gathered from young-fellow friends of mine coming back, a picture of just such young Americans as you will find there on strike, at the cotton mills at Danville. A kind of gaiety going on, in spite of hell. To the average man in the trenches—I mean the common soldier, let him be English, American, German, French, what not—I dare say there wasn't much thought of winning or losing the war. They must have been quite willing to let the heavy thinkers, the Wilsons, Clemenceaus, the Lloyd Georges,[12] figure out the purposes of the war and all that. What I fancy about them is that they had consciousness only of the thing in front of them. "It's no use grouching," they must have said to themselves, "I may be dead tomorrow. But there are these others here, Jim and Bud and Joe and Frank. If I can get a grin out of one of them it will help just that much."

There is always this feeling when you (being a man like myself . . . a middle-class man really, although you are a writer and do not buy or sell anything) come into a hall where there are a lot of workers, strikers congregated. They cheer.

There they are, sitting or standing in the room. It is always such a gloomy room, somewhere on a side street. The men and women, the strikers, packed in there. At Danville they had got a hall that had been used by the Ku Klux Klan and in a corner, propped against a wall, there was a huge cross, all arranged like the lights you see put up all over movie theaters, wired to make a fiery cross. They propped it against a wall in a corner and the people crowded in, some standing, as there were not seats enough. We went in.

I had been in some three or four hours. I had met a lot of newspaper men . . . bright fellows . . . talk of the strike and of the town. They took me out of town to a country estate, of Laurence Stallings, who collaborated on *What Price Glory?*[13] He had just had his tonsils cut out and we sat and looked at each other. "So that's you?"

"Yes." "That's you, eh?"

It would have been much better if the newspaper men had not taken me out there. A man who has just had his tonsils out doesn't want to see a fellow writer. Seeing fellow writers isn't such great shucks anyway, any time. We know each other too well. It would have been better if I had gone down there in the rain to the picket lines, stood around in the little temporary shelters, looking out at the great stone mills. I might have got more a sense of something I was after down there. I was sore at the people who were managing the strike that they had not arranged it in that way.

We did get to the hall finally.

You come into such a place. Let us say, just to make the point, that they have been told something about you. One of the amazingly charming things about Americans, and in particular about American workers, is a kind of humility in them that makes you ashamed. Why, they believe in you. They believe you can do something to help them. In Danville they believe in Mr. Fitzgerald. You ask one of the strikers down there, "What about Mr. Fitzgerald?" "Oh, he's all right. He's a good man," he'll say. These workers, mill hands, men and women, like poets really. They believe it will happen. They think it may happen at any time, any minute.

What do they believe?

They believe in people.

It may be because they are poor. They believe that in some queer way, some man having come along, let's say some fellow like myself, having made a speech . . . something of that sort . . . they believe all will change.

I dare say they have a sense of something. At Danville I was told something about cotton mills. They came in there a long time ago and the mills have been well managed. Let us say there was, originally, a million dollars invested. The mills have prospered and there have been big dividends made, stock distributed. Let's say the valuation has gone up to fifteen millions. There have been big salaries paid, a president getting seventy-five thousand a year and other officials as high as fifty thousand. What a lot of money really. Sometimes it seems to a man like myself that working people, who haven't any money and never expect to have any, do not really believe that our American civilization is a money civilization. They believe vaguely that there is just some kind of misunderstanding, and the queer part of it all is that they are right.

At any rate, at Danville, Mr. Fitzgerald and his fellows on their side have tried, from their point of view, to be decent. They own the houses in which the workers live and the strikers have been out for two months now. They might have thrown the strikers out into the streets but they haven't. A few have been thrown out recently.

At Danville the workers were striking simply for the right to organize. That is the main, the central idea. They have been told over and over how it is. "Look here," the labor leaders say to them, "capital is organized against you, all modern life is organized. No one of you has much chance, standing alone."

They know that is true. Modern people who so seldom go into any of our great American mills should go in oftener. The mills are terrifically well organized. They overpower you with the organization that has been built up.

You know well enough that, as an individual, a worker, you can't stand up against that. You are such a tiny little thing, such a minute cog in the great machine. "Stand together," the labor leaders say. "Let us stand together," the workers repeat.

There is so much confusion. You talk to almost any employer of labor about the right to organize. "How can you deny the right?" you ask.

"I can't. I don't," he replies.

He doesn't, either; that's the joke of it. "Why, I'll organize them myself," he says. "I'll let them have meetings. They can even make suggestions to me. All I want to do is to run the thing. I know more about running things than these fellows do."

The workers agree to that, but it doesn't work out. They get restless. What I myself fancy is that the average worker, having worked for one man for a long time as have so many of these people at Danville, Virginia, has a vague notion that if some fellow would come along and say just the right thing everything would clear up.

They are really modest people—these workers. "I can't talk myself," they say. They look about, hoping to find someone to do their talking for them. If someone would just get to the boss, say just the right thing to him. "I'm sure he is a good man," they say. "He doesn't understand how we feel."

So it goes on. The workers in such a mill go on strike. I said a moment ago that more people should go into modern factories but, when it comes to that, more people should go to strike meetings, too.

There is a way in which people, workers, when they go on strike, even when they are pretty sure to lose, get something, and it should be borne in mind that there isn't much these people get out of life. Labor hours are long. Life is a grind for them. Youth doesn't last long in a mill.

It is like this—modern men and women, modern workers, modern big mills, when there is no strike on, when things are just running on as usual, get very little feeling of each other. They are in the presence always, all day, every day, of a big, tightly organized thing. It makes them feel small. They lose the sense of each other.

Then a strike comes and, for a time at least, they get a rather fine feeling of each other. A man or woman, a worker, in ordinary times, is just a man or woman, but in a hall, while a strike is going on, he is, at the moment at least, a part of something like an army. He is, for a time at least, as big as the mills. He gets sharply the sense of others. Something grows warm in him. Hands reach out. Any American who has really been in at a strike while it is going on, before it wears out, while the spirit of it is at fever heat, will have an experience he won't forget.

He has perhaps been told by the newspapers that these people are dangerous. Why, they are people in love with each other, for the moment anyway. The feeling of isolation, so universal nowadays in our modern industrialized America, is gone. These people want only to stand shoulder to shoulder. They want to keep this feeling for each other. In a case such as that at Danville, they wouldn't mind really having the boss belong to their union, his running it, if they could feel he was one of themselves.

They can't feel that. Can you blame them? Should Mr. Fitzgerald expect that? Can any man, running a factory, really feel that a company union is a real union?

You come into such a place, an outsider. You are to make a speech. How futile really. What can you say?

You can say you hope they will win.

What?

Why, just the right to go on being as they are at that moment, all one, organized, feeling close to each other. You feel the struggle of all men against the control of all life by the machine.

They are men and women and, while I am on this matter, I would like to say something for the men and women who run these strikes. It is a heartbreaking job. You are always going about to little halls, seeing people such as I saw at Danville, people struggling for some right to live. You feel them almost inevitably doomed to defeat just now. It gets you.

There they are. They crowd into the little halls. They cheer you when you come in. Faces peer up at you. There is hope, love, expectation in the eyes of the people. At Danville, in the front row, there was a young fellow with his girl. He reached over stealthily and took her hand. Old men, heads of families, were there, and tired old women workers. A thousand eyes looking up at you. A kind of love grips you at the throat, but how utterly futile you feel, how ashamed. They so believe in you, or in someone like you, some talker, some writer, some leader, some poet who is to come and make what they want understood to their boss, to all bosses.

Well, you do nothing. You say a few words. You go away. You go back to your hotel. Some man comes in and offers you a drink. It is a pretty heartbreaking matter—this situation of most industrial workers in America.

---

## Lumber Camp

Another area of labor that attracted Anderson's attention was the lumber industry, a mainstay of the southern economy. This time, however, his interest was not so much in the organized industry as in the process of harvesting timber and those who performed the task. He wrote two sketches on the subject, neither of which was published. One, "Lumber," was set in the mountains of West Virginia, the one printed below, in Georgia. The latter contains a personal angle; "Little" David is the son of John and Caroline Greear, Anderson's hosts on his initial trip to Virginia in the summer of 1925. The family had moved to Helen, Georgia, where John worked in the lumber business and Caroline ran a boardinghouse.

Passages of "Lumber Camp" detail the actual harvesting of trees, which Anderson regards as a kind of rape of the land. He is not the only one with these feelings. The lumbermen themselves feel a genuine pathos, knowing the importance of satisfying the need for lumber while at the same time experiencing sorrow for having to destroy what nature had so bountifully created.

This text is from a rough manuscript written on lumber-company paper while Anderson was visiting the Greears in April 1930.[14]

Little Dave, "the white-haired wonder . . ." that is what the lumber jacks called him . . . he has been water jack up in the woods during the summer before . . . took me back up into the Georgia lumber camp in his father's car.

It wasn't much of a car. Dave recognized that. It had been bumped too long and too hard over mountain roads, over lumber roads. It threatened every moment to come to pieces. Dave's father had a good many kids and I dare say his income wasn't so large. "She won't hold, won't get us there, will she, Dave?" I said to the boy. He was an American kid. Three times the car balked on us. She seemed to be quite dead. He got out and fixed her.

He fixed her once with the tin foil off my package of cigarettes, reestablished some flow of electricity that had been stopped.

"You're a good mechanic, aren't you, Dave?" I said, my voice filled with admiration.

"We have to be, the kids of our family, if we want to get anywhere," Dave said. He spoke with a slow soft southern drawl, dragging his words as his father did.

Dave's father is an engineer and lays out lumber railroads. It is some job. The man who does it has to know timber, he has to know surveying and practical engineering. A lumber railroad must keep below the timber.

He is a man who picked up his own education in his craft, got it out of books at night. There was something of Abraham Lincoln in him, the father. You thought of earlier Americans, men concerned with government and religion, serious men who could nevertheless laugh heartily, outdoor men. He was reading Wells' *Outline of History* when I was there and his kids were reading it. They were all hot on education, the kids of that family.

In a lumber boundary they depend upon the engineer first of all to go look over the ground. Most of the timber left anywhere now in America is in the hills. All the cream, the timber that lies out on the flat open country, has long since been taken.

The timber is in the hills and even up there the valleys have been cut over. The good timber left is straight up the mountain sides or it is in the deep rocky gullies that gash the hills.

Your engineer, with perhaps another man from the lumber company, a practical woodsman, must feel his way back up into the country.

There will be dense laurel and thickets growing often ten or fifteen feet high. When you get into that you can see nothing.

There the trees are, back up in there. Men are taken along to do what they call "swamp it out." They cut and slash, these men, laying low the flowering bushes, slashing out the young trees.

Bonfires are built everywhere. If it's a laurel country, as in the north Georgia hills into which I had now come, the brush will burn green.

What all this country calls laurel is really rhododendron. The great soft leaves are loaded with oil.

There are bonfires everywhere, the country being cleaned up, fires crackling far into the night, the air loaded with rich smells.

A keen sense of destruction going on too. The lumbermen themselves feel that. Talk to one of them an hour and the subject will come up.

"Well, you take a hill country like this . . . you cut the trees out.

"You clean the country up—take out the laurel and the ivy. You slash out the young trees. You have to get to where the good timber is, you have to make a way to get it out," they say always a bit apologetically. They aren't apologizing to you. They seem almost apologizing to the green hills. "I've got to do it to you. I can't help it," they seem to be saying.

"It's a grand country, eh," they say. They know in their hearts what it will be like when they have gone on.

A long long desolate time. Maybe the country will recover, maybe not. [ . . . ]

When I was going up into the lumber camp with Dave, the Georgia hill boy, we came first of all to great stretches of cut-over land, hillsides cut over, gullies climbing up out of the valleys already slashed out, places where the lumberjacks had been ball-hooting logs[15] down hillsides, smashed logs that had split when they hit, sticking straight up like gigantic beanpoles out of the piles of cut, brown and dead rhododendrons (that thick soft bush, making white the hillsides with its great blossoms before the lumbermen came), torn young trees, barked and dying . . . when we saw all this, the road we were following paralleling the narrow gauge lumber railroad Dave's father had built, when we were being bumped over buried tree roots, driving through forests of stumps, I was thinking of a land, a vast hilltop tableland of my own Virginia country.

Dave knew about that country too. He was a child there and would soon be a young man. His father had been up there. His father had helped timber out that country too.

There was a great upland country there that had once been one of America's finest stretches of timber. Now it was dry and desolate, thin soiled and burned by wind and sun. Neighbors of mine, older men, came to my own house in the valley sometimes at evening to speak of it.

They spoke with a certain awe of what the Virginia hills had been. They were long lean men and some of them had lumberjacked it for years. They spoke of the great forest that had once been on the upper plateau. "I can't bear it, going up there now," one of them once said to me. He spoke of soft moss into which a man sank to his boot-tops, of springs bubbling up, of the dark quiet under the tall trees. They, the trees, "were as big around, some of them, as the sitting room of your house here," he said.

"They went far up into the sky.

"There were bears up there and foxes and, when my father was alive, packs of wolves.

"It made a man want to pray to go up there. It made him want to sing.

"You know what it is now. I hate to go up there."

Millions and millions of acres of that kind of cut-over land in America. There is no soil on such land anymore. The upper plains are cut by deep rain-washed gullies. Even the bushes won't grow.

"Where did it all go—the rich deep soil?"

"Well, down the rivers and the creeks," the mountain men say.

Why, it is the story of the cotton barons of the old South told over again. It is the story of the industrialists too—human lives wasted like that.

To produce goods—to produce timber.

You can't blame the lumbermen—they are doing what everyone is doing.

------

# Sugar Making

"Sugar Making" is written in Anderson's best impressionistic vein, its rich images allowing the reader to experience the subject on a level involving all the senses. This was decidedly different from the approach taken in the Elizabethton or Danville pieces, where he was dealing with weighty social issues. Here we are given details on the actual processing of sugar cane, but they are presented incidentally. The primary object is to have the subject felt and savored. Black workers were involved in the manufacture of sugar far more heavily than in the textile and lumbering industries. In this sketch black laborers are the dominant force, and Anderson is careful to indicate that he is speaking of those whose lives are primarily physical and whose songs are part of an oral, rather than a literate, tradition. There is a dreamlike quality to the piece, as Anderson acknowledges at the end of the first section. The final image, of the jealous woman chasing another with a cane knife amid the sweet smells of sugar, evokes a vivid surreal quality.

The text, never published, is edited from a manuscript that Anderson wrote after visiting a sugar refinery near New Orleans in March 1930.

In the big sugar refinery back of the levee by the river there are many strange moving shapes. There are great retorts in there, vast boilers.

There are cane crushers, cane shredders, cane choppers.

The cane comes in from the fields in cars that run on narrow tracks. The fields are flat. They run straight back from the levee of the Mississippi to the swamps. The fields are a mile, two miles, three miles, five miles deep.

The fields lie below the level of the river. They lie back of the levees.

Think of flat hot fields. Think of a hot mist arising in the early morning. Think of Negro men and women trudging to the fields in the morning.

Think of Negroes sweating. Think of mules sweating.

Think of row after row of little unpainted cabins in "the quarter."

There is a little low step before each cabin door. Late in the evening and on Sundays old Negro men and women come out of the cabins to sit on the steps in front of the cabins. Men and women both smoke pipes. The ground in the street is hard baked clay.

If you want to hear Negro spirituals do not go to the quarter. Go to a theater in New York or Chicago.

If you live in a Middlewestern town go to a lyceum concert. An American woman, with Polish blood in her, who has never been South, will sing you "Swing low, sweet chariot." Or she will sing you "Can't hear nobody pray." A group of young Negroes from a Negro industrial college may come to your town and sing these songs. They want to get money from rich white people for their college.

In the Negro quarters on the big sugar plantation the tired old Negro men and women sit on the steps before the cabins and smoke their pipes. There are fat middleaged wives there too. They come out of cabins and walk away toward the levee, their big hips rolling.

There are beautiful young Negro men, tall lean ones. They go in the evening to the levee too. The young Negro bucks and the wenches walk with a rolling swagger. Life gathers up through them warmly. There are cries from the darkness up there on the levee. A high-pitched feminine Negro voice cries, "Now you quit that, nigger. Now you quit that."

There are many voices up there on the levee, low voices, loud voices. The moon comes up. In the far South the moon is golden yellow. Stay down below the levee, sit on the gallery of the big house, where once the master of the plantation lived, smell the damp river smells.

The big sugar refinery is just over there. You can hear the grind and the roar of it. It is full of twinkling lights.

A sour sweet smell comes from it.

A sour sweet smell comes from the Negro quarters where old men and women sit on the low step before the cabins smoking the evening pipes.

I saw a young Negro woman, almost white. She had a slender lithe figure. Her face was ugly and degenerate. She had sullen eyes.

I saw the hands of old black men and women, marvelous alive old hands.

I saw a young Negro wench with golden yellow-brown skin and big quiet dark eyes.

I was standing in the warm darkness, unseen at the edge of the quarter.

It was night, a soft quiet moon-lit southern night. The old people sat as I have described them. There was a low murmur of soft voices. Children, tiny black, brown and yellow children, were rolling on the hard baked ground. Clouds of mosquitoes came into the quarter from the swamps beyond the flat cane fields. The black, brown and yellow people did not mind. The mosquitoes drove me half mad but I stayed, dancing, slapping my neck, my face and hands in the darkness.

There was the scene before me, the streets of the quarter at night. It is good to stand unseen thus looking into other people's lives. I am a Jack the Peeper.

A child cried in one of the cabins. There was the big factory, almost within a stone's throw. Dim figures could be seen walking on the levee. Couples walked across the face of the yellow moon that was hanging low over the levee.

When I walks that levee round, round,
When I walks that levee round,
When I walks that levee round,
I'se looking for that bully, must be found.

Young brown, black and yellow lovers were courting up there.
There was the sour sweet smell of Negro life.
There was the sour sweet smell of the Mississippi.
There was the sour sweet smell of the big sugar factory.
The soil smelled sour and sweet.

A Negro woman, a tall lean young wench, came running out at a cabin door. The light from inside the cabin streamed out on her. She passed through a little flood of light from an open door.

There was a great cut on her face and neck. Blood ran from it.

She ran. She ran past where I stood. Another tall lean lithe young wench was after her with a cane knife.

The one who was cut had kinky hair. She ran silently, passing close to me. She was making a queer little noise. "O, O, O, Lord save me," she cried.

The other wench, the one who pursued her, had straight black hair. It streamed out behind her as she ran, with the long wicked-looking cane knife uplifted. The cane knife is used to cut the tall sugar cane in the sugar harvest time.

She also ran close to me. Her breath came in short little gasps.

The two figures just ran like that, out of the light from the doorways in the quarter into the cane fields, toward the distant swamps.

There was no story I ever heard. I stayed about there for days later but I heard no story. One woman followed another like that, both running furiously, across the flat fields, along a road that ran between rows of young cane in the flat fields, one bleeding from a deep cut in her cheek and neck, the other with an upraised knife, her hair streaming out behind.

They ran until their figures became dim and lost in the distance.

The swamps beyond the cane fields are dim dark places. Poisonous snakes and lizards live there. The cypress trees push their way up out of the black stagnant water. The knees of cypress trees push up out of the dark stagnant water.

There are clouds of mosquitoes.

In the swamps there is a sour sweet smell.

It may all have been a distorted dream.

I went to sleep in the big house that had been the master's house. There were screens at all the windows and doors in the big house and the beds were soft.

I could hear the great wheels grinding in the sugar factory. I could hear the sustained sound of wheels.


*The Factory*

In the factory they ground cane from the fields in season but when there was no cane to grind, ships came to the factory door bringing ship loads of raw Cuban and Philippine sugar.

It was made into white snowy sugar, pure and clean.

They forced it through ground, burned, black bone dust and it came out white.

They put it into great cylinders and tossed it.

They made a sugar snow storm inside a great cylinder. You could look into the cylinder through a window. You saw a white sugar snow storm. You saw white flakes, white crystals of sugar broken into white particles. You saw them wind tossed, puddle tossed, wheel tossed.

You walked on and on through the great sugar factory and saw fat retorts. You saw great vats. You saw boiling heavy liquids.

Everything was clean. The floor was as clean as the table off which you will dine tonight.

The machinery was all dignified. The great wheels, as tall as a church, with cogs into the spaces between which you could lay your hand . . . the wheels had stately dignity.

The cotton factory of the South is gay, swift, dancing, cruel, but the sugar factory of the South is solemn and dignified.

When I was there they were not grinding cane from the fields but were making white sugar out of raw Cuban sugar.

More tariff please.

Please, more tariff.

The machinery that in season handled the cane from the fields was still.

The great belts that carry the cane to the grinders.

The great cogged wheels.

The choppers, the shredders.

The tearers, the squeezers.

All these were standing in half darkness at night and were very dignified.

A few workers, watchmen, were in this still part of the great factory that night, walking about under the great wheels, under the great belts, as broad as sidewalks, under the rollers and squeezers, under the shredders and choppers.

There was a sense of stately dignity. The great retorts had stately dignified shapes. They were like rich men who have grown old with dignity and have big expensive automobiles.

They were like fat rich old women heavy with jewels riding slowly through streets in carriages.

They were like fat old kings going to see their sons married.

The big wheels, the big machines, in that silent part of the factory, were clean like fat white old circus horses that go in processions.

The few workmen who walked or stood among the machines in that part of the factory that night were clad in clean faded blue overalls. They seemed to walk with special dignity.

I stood looking. I wanted a great drum. I wanted to beat a great drum. I wanted to beat:

Tum, tum.

Tum, tum.

As savages beat drums in swamps and forests in Africa.

As bands in circus parades beat drums while great fat sleek white and dapple grey horses cavort slowly, heavily, with stately dignity through the streets of towns.

This is the silent part of the sugar factory, where in the season when the cane comes from the field and is dumped from cars onto broad conveyors all these great ponderous machines become active. Then you may see the great wheels turning. There is a heavy clunking sound. Negroes shout.

There are tall lean young Negro men handling the cane. They do not sing "Swing low, sweet chariot" or "I can't hear nobody pray."

The cane comes in from the fields on hot days and nights. The young Negroes have hot blood in them.

They sing.

"You can't have none of my jelly roll" or "Shake that thing."

The great rollers move with stately dignity. All of the machinery for chopping, shredding, tearing, rolling, crushing, squeezing is heavy and dignified.

There is no sharp rattle.

There is no wild dance.

The machines are like fat old people stepping a minuet. They tread heavily, slowly. A flood of warm sweet juice runs down into fat tanks and retorts, pumps go chug, chug, heavily.

The sugar factory runs on and on. It never stops. Sugar makes candy. It is put into coffee. It makes moon whiskey.

All the air is heavy with raw sugar smells. All the year round, in the ever busy part of the factory, the retorts boil, sugar is forced through burned bone to make it white, it is pumped here and there.

It goes into the huge cylinders to be rolled and tossed. You may see the white whirling snow storm, looking through a glass window as into a room on hot nights in June, July or August.

The white crystals of powdered sugar pour out into barrels and bags into cartons.

Girls seated in long rows label it and seal it. There is a cloud of powdered sugar. The raw brown sugar arrives in ships from Cuba and the Philippines and goes out again by ship and train, clean and white, neatly labeled, in white bags encased in brown bags.

Over all the country, day and night, all the year, a heavy sweet smell.

It is a half sour sweet smell. It creeps out over the river. It goes across the low flat fields to the swamps. It is in the big house where the master lived in the old days, the house with the great galleries and the fat stately white pillars. It goes into the Negro cabins, into the rows of neat little frame houses where the white workers live.

It is in their beds.

It is in their hair.

A Negro wench, pursuing another wench who has been fooling with her brown man, waving a wicked heavy cane knife, running across long flat fields into the darkness toward a distant swamp, runs through heavy sour sweet smell.

[ . . . ]

---

## Tobacco Market

"Tobacco Market" originally appeared in the *Marion Democrat* on February 3, 1931. It recounts an actual visit to a tobacco auction at nearby Abingdon, Virginia. Unlike "Blue Smoke," the broad-ranging sketch on the tobacco industry included in *Puzzled America*, "Tobacco Market" offers details on how such auctions are conducted. It also contains touches of humor and a characteristic glimpse of human drama in the person of the hypothetical small farmer whose fortunes are hostage to the powerful forces that drive the tobacco market in the South.

This text is edited from a typescript that Anderson later adapted from the newspaper article.[16]

A day at the great tobacco market at Abingdon, Virginia. The market begins at 9:30 in the morning and lasts usually until 3:30 or 4 in the afternoon. There are two big floors at Abingdon and the market moves from one to the other. We arrived shortly after noon when the market was in full swing.

The town was full of farmers who had brought in tobacco. They were selling at one of the warehouses and arrangements were being made to move to the second big floor in another house on the next day.

This particular Virginia market has been through a lot of difficulty but has got itself firmly established now. It is a big market this year and promises to grow bigger every year. Now the farmers are coming there from counties in eastern Kentucky and Tennessee, from North Carolina and from all Southwestern Virginia.

Such markets are not easily established. There is a big investment necessary and after being established the success or failure of the market depends a great deal upon the attitude toward it of both the sellers and the buyers. The buyers are the four great American tobacco companies, to whom ultimately most of the tobacco goes. They are makers of plug tobacco, of cigars, of pipe smoking tobacco and, most of all nowadays, of cigarettes.

Luckies. Camels. Chesterfields. Old Golds.

Obviously it is not to the interest of the big tobacco companies to have many small markets. At Abingdon, Virginia, in the hills of the Blue Ridge, a quiet old town, when the market was first opened some years ago, the amount of tobacco brought in was at first relatively small. It was difficult to get buyers in. The market failed as did the one nearby at Bristol, Tennessee, and a good deal of money was lost.

Still the market was well located. The nearest big markets were at Greenville, Tennessee, and at Asheville, North Carolina. The success of the market now is largely due to the persistence of two or three men.

To conduct a tobacco market requires a special kind of skill. First of all you must be a judge of tobacco in the leaf. There are so many things can go wrong for the raiser. It is one of the most trying of all crops to raise and to prepare for market. The market is not left altogether to the whim of the buyers but is to a certain extent controlled by the warehouse man. He at least tries to control it. He is himself in the market constantly bidding on every basket of tobacco put up. Great speed must be maintained. At this Virginia market the average sale is from three hundred and fifty to as high as five hundred baskets an hour. The auctioneer is moving swiftly from basket to basket. The baskets are set on the great floor in long rows. The auctioneer is chattering incessantly. It is difficult to understand him. At first you feel as though you had wandered into a Chinese laundry at an unfortunate moment. The Chinaman is sore at something and is letting go a string of Chinese oaths.

Six, six and a half, and a half, wha hoo—wee wan ah—wee woo—wee haa woo—at six and a half—sold.

There it goes, another basket containing perhaps a hundred, two hundred, three hundred pounds of tobacco gone into the great maw of one of the big tobacco companies.

The warehouse man has been struggling to hold up the price. He has approached the basket ahead of the auctioneer. His quick eye has judged it. Perhaps he thrusts in his hand and pulls a hand of tobacco out of the heart of the pile. He has made the first bid.

Now come the other buyers. They are keen-eyed young men. The great broad-bottomed basket, containing often some farmer's whole crop, has been sitting there waiting. The farmer himself is standing near. Perhaps his heart is beating anxiously. These young men come, these buyers. There are the paid buyers for the big tobacco companies and the others. There are speculators here. They watch. If they think a basket of tobacco is going at too low a price they also bid quickly. It is all done very rapidly. A dozen pairs of hands are thrust into the pile. The tobacco, so neatly piled in rows, is rolled and tumbled about. A nod or a shake of the head and all is over.

The speculators are not buying for factories. They are buying to sell again. Often a basket contains a mixed lot, some good tobacco and much bad. The speculator buys and repacks the basket. He calculates quickly that he can make money on that basket. He takes a chance. There may be ten or a dozen of these speculators hovering about the auctioneer, as well as the salaried buyers for the great companies.

The sale goes on quickly, smoothly, rapidly. A flow of words, restless, alert men moving forward from basket to basket. The fate of innumerable farmers is being decided thus.

There is to be sure the same thing going on in the wheat pit at Chicago, the cotton market at New Orleans and at other markets where the products of the farms are sold, but it is not often carried on in the farmer's presence as it is here. Here he sees and hears it all. He stands helplessly looking. Here before his eyes is a picture of what happens to everything the farmer raises. These are the middlemen he is always hearing about, reading about, the sharp-eyed buyers and sellers. Have you seen a well-trained and hungry dog standing by his master's loaded table? He sits silently there. Watch his eyes.

Outside the streets are jammed with wagons and trucks. There are other speculators out there. There are men, called "pin-hookers," who go from load to load, offering to buy the load. The pin-hooker also takes a chance. He sizes up the load—"I will give you so and so much." He is taking a chance that he can sell at a sharp advance over what he has offered the farmer. He is betting on his judgment too. Why, that is all right isn't it? A man must use his brains in this world.

There are men standing about out there or wandering aimlessly about. At Abingdon, Virginia, 7,800,000 pounds of tobacco were sold last year and it is predicted that between ten and eleven million pounds of tobacco will pass over the floors and under the hands of the buyers this year. It will all happen in a few short weeks. There has been such a congestion this year that often a seller, arriving perhaps from a distant country, has had to wait several days before he can get his tobacco on the floor. Farmers bring blankets with them and sleep on their loads. There have been bitter cold days and nights. Already this year one farmer has died from exposure.

There are amusing, half tragic tales told. Tobacco thieves are about. One farmer crawled in under the canvas that covered his load to sleep at night. When he awoke his truck was moving. He put his head cautiously out. Two Negroes had stolen his truck and were driving rapidly along the road toward another market at Greenville, Tennessee. The man who owned the tobacco kept quiet and at last the truck arrived at Greenville and the two Negroes went into a restaurant to get something to eat.

While they were gone he crawled out and managed to find a policeman. The two Negroes were arrested and the farmer with his load of tobacco returned to again wait his place in line at Abingdon.

The Virginia tobacco market is very like an old-fashioned fair. There are plenty of sharpers about. A man stands at the end of a truck doing some sort of card trick. Farmers gather about. There are all sorts of temporary lunch stands and fruit stands. The flash men are gathered in. They are hungry-eyed too this year. Here the farmer is getting money. Many thousands of dollars are being paid out in cash every day. Where there are many men with cash in hand you will always find sharpers ready to take it away from them.

A sharp young man took me in charge. He took me from pile to pile, pulling out hands, showing me what made desirable tobacco and what made tobacco undesirable. He explained the ticketing of baskets, the method of book-keeping, the buying and selling methods, the charge made by the marketing companies. As he had also been connected with other markets in other Virginia and North Carolina towns, he told me about them.

He explained also the methods used by the speculators, showing how these men worked over the baskets, hoping to get a better price than they had paid. He took me to the packing rooms.

There are four great sections to the packing rooms, representing the four great American companies, and men were at work packing the tobacco into great hogsheads. All tobacco bought during the day is packed and shipped on the same day. There are no curing plants at Abingdon and the tobacco goes to these before being packed away in storage warehouses. Some of it is of course exported. Tobacco bought this year will not go into manufacture for perhaps three or four years. After being put through the drying plant it will be stored away.

There are these men, these farmers, standing about. What a feeling of disorganization, of futility. Look at the tired, discouraged faces. Many of the men are weary from long waiting. Finally each man's turn comes. His baskets of tobacco are sold. After days of waiting the sale takes but a few seconds.

What pregnant seconds. There he stands, quietly to one side, that man, that farmer. Often he is poorly dressed. He is tired. All year he has been waiting for this moment. He has laid out and burned his seed beds in the spring, has set his plants, has tended them, harvested them, cured them in his tobacco barn. He has carefully sorted the tobacco. Some do this well, some do it badly. There are those who try to hide the poor tobacco deep down in the pile—"nest it," they say.

The auctioneer comes. Now the buyers are there. It is all over in a few seconds. What hopes that farmer has had. Perhaps he knew his crop was not so good but still he hoped. He told the wife—"If I have luck." The wife and he were lying in bed talking on the night before he set off. There are dreams of sending the children away to school, of new dresses for the wife, new shoes for the children. One load of tobacco has been sold on this market for as high as $2,500. That man standing over there last year got eight hundred dollars from an acre of tobacco. It meant, of course, long hours of intensive work. The market, on rare and fine baskets, has this year gone as high as thirty-four cents. It has dropped as low as one cent.

There is everything in these few words pouring from the lips of an auctioneer. A man may be made or broken here in a few seconds. The year is a success or it is worse than a failure.

There is an inner cry—"Wait. Wait. For God's sake, don't be so fast.

"Don't be so careless, so casual. For God's sake, that is my blood there.

"My life has gone into that basket of tobacco. Stop. Wait."

No words said aloud.

It happens. The auctioneer passes. There are a few hurried words, a few nods. The farmer does not have to abide by this decision. What has been offered is written on a ticket and the ticket is lying there on the basket. He can tear it up. He can try again. And not all of these farmers are silent. There is a wit among them. The buyers stop buying for a moment. They drink Coca-Cola and smoke cigarettes. A farmer laughs. This is not a southern Negro's laughter. It is a southern white man's laughter, something bitter in it. "Come on, come on," he calls. "Get busy. You got a lot of tobacco to steal yet today." The amazing, the pathetic, the stirring thing really about men is that, no matter how much they are licked, they do try again. The farmer who is defeated this year will be back at it next year. There may be a lump in the throat, a moment of desperate depression or of elation, and then, with what money he has got, the American farmer drives off, to try it again.

# 5 A New South

From the mid-1930s until 1941, the year Anderson died and the year of Pearl Harbor, the South underwent sweeping changes. Labor troubles were no longer the primary focus; they had been supplanted by the widespread effects of the depression. New Deal programs were providing employment and performing useful civic tasks. The TVA was transforming the economy of several states. Despite the repeal of prohibition, illicit liquor was still a mainstay of the southern subculture. This became the subject for *Kit Brandon* (1936), Anderson's final novel. His outlook during this period was optimistic on the whole. During much of 1934 he had made wide-ranging travels over the Southeast observing conditions in the region and writing monthly installments for *Today* magazine. Many of these he collected in 1935 into a volume, *Puzzled America*. "We do not want cynicism. We want belief," he states in the introduction. "Can we find it in one another, in democracy, in the leadership we are likely to get out of a democracy?" The question is rhetorical; however, to read *Puzzled America* through is to see an evolution from concern and disillusion to hope.

The late 1930s were also favorable for Anderson personally. Having married Eleanor Copenhaver in 1933, he enjoyed a domestic happiness he had not known in his previous three marriages. Though less productive as a writer, he worked for several years on his memoirs (published posthumously) and on other literary projects as well. Like many Americans, he expressed revulsion over the rise of fascism in Europe in the late 1930s. He believed that life in America, as gauged by the region he had chosen to live in more than a decade before, was an essentially good life. It is fitting that what may have been his last writing for publication was an editorial that he dashed off for the student newspaper at Marion College. In this brief essay, which has the eerie title, "Chance Rules Us All," he recounts the circumstances of his first coming to southwestern Virginia and observes: "By that odd chance all my life has been changed. I was lucky."[1] Chance brought an end to Anderson's life in a peculiar way. Having swallowed a toothpick, he developed peritonitis soon after embarking on a voyage to South America and died in Colón, Panama on March 8, 1941. Numerous funeral plans were discussed, even burial at sea. However, he was brought back to Virginia and placed in Round Hill Cemetery, on a high knoll overlooking Marion. It was the spot he himself had chosen for the end of his odyssey.

## This Southland

From time to time, Anderson attempted to synthesize the various Souths he had discovered into a unified vision. It was impossible. There was simply too much diversity—geographical, ethnic, demographic— among the states, too many social changes happening too rapidly. "This Southland" does, however, focus on a common denominator: the agrarian economy. Anderson was struck by the exploitation that had taken place within this economy over many decades. The Civil War had left it devastated; much of the former aristocracy was now a decayed minority. Northern industry had come into the region, transforming the natural countryside with unsightly factories and ugly mill towns while paying meager wages to local workers. A new type of money-grubbing southerner was now beginning to appear, and this threatened further subjugation in the form of continued low wages and substandard living conditions. The poor southerner had fallen victim to all these forces.

Implicit in these observations is a feeling that wealth has been unfairly distributed in the South. Such a "vast agrarian section of the country, a section . . . that should be a garden, that should be rich," instead has vast numbers of its population still struggling in near poverty. Although the sketch was apparently written in the mid-1930s, when the New Deal programs that Anderson so heartily endorsed were beginning to make an impact, he sees little hope that these will have much effect on an entire regional economy with its long tradition of agrarian struggle.

"This Southland" was apparently never published; the text is edited from a typescript.

How are you going to get it as one picture? There are the plains of Texas; Tidewater, the Southside, the Piedmont . . . of Virginia; the lowland and upland countries of North and South Carolina; Arkansas and Florida; the lower Mississippi (the sugar bowl); the Cajun civilization in the country about New Orleans.

New Orleans itself (oh sweet tolerant city) . . . put it over against Birmingham; Natchez, Mississippi against Greensboro, North Carolina. It is a vast puzzle.

You use the words "Poor White." What do you mean? Do you mean the spay-footed swamp boys from down New Orleans way, the hill men of Southwest Virginia, Kentucky, Tennessee and Missouri or the Georgia and Florida Crackers of the great hot South basin?

It is like all America, a changing thing. In New Orleans and Mobile the river packets have almost completely disappeared. When I first began going South, twenty years ago now, the little packets and some of the big ones still loaded near the banana wharfs in Mobile and at the foot of Canal Street in New Orleans. There were the singing ragged Negroes. You could go up-river, from Mobile to Selma and back, a six-day trip, for twelve dollars, room and board furnished. You got Negro song, not as you hear it in northern concert halls, but against background of river, rain and woods.

Oh what I owe to the South, the months . . . in the aggregate years . . . spent loitering there, the piney-woods country, Negroes singing under pine trees as they brought in the turpentine, bare-footed on the sand shores of the gulf down below Mobile, the strange trumpet call of bull alligators in swamps, red birds flitting across roads in Alabama and Mississippi . . .

Friends made, Julius Friend, Jack McClure, Weeks Hall, in that strange old house he brought back to new life up on Bayou Teche, Natalia Scott, Wharton Esherick, a Yank like myself, with whom I went painting, quarreling and talking for a long winter in the piney-woods . . .

Bill Faulkner, the talented one . . .

I could go on naming them. There were the two Southern women, with the huge plantation, some five thousand acres, inland in Louisiana. There were old Negro men and women among the tenants who had never been off the plantation. Groups of them came up to stand before the door of the big house to sing in the evening.

You get all kinds of strange contradictions. Your northerner thinks of the South as all one thing. What is there in common between Savannah, Georgia and Knoxville, Tennessee, between North Carolina and southern Mississippi—down in the deep black belt? At Savannah the southern woman who sits beside you at dinner says, "But how can one of you Yanks ever know the South?"

You ask her, "But have you ever been in a North Carolina cotton mill town, in a cypress lumber camp down in the swamp country, in the hut of a tenant farmer in Alabama?"

"But those places are not the South. This is the South.

"In New Orleans . . . this is the Real South.

"In Natchez, Birmingham, Charlotte . . . this is the Real South."

They do all seem to have one thing in common. Some three weeks ago I drove for three days with a country doctor in the heart of the South Carolina cotton country. The doctor was one of those men you keep meeting [in the] South. He was poor, lived in a broken-down house, an old Negro man taking care of him. He never sent one of his patients a bill. He was gentle, patient, mentally awake, knew what was going on in Washington, took a New York paper. In his library were the works of Balzac, George Moore, George Borrow, Turgenev, Hardy, Mark Twain. He was the sort of man an organization like the modern KKK would never dare fool with. I said to him . . . "You are of the best blood of the South, eh?" and he laughed.

"Did you ever know a southerner who was not of the best blood of the South?" he said. He was one of that type of southern men like Judge Chamlee of Chattanooga who dared take part as a defense lawyer in the Scottsboro case, along with the communist lawyers and that shrewd criminal lawyer Leibowitz from New York . . . Chamlee being in no sense a communist . . . one of the kind of men like Judge Horton of Alabama who threw a Scottsboro conviction out of court.[2] There are such men in the South.

The South Carolina doctor helped educate a little. We had found each other through a chance meeting and a mutual love of the old writer, George Borrow. The Borrovians hang together. His was a particularly poor section and he was bitter about it. He spoke of the strange new emotional shifts going on in the South just now . . . the southerners almost without exception being political democrats . . . it didn't mean they were economic democrats . . . the money-makers growing more and more resentful of some of the Roosevelt policies . . .

For example this paying a decent wage for a decent day's work to CWA workers.

"But are there money-makers in this land, in this country of tenant farmers, white and black, your patients?"

"Yes." He had a bitter little laugh. He was a nervous, alive, shrunken little old man. I had been told that his wife had died young and that he had never remarried. In his little southern backwoods town he would have been the only man who ever looked into a book. Plenty of time to think as he drove over country roads for years in a buggy and then in a car. His Ford was ten years old. "There are men who will make money in hell," he said.

I got from him an inkling of a new class coming up in the back country in the agrarian South. "The gentleman on the land is going or gone," he said. There was a new type of man getting to the front. "Even at eight or nine cents a pound money can be made on cotton if you pay your labor nothing."

He spoke of Negro women picking cotton at thirty cents a day. You do not need to have share croppers or tenants. On any big farm in the South there are little shacks stuck around on the land, often without floors and windows, one to every twenty-five or thirty acres.

Many of the people are desperate. Give them any sort of shelter, just enough money to buy any kind of food, a little corn meal, fat pork, some collard greens . . . two dollars a week and a house for a family.

Drive 'em. Drive 'em.

So many are ignorant. They will take what they can get. They'll take anything.

It was, the country doctor thought, up out of this class, bound to the land, children undernourished, aroused often by equally ignorant preachers out of their own ranks, that there came materials for such organizations as the KKK. They were the men who did the lynching. The doctor understood his people. "They have been so beaten down for so long. A man never gets so low in life but that he must assert his superiority over something. He must hate. He must. He must. At times the killing of a Negro man brings a kind of joy."

The doctor having also in him a kind of faith. He kept telling me something I had long sensed. "You laughed at me about the best blood of the South," he said one day as I drove with him. We had just passed a particularly poor shack, two girl children and a boy child, all in dirty ragged clothes, hanging over a fragment of broken-down fence. We met a man in the road, also ragged, shambling along toward the shack.

"How-de-doo."

"How-de Jim."

"There," the doctor said, "you saw him. You saw his children." The great grandfather of the man had been a big land and slave owner. "There's your aristocracy," the doctor said. "Jim can't read or write. He doesn't know who his grandfather was. What difference does it make to him? He's one of the lost ones. His wife's dead, died of poor food and child bearing. She was a patient of mine."

A new class in power, hard-headed, money-minded men. A son of Jim's might turn out to be such a man. They made money by driving the people mercilessly, robbing them. They were buying up land. They could make money on cotton land no matter what the price of cotton.

The cotton allotment wasn't going to work. It took care of just such men. Not all land owners were of that sort but that sort were growing in numbers. The allotment meant planting less acres to cotton. What was to become of the little tenant farmers thus thrown off the land?

I asked a woman land owner. There are a good many women running large farms. "I'm going to take care of mine," she said.

"Then it is left pretty much to the good nature, the charity of the land owner?"

"Yes," she said.

My father, who was in the Civil War and who afterwards talked of it endlessly always spoke of southern men . . . half affectionately I thought . . . as "rebs."

"So there the damn rebs were, coming out of the woods. They came at us yelling."

You don't speak of them as "rebs" when you are in the South but occasionally the word slips out. You don't speak of the rebellion. You say, "the war between the states." "You Confederates," you say. The Civil War does, in some odd way, live on. It is still the American epic.

They do not hesitate much about calling you a yank and that is confusing. Let's say you come out of the Middlewest. You always thought, you were taught as a child to think, of the New Englanders as yanks. You want to say, "No sir, and it please you, I'm a middlewesterner not a yank." You keep thinking, at least the Middlewest and the South should begin to get some kind of understanding now. Both countries are essentially agrarian. The agrarian question won't be settled for a long long time. They should be fighting on the same side now. Iowa and Alabama should understand each other. Old hurts last a long time. Both the North and the South are still paying for slavery. The North was so patronizing, talked in such a high moral tone. Think of the hypocritical moral tone of northern politicians during reconstruction.

And the South has been bull-headed and stupid. Think of Alabama and Iowa traditionally belonging to opposite parties.

For the southern story is an agrarian story, a soil story. It remains that. You forget that going south, as most northerners do go, along the big paved highways, through North Carolina, parts of South Carolina, sections of Tennessee, northern Alabama and Georgia. From Greensboro in North Carolina clear to Atlanta, along the line of the southern Railroad, there is one bright, big, busy town after another, labor gathered in from all the back country, High Point, Salisbury, Kannapolis, Concord, Charlotte, Gastonia, Spartanburg, Greenville, Anderson and on into Atlanta, smoke stacks and the characteristic water tank atop the cotton mill never out of your sight as your car runs rapidly along smooth cement highways.

The towns are pretty much mill-owned, the houses in the towns mill-owned. There are bright, attractive mill towns and ugly, sordid ones. At night the lights from the mills gleam across the hills and across the long, flat stretches. Let's say you take the drive on Saturday, or come into one of the towns nowadays anytime after three-thirty in the afternoon. The streets of the towns are crowded with cars . . . many new ones these last few months. Now the mill workers are having a little leisure. There are plenty of good-looking girls, gaily dressed. Young men mill workers are playing ball in vacant lots.

More than once in the past I have cursed the mill owners and some of the mill managers, sometimes to their faces. There is the deadly sameness of the houses in many of the mill towns. I have spoken of the long hours, women and children bound to the fast flying machines for long hours, often at night, the nerve strain, breaking down of nerve fibre young, destruction of human material in the mills but the mill owners and managers always had an answer for me.

"These people came from the ranks of the tenant farmers of the South from among the Poor Whites of the hills. Go visit them in their homes. See what they have there. See what educational opportunities they have, what kind of food they have."

At least in the big towns there were schools. The work of men like Parker of Greenville and others of his kind did count. Manufacturers like Harold Hatch did feel their responsibility. Some of the mill villages are bright and charming. It is true that when some of the industrialists came into some of the towns, they did come, in the minds of the people, almost as saviors. There were meetings held in the little churches, prayers went up. "Save us. Save us." The North still owes a big debt to the South for the cruelty of reconstruction.

It is a little absurd to think of Greensboro in North Carolina and Greenville in South Carolina as being in different states, having to go for their laws to different state legislatures. They are so alike, present so clearly the same human problems. Greenville is so much closer to Greensboro than to Charleston. It is better, if you are trying to think of the South, to think of the whole upper, heavily industrialized section as one state.

It might be called the "Southern Industrial State."

Put against it the "Southern Agrarian State" and it [is] as Texas to Vermont, the whole huge Russian state as against little England.

There will be patches of industry in the great agrarian state. Southern farmers cultivate cotton within sight of the cotton mills in the Industrial State. It would, however, seem more intelligent if we could some day make some new state lines. There is such a thing as regional needs. Industry has made pretty much of a farce out of the old notion of state's rights.

The big industrialist is, after all, a shining mark. If he lives an isolated life in a great house, if his wife pays Hattie Carnegie seven hundred dollars for a dress, if his daughter is a fool and drives past hungry mill workers in a Cord car . . . well, after all we know it, we see it. When a certain mill owner taught children, employed in his mill, to sing a song, telling how much they loved him, what a big, broad, sweet man he was and the children did it publicly . . . when another mill owner's wife said publicly she'd as soon sit down with a Negro as with one of the girls employed in her husband's mill . . . after all it was known . . . there was a laugh, running through houses and through mills. It may have been on the wrong side of the mouth but it was a laugh.

But what about the other fellow, the new type of successful agrarian spoken of above. I saw plenty of evidence of his presence everywhere in the South. I heard stories of Negro women cotton pickers working for him for thirty cents a day, whole families, white and black, for two dollars a week. He isn't big enough to get into the newspapers, he with his three hundred to a thousand acres.

He is there, he is crowding out the old-style gentleman farmer. You know about the old style. Of the old families, the ones once in power in the South, in an amazing number of cases there are no men left. Someone should give a real story of the Civil War some day. There is an inside story.

The story is one of rapid disintegration of southern armies toward the end of the war, when defeats began to be a little common. After all the old slave owning, land owning class, out of which came the pre–Civil War political leaders, the leaders in all phases of southern life, were but a small percent of the people. The Poor Whites, already a dispossessed class, had to make up the rank and file of the southern armies. There [were] some marvelous fighters and stickers among them. There were a good many in it half-heartedly. After all Lincoln in his pronouncement that any kind of slavery degraded labor had an appeal he could make to the common man that Jefferson Davis never had. You have to remember Alexander Stephens'[3] pronouncement that the corner-stone of the Confederacy was slavery.

But the sons of the old land owning families, the old "aristocracy," so called, didn't desert. They stayed, most of them, and got killed and those who came home came to a ruined country. The North didn't do much to help them readjust. It didn't help the Negro to readjust. Everyone was left out on a limb. A lot of the young men, those who had any spunk, went north. They have been doing it ever since. Where do you suppose all of the young southerners in New York and Chicago come from? They aren't the sort who can make money on cotton land with cotton nine, ten or twelve cents a pound.

Leaving, as I have suggested, in an amazing number of cases women to run, or try to run, the old places and to try to carry on something resembling the old life.

Plenty of the old sense of responsibility in many of these. Why should the long dispossessed Poor White or the Negro who never possessed feel responsibility? The world pays bitterly always for degradation of labor.

You would get . . . it is inevitable I think . . . you have got, growing in numbers, this new kind of land man growing in numbers and in power in the South. You have a man who knows how to make money on the land under the hardest kind of conditions. It is a kind of man bound to push to the front in a certain kind of civilization. Press a whole class . . . the Poor White . . . down and down long enough . . .

The North certainly hasn't helped. High tariff walls haven't helped certainly. We of the North have been up to our own little game. We have been satisfied with a romantic picture of the South and with the chatter of our own professional southerners.

Get yourself a little land. Press your labor down and down. You don't need much education to outfigure ignorant Negroes and whites . . .

It's true I have seen the same thing going on in northern coal mining towns. I have seen it in steel towns and in northern textile towns.

And here it is on the land, over a vast agrarian section of the country, a section of the country that should be a garden, that should be rich. It puts the problem in a new light. President Roosevelt can call into his office the big steel man, the auto maker, the cotton mill owner, but he can't call these little ones.

My point is that the problem of the South is an agrarian problem. I think most southerners will agree.

---

# Paying for Old Sins

The main objections that Anderson voices in the following book reviews are against clichés used by both white and black authors who write about the South. For him Carl Carmer was the typical Northerner-come-South, that is, he expressed the region in stereotypical terms that he thought his readers would find charming. Likewise, Anderson chides Langston Hughes for his one-dimensional treatment of whites. Anderson had lived in the South for almost a decade when he wrote these reviews (they were published in *The Nation* in 1934). Having made an honest attempt to confront southern subjects honestly and thoughtfully, he naturally found fault with the limitations he saw in these two volumes.

On the other hand he praises Hughes for his depiction of black characters, although he offers little elaboration on what makes these characterizations effective. An interesting supplement to these remarks may be found in some of Anderson's published letters to Jean Toomer, author of *Cane* (1924).[4] In these he speaks of the need for an authentic black literary voice, something that he himself, being white, could never hope to articulate. In noting that Toomer—and, one assumes, Hughes as well—has this ability, Anderson cautions that this voice must not become tainted by whiteness, nor should it exaggerate its inherent blackness in a self-conscious way.

*Stars Fell on Alabama.* By Carl Carmer. Farrar and Rinehart. $3. *The Ways of White Folks.* By Langston Hughes. Alfred A. Knopf. $2.50.

Carl Carmer went to Alabama a bit too anxious to please. He is so sunny and good-natured about everything from grits and collard greens to Scottsboro that it rather makes your bones ache. These Alabamans are so persistently and so confoundedly cute, even in their cruelties, the aristocracy is so aristocratic and the niggers so niggery. Thank you kindly. Hand me the Bill Faulkner.

Sample, page ninety-three: "We had planned a few days' tour before the visit Mary Louise had planned was to begin. An hour or so after we had started we had seen the red-gold of the dust turn to white. Below that white surface black soil—the Black Belt from whose dark and fertile land rose pillared glories with names that are poems—Rosemont, Bluff Hall, Gainswood, Oakleigh, Farmdale, Snow Hill, Tulip Hill, Winsor, Chantilly, Athol, Longwood, Westwood, Waldwie."

Poems man? You do not make words poetic by asserting they are poetic. Where is your poetry?

The book promises well. There is poetry in the title and the foreword excites. And then, too, Farrar and Rinehart have made the book well. Physically it is beautiful and Mr. Cyrus LeRoy Baldridge has made some drawings that are charming, but for me the book doesn't come off. I have already seen that some critic has said that it was not made for home consumption and I think he is wrong. I think the southerners will love it, particularly the professional southerners of New York and Chicago. Mr. Stribling[5] you are quite safe. This man will never steal your Alabama from you.

Nerts, say I. All this fuss because some Alabama farmer invites you to supper. It always did annoy me, this business, some Yank going South.

No one shoots him. A Negro woman brings a cup of coffee to his bed in the morning. He eats hot bread. The hotel rooms are dirty. Now he is off . . . "Oh this gorgeous land, home of old romance," etc., etc. Not that it isn't all true enough, if you could get below Alabama life, down into it . . . Indiana life for that matter . . . what makes people what they are, the real feel of the life around you, get down into you, become a part of you and come out of you.

I don't think Mr. Carmer does it. He skirts it now and then and when he becomes what he really is, a very competent gatherer-up of names of fiddlers' tunes, collector of folk tales told by others, etc., the book begins to have real value. He should have confined himself to that work. The man is not a story teller.

And, as I have said, this other business, this damned half apology before southerners for being born a northerner, this casualness about southern cruelty. There is an innocent school teacher taken out to a tree and hanged because he had a relative who was a murderer. "Give me a cigarette. Let's go down to Mary Louise's house. These Alabamans are so cute, don't you think."

There is one favorite southern tale I didn't find in the book. It is about the white farmer who came down to the cross-road general store. Several other white farmers lounging about. "Well," he says, "I killed me a nigger this morning." Silence. He yawns. "Boys," he says, "I bet you that nigger will go three hundred pounds." To make his book quite perfect, Mr. Carmer should have got that one in. It is so cute.

*The Ways of White Folks* is something to puzzle you. If Mr. Carmer goes one way, Mr. Langston Hughes[6] goes another. You can't exactly blame him. Mr. Hughes is an infinitely better, more natural, story teller than Mr. Carmer. To my mind he gets the ball over the plate better, has a lot more on the ball, but there is something missed. Mr. Carmer is a member of the northern white race gone South, rather with jaws set, determined to please and be pleased, and Mr. Hughes might be taken as a member of the southern colored race gone North, evidently not determined about anything but with a deep-seated resentment in him. It is in his blood, so deep-seated that he seems himself unconscious of it. The Negro people in these stories of his are so alive, warm, and real and the whites are all caricatures, life, love, laughter, old wisdom all to the Negroes and silly pretense, fakiness, pretty much all to the whites.

It seems to me a paying for old sins all around, reading these two books. We'll be paying for the World War for hundreds of years yet and if we ever get that out of us we may still be paying interest on slavery.

Mr. Hughes, my hat off to you in relation to your own race but not to mine.

It is difficult. The difficulties faced by Mr. Hughes, as a story teller, are infinitely greater than those faced by Mr. Carmer. Mr. Carmer has but to take the old attitude toward the American Negro. "They are amusing. They are so primitive." If you go modern you go so far as to recognize that Negro men can be manly and Negro women beautiful. It is difficult to do even that without at least appearing to be patronizing. You begin to sound like an Englishman talking about Americans or a Virginian talking about a Texan. Even when you don't mean it you sound like that.

The truth is, I suspect, that there is, back of all this, a thing very little understood by any of us. It is an individualistic world. I may join the Socialist or the Communist Party but that doesn't let me out of my own individual struggle with myself. It may be that I can myself establish something between myself and the American Negro man or woman that is sound. Can I hold it? I am sitting in a room with such a man or woman and we are talking. Others, of my own race, come in. How can I tell what is asleep in these others? Something between the Negro man and myself gets destroyed . . . it is the thing D. H. Lawrence was always speaking of as "the flow." My neighbor, the white man, coming in to me as I sit with my Negro friend, may have qualities I value highly but he may also stink with old prejudice. "What, you have a damn nigger in here?" In the mind of the Negro: "Damn the whites. You can't trust them." That, fed constantly by pretense of understanding where there is no understanding. Myself and Mr. Carmer paying constantly for the prejudices of a whole race. Mr. Hughes paying too. Don't think he doesn't pay.

But story telling is something else, or should be. It too seldom is. There are always too many story tellers using their talents to get even with life. There is a plane to be got on—the impersonal. Mr. Hughes gets on it perfectly with his Negro men and women. He has a fine talent. I do not see how anyone can blame him for his hatreds. I think "Red-Headed Baby" is a bum story. The figure of Oceola Jones in the story "The Blues I'm Playing" is the most finely drawn in the book. The book is a good book.

# The TVA

When Anderson and his friend Roger Sergel of Chicago visited the
vast Tennessee Valley Authority project in the late winter of 1934, the
Roosevelt administration had been in office less than a year. Anderson
was on assignment for *Today*, a pro-Roosevelt magazine to which he
would contribute more than a dozen articles from 1933 to 1935. "The
TVA" contains references to such New Deal programs as the NRA (National Recovery Act) and the CCC (Civilian Conservation Corps)
about which Sergel had expressed some skepticism—until he saw firsthand the effort to harness the power of the mighty Tennessee River.
Anderson estimates the future worth of the TVA in human terms. If the
project can raise the standard of living, preserve the environment, and
rechannel natural resources, it will benefit the people of the entire region, who are "the oldest American stock we have." In a larger sense,
however, the TVA represents the success of government (i.e., the policies of the Roosevelt administration) to reach out to the needs of everyday people, or at least it is a beginning toward that end. (In its initial
appearance in *Today* the sketch was titled "A New Chance for the Men
of the Hills."[7]) It is also an acknowledgment of how modern technol-
ogy can improve the quality of modern life.

The text is from *Puzzled America* 54–65.

There is the Tennessee River. It starts up in the Blue Ridge country.
Little rivers come racing down, the Clinch, the Holston, and others.
The Tennessee is a hill-country river, working its way down valleys,
under big hills, little hills, now creeping west, now south, now north—
Virginia, West Virginia, Kentucky, Tennessee, down into northern Alabama. The hill country of north Georgia is in the TVA sphere of influence. That is what this TVA thing is, "a sphere of influence."

It is something to dream and hope for, this land drained by the Tennessee. There are a few rich valleys, growing blue grass. There are mountain ranges. Once all these mountains and hills were covered with magnificent forests. It was one of the two Morgans who are in charge of this
vast enterprise with David Lilienthal, H. A. Morgan,[8] the land man, the

folk man of the project, who talked to me of that. He was president of the University of Tennessee before he got into this thing and he is a land man.

He talked for an hour and I got a sharp sense of the land-loving man. There was the story of how the hill lands had been robbed. No use blaming any one. The big timber men came to denude the hills. Then the little ones with the "peckerwood" mills[9] came to clean up.

The farmers were left on the hills. Traditions grew up about these people. John Fox wrote of them in *The Trail of the Lonesome Pine*. Not so good. Jeeter, of Erskine Caldwell's *Tobacco Road*, is nearer the real thing.[10] They were of the feud country, a pretty romantic lot, in books and stories. In real life they were something else—in real life it was a pitiful rather than a romantic story.

It was the story of a people clinging, year after year, to little hillside farms. Every year they got poorer and poorer. Some of these men went out of their hills to the coal mines and later to the factory towns that had come into the hills, but many came back. There is the love of his own country in the hill man. He does not want to leave the hills.

The depression brought the hill men back faster. I went into little upland valleys where a farm of thirty or forty acres might once have sustained one family. (It would have been poor enough fare—hard enough living for the one family.)

But now, often, on such a farm I found three or four families. Sons had come back to their mountain fathers, bringing wives, bringing children. They had built little huts—often without windows.

"At least here, on my father's land, a little corn can be raised. There will be a cabin floor to sleep on at night. It is less terrible than walking among the out-of-works, in some industrial town."

There is a story of an Englishman coming into the hill country, going among the hill men. The Englishman was stunned.

"These hill men are English," he said. "I don't like it."

"You don't like what?"

"I don't like their failing; I don't like to think of Englishmen as failures in a new land."

It is a land of tall, straight men—the kind of stock out of which came Daniel Boone, Andrew Jackson, Andrew Johnson. They have fine looking children, these men. The children fade young. The women fade young.

There is bad diet. No money. The soil gets thinner and thinner with every passing year. Most of this hill land should go back into forest. Every rain that washes down the hillsides takes more of the soil away.

Suppose you put the hills back into forest, what are you to do with these people? Are you to herd them down into industrial cities, where there are already too many men out of work, living on charity?

You have to think of the fact that what we call the modern world has pretty much gone on past these people, as it has gone completely past the tenant farmers, farther south. There are these mountaineers, millions of them scattered over a vast territory, touching several states. These are not the foreigners of whom we Americans can say so glibly—"If they do not like it here, let them go back where they came from." These men are from the oldest American stock we have. It is the kind of stock out of which came Abraham Lincoln. Robert Lincoln, his father, and Nancy Hanks, his mother, were poor whites of the hills.

And there is all this other stuff about us of which we Americans are so proud, our well-equipped houses, motor cars, bathrooms, warm clothes—what we call our American standard of living. All these things not touching these mountain people.

They are clinging to their hills in one of the most beautiful lands in the world.

"Can we take what they and their hills already have—adding nothing—find the riches in their hills—and give these men modern life? If this modern mechanical life is any good, it should be good for these people."

There is wealth in the land on which these people have tried to live. It is a new kind of wealth, the wealth of the modern man, of the modern world. It is wealth in the form of energy.

Power—the coinage of the modern world!

There is plenty of power—the private companies have only got a little of it so far—flowing silently away, along the Tennessee, along the rivers that come down out of the hills to make the Tennessee.

Long ago, I'm told, army engineers went through these hills. They drew up a kind of plan, having in mind the use of all this wasted power in case of war, power to be harnessed, to make munitions, to kill men.

There came the World War and the building of the Wilson Dam at Muscle Shoals. That is where the Tennessee, in its wanderings, dips down into northern Alabama, thrusts down into the land of cotton. It is something to be seen. All good Americans should go and see it. If the

Russians had it there would be parades, special editions of illustrated magazines got out and distributed by the government.

There it is, however, completely magnificent. You go down, by elevator, some ten stories, under the earth, under the roaring river, and walk out into great light clean rooms. There is a song, the song of the great motors. You are stirred. Something in you—the mechanically-minded American in you—begins to sing. Everything is so huge, so suggestive of power and at the same time so delicate. You walk about muttering.

"No wonder the Russians wanted our engineers," you say to yourself.

The great motors sing on, each motor as large as a city room. There is a proud kind of rebirth of Americanism in you.

"Some of our boys did this," you say to yourself, throwing out your chest.

The Wilson Dam never was made to impound much water. The idea was to take the power directly out of the swirl of water rushing down over the shoals.

But sometimes it doesn't rush. Dry seasons come, far up-river and in the little rivers. The forest-denuded hills do not hold back the water after rains. Every time you build another dam upriver you get power out of the new dam and you increase the power at Muscle Shoals. They are building two dams now, each to make a great lake, the Joe Wheeler, some twenty-five miles above the Wilson, and the Norris, far up-river, a day's drive, near Knoxville. They will both make great lakes, the shore line of the Norris to be some nine hundred miles, it to be at places two hundred feet deep.

Power stored to make a steady stream of power—power from the Wilson being used to build the Joe Wheeler and the Norris—the river being made to harness itself. There is a new kind of poetry in that thought.

These, the first of perhaps a dozen dams to be built along one river— power aplenty for great stretches of country far outside the sphere of influence of the present TVA.

The power to be used, to give an opportunity to small industries, reduce the power costs in towns over a wide country, make electrical power available in homes where it cannot now be used—the money coming in to go back into the country out of which the power came.

Denuded hills to be reforested, soil washing stopped.

This soil washing, going on in every denuded hill country, filling your lakes with mud after you build your dams, utterly destroying, making a barren waste of wide stretches of country. It's hard to dramatize the slow, steady year-after-year eating away of soil richness. Whole lands have been destroyed by it, made into deserts. The government foresters, working with the CCC[11] boys, are like wronged children in their eagerness to make their work understood. "Tell them about it. Please tell them," they keep saying. They follow you around eagerly. "You are a writer. Can't you tell them? Can't you make them understand that we are builders? These CCC camps. We are taking these city kids and making builders of them. The boys in the camps begin to understand. Please make every one understand."

Engineers and foresters going at night, after the day's work, to country towns in the district, to country school houses, lecturing, explaining. I found in these men working on the TVA something I have been hungry to find, men working at work they love, not thinking of money or promotion, happy men, laughing men. They think they are saving something. They think they are making something.

I went into the TVA accompanied by a friend,[12] a business man who lives in Chicago. Formerly he was a college professor. Once he wrote a beautiful novel that got little or no attention. He was poor and went into business. He succeeded.

But like a good many American business men, he wasn't very happy in his success. When the New Deal was announced he went in for it, head over heels.

He was strong for the NRA,[13] but recently he has been skeptical. I had written him, telling him that I was going to look at the TVA, and he wanted to go along. We met in Knoxville and spent most of the first night in a hotel room, talking.

He was discouraged.

"It isn't going to work," he said. He was speaking of the NRA. "They are trying to fix prices now. The small man is doomed." He is himself not one of the small men. "You can't stop the chiselers. You can't. You can't."

We went to look at the TVA. We did look. We listened. We went down among the workers on the dams. We went into power houses, visited men in their offices. Sometimes we were accompanied by enthusiasts, engineers, foresters, and others, and often we were alone. We had our own car.

We kept talking. We kept looking. A change came over my friend.

"So this is the South," he said.

He had the northern man's point of view. To the southerner the South is the deep South. He began talking of the TVA as the South's opportunity. In spite of the fact that my friend was once a college professor, he is an educated man. He knows his American history.

"Look what we northerners did to the South," he kept saying as his enthusiasm grew. "And now this."

We took our look at the TVA, the immediate sphere of influence, and pushed on down into the deep South. We got into the back country, going by back roads.

Men were plowing in the southern fields. There was the thing, always a new wonder to the city man, the patience of men with the earth, the way they cling to it. We were in a poor district. They are not hard to find in the back country of the deep South. There were these miles of back roads, deeply rutted, even dangerous, bridges fallen into decay.

"It is a kind of inferno," my friend kept saying. We had just left the land of new hope, men busy, the strikingly charming government-built town of Norris, at Norris Dam, going up, men laughing at their work—

Memory in us both of a lunch had with a dozen foresters in a town in the heart of the TVA—the town sitting on land that would presently be a lake bottom—the laughter in the room, the anxiety of the men that their story be told straight.

"Don't talk too big. Don't promise too much. We may be stopped."

That against the land of desolation, of no hope—the poor farmers, getting poorer every year. The cotton allotment in the South wasn't going to be of much help to the people along the road we had got into. It would go to the land owners, and not one out of ten of the little farmers, white or black, along the road we travelled would own the land he was plowing—

Poor little unpainted cabins half fallen down. Pale women with tired eyes. Undernourished children playing in bare yards before the cabins.

"There are too many of these."

We had got into an argument. My friend had lived his boyhood on an Iowa farm.

"You have places as bad as this in your Chicago," I said, not wanting him to think all American misery was in the South.

"I know, but not on the land! In the end, everything comes back to the land."

"The people who cannot love the land on which they live are a lost people."

"It is right that all America should try this experiment in the South," he said. There were the one-mule farmers patiently plowing the land beside the road.

"It is wonderful the way man goes on. In spite of defeat he goes on," my friend said.

Two old men came out of a strip of pine woods. They were toothless, bent old men, southerners, poor whites, going along the road in silence. We passed them.

My friend leaned out of the car. He was excited.

"Hey!" he called.

The two old men stopped and stared at us. I stopped the car. My friend hesitated.

"Drive on," he said. He turned to me and laughed. "I wanted to tell them something. I can't," he said. "It would sound too silly."

"What?" I said.

"Something new in American life is begun back there, and it mustn't be stopped," he said. I thought it was the feeling, alive in him, as it is still curiously alive in so many Americans, alive in spite of greed, chiseling, desire for fake money, bigness. The feeling of men for men—desire to some day work for others. The TVA may be a beginning.

---

## They Elected Him

In his profile of Rush Holt, a recently elected U.S. senator from West Virginia, Anderson's method is more journalistic than artistic. He has obviously followed his subject on the campaign trail and has seen him in action on the floor of the state legislature. Yet he still relies on familiar techniques such as colorful anecdote and hypothetical dialogue. Obviously, Holt was the kind of politician that Anderson admired—bright, independent, hard-working, honest, progressive, and prolabor. Holt's youth (he may be too young to be seated in the Senate) seems to suggest to Anderson the rebounding energy of the American political process as represented by the Roosevelt administration.

The text is from *Puzzled America* 183–98.

To an older man, any older man, going into West Virginia any time within the last three or four years, there would have come at once a prejudice: "Who is this Rush Holt, everyone in West Virginia is talking about?"

"So here is another of these 'flash' young men." Such young men, often by circumstances thus pushed up, these young Napoleons! The older man remembers that it was in the hills of West Virginia that the young George McClellan got his start as a warrior, the young McClellan who later, hailed as a young Napoleon, was suddenly pushed up to command of the Army of the Potomac. How it all went to his head. He was the great one. He kept Abraham Lincoln waiting in the hallway of his house. "I haven't time to see him now. I'm busy." A few quite amazing victories in the hills of West Virginia early in the war, and then that. Will the same thing happen to Rush Holt?

It is a fair question because what Rush Holt has done in West Virginia is something new in American affairs, and certainly new in West Virginia. Do you know West Virginia? You should. It is one of the most interesting states in America.

It is a land of mountains and swift-flowing rivers, of big water-power companies, gas, oil, and coal.

Coal, plenty of coal.

They have been taking it out of the West Virginia hills by the millions of tons, shovelling it out, using the latest mining machinery, blowing it out of the hills by the acre, any way to get it out quickly and at the lowest possible cost.

Plenty of good mines ruined when they were but half worked out, plenty of men killed in the mines because of cheap, hurried timbering. The waste of power and wealth in coal in the country is like the huge land waste in America. It is one of the crimes of America. Any man who travels over this country and does not see everywhere the necessity for a new regimentation is blind. Individual liberty means, too much, liberty to destroy.

Although West Virginia is a land where millionaires have been made rapidly, coal, oil, gas, waterpower, lumber, and industrial millionaires, it has also made plenty of poverty. There are a hundred thousand coal miners in West Virginia, men in the big mines, the little mines, the wagon mines. A few years ago around Weston, where this new man, this new West Virginia leader, Rush Holt, came from, they struck gas. It was so plentiful and so cheap that for a time, for a few years, they sold it to you for twenty-five cents the fire. You turned it on, left it on, threw the windows open to cool the house. What difference did it make. The biggest, highest-powered gas well ever blown off in America was blown off near Weston.

Go into West Virginia now and they'll tell you. Older men will tell you an old American story of the days of the opening up of the country—the coal mines being opened up, one after another, each new mine bigger than the last, the water-power companies coming, old Mother Earth belching forth her gas, the old lady being more and more wounded and hurt. Blood flowing out of her wounds.

On every side new millionaires being made. Get yourself a piece of mountain land. Dig down into it, bore down. You may be the lucky one. This is a free country. Every man has a chance here.

Over in the neighboring coal and power state of Pennsylvania they had the same thing but also something else. In Pennsylvania there was always the background of solid German and Dutch farmers. Drive west from Philadelphia into the land over about Lancaster and York. It is one of the sweetest, richest farming sections in America and every year it grows richer.

But there is nothing like this in West Virginia. It is a land of riches and poverty. Never, in all my wanderings over America, have I seen such desolate towns. They send a shudder down the spine. "Are children raised in these black holes?" you ask yourself. "Do boys and girls grow into manhood and womanhood here?" You stop your car on one of the paved highways above such a town. There is the mine, that black hole in the side of the mountain above the road. Coal, thousands of tons, comes roaring down a runway to the tipple. Below there is a river, and the rivers of West Virginia are very beautiful, and beside the river a mining town. Often such a town will be quite empty, the mine worked out, the houses, so poorly, so shabbily built in the beginning, now with roofs sagging and the doors and windows gone.

But you have stopped by a town still occupied, a mine still being worked. There is a railroad along the bank of the river, below the town, and beside the railroad, a long row of coke ovens.

The coke ovens are pouring forth black smoke. The wind blows it down over the town. It lifts and falls. Although you have stopped your car within a few hundred yards of the spot where the town used to be, the town itself is often quite wiped out. Only a dense cloud of black smoke lies over the place where it once stood.

It is a matter of black wonder to the man out of the open country, away from these hills. He keeps asking himself—"Can ordinary human life go on here, in this black land?" It does. Now the smoke lifts. So life goes on here as in any American town, a little clean New England town or an Iowa corn-shipping town. See, it is fall now and a group of boys—half men, in their football togs—are in a vacant lot running off football signals. Red Jacket, home of the famous Yellow Dog Contract,[14] will be playing the schoolboys of Matewan next Saturday. Laughter and cries out of the black smoke down there.

Here comes a young man, a young miner, down a path in the scrubby wood that leads up into the hills, his arm about the waist of a young woman. They'll tell you these West Virginia miners are not Americans. It's a lie. Many are American to the bone.

The onlooker remembers stories he has been hearing, stories picked up from the lips of coal miners in company stores, in a coal miner's house where three or four big-bodied miners sat smoking their pipes about the kitchen stove after the day in the mine. "How about a little more of that beer, Jake?" Stories of fights in the mines, on the streets of the mining town. Stories of the old Hatfield-McCoy feud of Mingo and McDowell counties, over on the Tug River, at the edge of Kentucky, land where almost every man you met on the streets of a mining town went armed. Men shooting their way into power. Men keeping power with shotguns and rifles. "We were lying up above town in the hills; when the thugs came down the railroad track we gave it to them. We got eight."

Strangers coming into such a town, travelling salesmen and others were often stopped on the street. Or a merchant told such a one, "Say stranger, let me tell you something. If you've got any opinions keep them to yourself. Keep your mouth shut while you are in this county."

The young man, Rush Holt—now suddenly pushed up, largely by labor, to be the outstanding leader in West Virginia. His first name is Rush—he is aptly named—he's a fast one all right, has been fast since he was born, twenty-nine years ago. He did not come out of a mining town, but out of the rolling hill country some hundred and fifty miles northeast of Charleston, up near the Pennsylvania line. His people, on both his father's and mother's side, have been there in that country a long time. They were there and Weston was an old town before the Civil War, when West Virginia was a part of old Virginia. Old Virginia built a huge stone hospital up there. West Virginia wasn't so rich then. The forests hadn't been cut away, but few of the mines had been opened.

It was a land of hill people, and here is something interesting. Hill people are proverbially an independent proud people and coal miners are not meek. There is nothing of the pale factory hand about your coal miner. In the first place, the very nature of the miner's work makes him a proud, a highly individual man. The miners do not work in large gangs, under the eye of a boss, but commonly by twos, in little rooms down under the ground. They work always in the face of danger. Each man must depend absolutely on the courage and coolness of his fellow. See the miners coming out of the mines at evening. Their faces are black. The coal miner's lamp is in the caps. There are white men and Negro men, now all black. See them as they walk in the streets of their towns. "Go to the devil. I'm a man. I do a man's work. Just because I am black and dirty and do black dirty work, don't expect me to kowtow to you." Between the native mountain man and the coal miner there is something in common and, for that matter, a great many of the West Virginia coal miners come out of the hills.

And so there they are, the coal miners, and there are the Holts of Weston. The Holts are a tall, lean, good-looking race. And what striking individuals. Rush Holt's grandfather, although he was a Virginian, was a northern sympathizer when the Civil War came, but when his son, Matthew Holt, ran away from home and enlisted in the northern army at thirteen, then the old man went and jerked him out. "If you are going to fight, I'll tell you who and when to fight."

"No, you will not. I'm only thirteen now, and you can get me out of this war, but I'll find my own wars."

He did. Rush Holt's father, Doctor Matthew Holt of Weston, West Virginia, has been in a fight ever since. Now he is the independent mayor of the town of Weston. The Civil War is the only fight in a long life he has missed. He became a doctor and didn't marry until he was forty-eight. His son Rush, at twenty-nine, isn't married yet. He'll be a catch when he gets to Washington, this young senator.

And I dare say that almost every normal town in America has a character like Matthew Holt. He would have lived until he was forty-eight at the town hotel. He was a doctor and a good one, and all day rode around the country, curing people and getting into arguments. He would have read Bellamy's *Looking Backward* and the books of Bob Ingersoll.[15] As he spent most of his days driving about the country in a horse and buggy, he would have become a bit horse crazy.

"Well, why not. I'm not married and have no kids. I make money. Why not spend it on horses?" He would have been fond of fast trotters, and had some good ones in his stables, taking them about the country to the county fairs.

And when not driving a fast horse, he would engage in an argument, in the town drugstore or on the courthouse steps.

He would have been the sort of man who got into every fight that ever started in that fighting country. Like his son Rush, he would have been a smiling fighter, not hating the men he fought, never hating. What is the use wasting energy in hating? A country doctor finds out about other men. He is engaged in a bitter fight with Jim Smith today—the fights are always about ideas—Doctor Matthew Holt, an old man now, would have been strong for woman's suffrage before the women of his town had ever heard of it. He would have been for birth control before Margaret Sanger[16] was born—he is in a bitter fight with Jim Smith today but tomorrow night Jim's baby will be taken ill suddenly, and there is Doctor Holt by the bedside. There is something nice in his voice now.

"Take it easy, Jim. Don't worry. We'll pull her through."

Such a man, well-hated sometimes, sometimes deeply loved. When the World War came on, he was already an old man, married now and the father of six children—his wife, the Scotch woman, Chilela Dew— the Dews also a professional family, all school teachers, or doctors, or judges—a great-aunt of Rush Holt's was the first woman in West Virginia to pass the state medical board and to get a license to practice medicine in the state—when the World War came on, old Doctor Holt was against it. He saw it then as we all see it now. He fought openly against it and one night, when he was returning from the bedside of a patient, a mob set upon him. He had his wife with him in his car, she also was an old woman now, and one of the rocks, thrown by the mob, clipped her on the head. It didn't kill her. They don't kill easily in that family.

But the old doctor didn't quit fighting, and he had help. A crowd of men came to the front. They didn't agree with the old doc, but he was the old doc. Tall men from the hills came down with their rifles and marched up and down before his house. They set a guard over him and his house. "We don't agree with your damned opinions, doc, but you go on fighting. We'll stand by you." It was Voltaire's pronouncement taking an American form. "I don't agree with a damn word you say, doc, but I'll fight for your right to say it."

The doctor, Rush Holt's father, did keep on fighting, sometimes having the whole town with him and sometimes having it against him. He fought the gas companies, the power companies. Only two years ago, at eighty-four, he put up for mayor. He wasn't on either the Democratic or Republican ticket. "All right. I'll run. If you want me for mayor, write my name on the ticket." They did. He got more votes than the two regular candidates combined.

I have already said that young Rush Holt was fast. I rode with one of his brothers in a car. We went along over the mountain roads at sixty but he apologized to me. "Rush drives faster than I do," he said.

Rush was out of high school at fourteen and went down to the University of Cincinnati. He was wearing short pants yet and they wouldn't take him, but the University of West Virginia would. They thought, down at Cincinnati, that he was too much the child.

They thought the same thing when he got into the state legislature and also when, at the request of the working men of his state, he put up for the Democratic nomination for Senator. In the newspapers of the state, they put cartoons showing him riding about in a kiddy-car. A newspaper man at Charleston told me an amusing story.

"When he first came down here, to the state legislature," said the newspaper man—most of the newspapers of the state had been either against Rush or had been mild supporters in the fights he had made in the state—fights against the power companies and the big corporations—but the newspaper men, the leg men, have been for him to a man—the newspaper man laughed—"he came down here and there was a question of seats on the floor of the House. Rush went to the man who arranges about the seats. 'I want to be up front. I guess I'll be doing quite a lot of speaking,' he said."

That and the other story—when he was swept into the Democratic nomination for the United States Senate, defeating seven other older and more experienced political figures. They told him he couldn't get into the United States Senate.

"You have to be thirty, and you will be only twenty-nine."

"Oh, I don't know," he said. "Henry Clay got in at twenty-nine."

It is a laugh. It is something good. My own impression of Rush Holt, got before I ever saw him, on other trips into West Virginia when he was being talked of in the state, wasn't very favorable. "So, another young genius," I said to myself. "Very likely he'll be a young smart-aleck."

Then I went and watched him at work on the floor of the legislature of his state. I went unannounced to some of his political meetings. I followed him into the rough country, into McDowell and Mingo counties, saw him at miners' meetings. By this time, having begun to sense his power with the voters, his opponents had begun to call him a Communist, a Socialist, an atheist.

"See, he don't believe in God," they cried.

"I'm not running against God," he replied.

He did it smiling. He did everything smiling. He is a smiling young man. When he was in the state legislature, I saw, as any man sitting and watching could see, that his power in the state was due largely to knowledge. Young Holt had simply been a lamp-burner, a student. He had come from a race of men who were all students and he was running true to form. It was said of him, by newspaper men and by other members of the state legislature, when he was in Charleston as a member of the lower House—he jumped directly from that to the Democratic nomination for the United States Senate—"He knows more about the laws of this state, what they are, what they mean, how they got on the books, who put them on the books, than any man we have ever had in the House."

It was a year ago that I sat in the West Virginia State House, the Legislature being in session, watching him at work. Other members of the House kept running to him. "What does this bill mean? Explain it to me."

He did explain. When the House wasn't in session, he got into his car and, running over the state, explained to the voters. He went into a hundred county-seat towns, explaining and explaining. As every one knows, most members of most state legislatures are of a certain type. They are country lawyers. They do not get down to the state capitol very often. When they go down, as House members or as members of the state senate, there is always a lot going on.

Almost every night a party—this lobbyist or that lobbyist pulling a party. "Come on, boys. How about a little fun tonight?" A man doesn't have much time to get up on what is going on.

It takes a crank for that, a worker. It takes a man who wants to know.

And young Holt is that. I have watched him in the legislature of his state. I have talked about him to young men and old men, merchants of his state and workers.

He speaks to the voters of the complaint that he is too young.

"I can't help that," he says. "I got born as soon as I could."

Rush Holt, the youngster, made his campaign for the senatorship from West Virginia on facts. He is a fact hound. All of his speeches are an array of facts piled up. "Here is what my opponent says to you. Well, here is how he has voted." Not often needing written records, he has it all at his mind's edge, the exact time and place of every vote of every member of his state legislature, not only in his own time but far back of that. He has the records of the congressmen of his state, the senators of his state. He told them, when he first went down to Charleston as a young legislator, that he was going to do a lot of talking, and he has done a lot. He has come very near talking the state of West Virginia into something new, something it never was before, a state curiously aware.

Rush Holt has made it that, and he isn't a crank or a fly-by-night. If he goes to Washington to represent his state in the Senate and he will—he won't go as the young McClellan went after certain West Virginia victories to the Army of the Potomac—as a young Napoleon. He will go as a fighting young student, a very smiling and warm young man. They feel now, over in West Virginia, that they have got, in their young Holt, something pretty good and significant in American politics. If young Holt keeps his head, and I fancy he will—if he goes on as he has begun, he will be too busy, as a student, to get the big head—if he goes on as he has begun, the whole country will presently be liking and admiring him as he is now liked and admired in West Virginia.

---

# Hard-Boiled

The solitary hitchhiker is a commonplace figure in American literature of the depression era. Anderson often gave rides to such people—for instance, the young Irishman in the "Piney Woods" sketch in Chapter 3—mainly because of a life-long passion to learn the personal stories of people that interested him. The woman he picks up in Boone, North Carolina, has been badly scarred by having witnessed the murder of her father by her brother and hardened by abusive lovers. Yet she still has a certain resilience and cheerfulness. In a literary sense she is emblematic of a class of person in the South and elsewhere in the depression years in that she is a kind of vagabond, uprooted from home and wandering aimlessly. Having developed a hard, impassive shell, she accepts a small gift of money from Anderson without emotion.

"Hard-Boiled" was originally published in the *Marion Democrat* on August 30, 1932; and reprinted in *Direction* 1 (April 1938): 8–9.

She was obviously a female drifter. That is one of the things that happens. As you drive about the country you find both men and women drifters. It may be that this woman was not only drifting from place to place, from factory door to factory door, as men out of work do, but that she was also drifting from man to man. She may have been one of the kind who live with one man for a time and then drift on to another. There was something hard about her. She talked freely and boldly. As you looked at her, you felt that she had no roots that she had put down into the ground anywhere. She had no house, no garden, no town, but was surprisingly, amazingly cheerful. I picked her up in the road one day, near the town of Boone, in North Carolina.

There had been a tragedy in her life when she was a young girl. It may have changed her whole life. She grew up on a small tenant farm in the hills of North Carolina and, when she was still a young girl, her older brother killed her father. There were but two children in the family.

Her brother had been sent to prison for life. She told me about it as we drove along. At first she was reticent, staring at me when I spoke to her with her rather hard blue eyes, but gradually she grew more friendly. She realized that I wanted nothing from her and that I was interested. She told me all about the killing of her father by her brother as one might tell the story of an automobile wreck seen by an on-looker. The point is that the story did not seem personal to her. She seemed outside it.

"Well it happened. This is the way it happened." That was the way she told the story.

There are people to whom nothing is very personal. Her father could not make a decent living as a farmer. He had not remained on one farm but had drifted from place to place, always hoping he would be lucky and make a little money. The family had always been poor. Poverty strengthens one man while it weakens another. The father had got ugly-tempered.

There was the brother who still lived at home and he also was always broke. Like the father he was a dissatisfied man. When he could get the money for liquor he got drunk. He often came home drunk.

He was half drunk on the day when he got an axe and killed his father, did the act for which he was sent to prison for life. The woman in the car seemed rather to enjoy telling of the killing. She described the scene, herself standing by the door of a mountain cabin and looking on.

It was raining. It was winter when it happened. You knew, listening to her although she did not say so, that it was a poor miserable house. No doubt the roof leaked.

Her father would have been, as suggested, a southern poor white, living in a little shack. There would have been a few sad-looking chickens in a yard and a sad-faced woman, the wife and mother, somewhere in the house. The brother was somewhat older than the woman I picked up. He was in the house, lying on a dirty bed. He had been sent off to a town ten miles away on the day before. He took a little money to get supplies. The woman said her father had rheumatism and couldn't go. The young man had spent the money to get drunk. He had come staggering home late that morning.

The father was angry and ill-tempered and went about the house and the yard cursing the son and at first the son had answered but later he had grown silent. The son was larger and stronger than the father. The father kept it up . . . a chance for his hatred to escape. It might have been land hatred. That would have been it. He hated the land because he had worked on it all his life and had got nothing. He had drifted from place to place, the land he worked always belonging to someone else, half the crops taken by someone else. He was always in debt.

He was getting relief by taking it out on his son. On the day before it had been the wife and tomorrow it might be the daughter. The father sat down on some steps at the rear of the house and stared into the hills. He kept cursing the son.

So the son killed him. He got up from the soiled bed and went barefooted across the room of the cabin. There was an axe leaning against the wall. He got it. He went softly out of the house past his sister, pushing her aside. "I didn't scream," she said, telling of it, "I didn't do a damn thing."

"Didn't you care?"

"Oh, not so much. Dad was dad."

The son had split the father's head open and she seemed to like describing the scene. It had been an exciting event for her—she and the mother running and screaming in a mountain road and then later going to court. They became the center of attention. They had to go, day after day, to the courthouse at the county seat, ten miles away, for the trial of the son and brother and something happened there too. The woman told about that. She and the mother had been brought to town as witnesses in the trial of her brother. The woman talking to me—in spite of a sort of heaviness, roughness, hardness really—had the thing our talkie actresses so desire. She had "It." [17] One day when she was in court, during her brother's trial, a young man of the town got a chance to whisper to her. She might have been quite comely then. He was a bold tough young man of the North Carolina county-seat town. "Will you be in town tonight?"

"Well!"

She wanted to stay in town. She was already wise. If she could make a little money she might get a chance to go to the talkies. There was even a chance for a new dress. She didn't yet know much about the handling of such matters, how to approach a certain question, but the young man took a dollar bill out of his pocket and, holding it in his hand, showed it to her and made a movement with his eyes. She herself told me all this. She told it as she had told of the killing of the father.

So she stayed in town. She made no explanation to her mother that night and never did. The mother was afraid of her. Life had made the mother afraid of everyone.

A neighbor had brought the two women to town and when it was time for them to go home the daughter couldn't be found. The mother had to go home. There was a cow to milk and a pig to feed. The daughter walked up and down the main street of the county-seat town and presently the young man who had spoken to her appeared and took her to a car. There has always been, in society, a certain type of woman, working at an old old trade. This is the way they begin. There were three men in the car. They took her into the country and afterwards they cheated her. She was green then. They didn't give her a cent, she said. They laughed at her. She swore viciously when she told of it.

I left her in the main street of another North Carolina town. "Have you any money now?" I asked.

"No," she said quite cheerfully. She had herself. She was young. I gave her fifty cents. I wouldn't call it a generous flourish. Perhaps I was merely being a moralist. "It may mean one less assault," I thought. It seemed to me that all of her relations with men had been assaults. I didn't say so and she did not thank me for the money. She took the fifty cents and after staring at me with her strange hard eyes walked briskly and cheerfully away along a street of the town.

---

## City Gangs Enslave Moonshine Mountaineers *and* from *Kit Brandon: A Portrait,* Chapter 5

Sometime in early 1935 Henry Morgenthau, Secretary of the Treasury in the first Roosevelt administration, asked Anderson to go over to Franklin County, Virginia, some fifty miles distant, to assess the conditions behind an immense trial that was about to take place in the federal court in Roanoke. Thirty-four persons were being tried for conspiring to violate the Internal Revenue Service laws of the United States in one of the largest contraband liquor operations in the nation. Even though prohibition had been repealed in 1933, this enterprise had continued to flourish largely because of big city syndicates coming to the mountain men for their product. The article that Anderson wrote on the trial is somewhat atypical of his feature sketches in that it contains numerous statistics defining the enormity of the illicit industry in this remote corner of the rural South. However, one point he makes of these facts is that once again the small producer was being manipulated and, of course, exploited, by larger interests.

As for actual individuals involved in the case, the one who attracted Anderson's particular interest was Mrs. Willie Carter Sharpe. A girl from the hills who had worked as a dime-store clerk, she had become involved in moonshine distribution and married the son of a liquor baron. On the witness stand she regaled the court with fabulous stories of driving powerful cars filled with moonshine and eluding caravans of state and federal pursuers, often speeding through the streets of towns at seventy-five miles an hour. Not only was her reputation notorious, her court testimony was riveting. She had attained a kind of legendary status, epitomizing the excitement and danger of bootlegging. She claimed that even blue-blooded Virginia women had asked to ride with her for the "kick" of it.

Morgenthau had asked Anderson to get the "human" story behind the case. It is told in the first piece by the emphasis on the role of the everyday "cobweb," the small operator engulfed in the larger network. It is told in yet another way in *Kit Brandon: A Portrait* (1936), Anderson's final novel, whose protagonist is modeled closely on Willie Carter Sharpe.[18] Anderson wrote of talking with her at length in an attempt to discern the woman behind the legend. Kit recounts events from her early life and her fascination with fast cars and the thrill of the chase; however, she is anything but a one-dimensional character. Her real desire is for the usual human needs—respect, love, a mate "with whom she could make a real partnership in living." In the chapter reprinted below some details from this background are included. But the main figure in this segment is Tom Halsey, father of the young man Kit was married to, and a fictional counterpart of the kind of bootlegging king that had been tried in Roanoke in the spring of 1935.

"City Gangs" appeared in *Liberty* 12 (November 2, 1935): 12–13. *Kit Brandon: A Portrait* was published by Scribner's in 1936.


## City Gangs Enslave Moonshine Mountaineers

What is the wettest section in the U.S.A., the place where, during prohibition and since, the most illicit liquor has been made? The extreme wet spot, per number of people, isn't in New York or Chicago. By the undisputed evidence given at a recent trial in the United States Court at Roanoke, Virginia, the spot that fairly dripped illicit liquor, and kept right on dripping it after prohibition ended, is in the mountain country of Southwestern Virginia—in Franklin County, Virginia.

Franklin is a big county and practically all mountains. It lies just south of the county seat, Rocky Mount, and some twenty-five miles due south of the industrial city of Roanoke and but a few miles from Lynchburg, home town of Senator Glass.[19]

These big towns and others, growing factory towns, Staunton, birthplace of President Wilson; Winchester, place of many battles during the Civil War, home town now of Senator Harry Byrd;[20] Lexington, home of Stonewall Jackson and the place where Robert E. Lee went to become a schoolteacher after Appomattox—a Lee was among others recently being tried in the United States Court—all of these towns lie in the famous rich valley of Virginia, the Shenandoah Valley. Lynchburg, as you go west from tidewater Virginia, is really the beginning of the mountains—Virginia's portion of the famous southern highlands, land of moonshiners and of the feuds.

Involved in the trial at Roanoke were some of the solid men of the big mountain county. There were merchants, automobile salesmen, liquor financiers, sheriffs and deputy sheriffs, a member of the state prohibition force, a federal revenue man—makers and more makers of moon—and the charge on which these men were tried was not alone that of liquor making, but of a conspiracy to beat the government out of the tax on liquor. Carter Lee, a grandnephew of Robert E. Lee, was up there, facing a possible prison term, and the South was shocked. He came clear. The jury declared he was not guilty. He is the prosecuting attorney of the mountain county and, of all the men indicted, he and two unimportant deputy sheriffs were the only ones who did come clear.

As to the amount of liquor made in the mountain county right on in the years after prohibition ended, some notion may be had by the figures given in the testimony.

Fred O. Maier, representative of Standard Brands, Washington, D.C., testified that 70,448 pounds of a single standard brand of yeast, such as is used in distilling, was sold in the county in four years. The yeast was sold in pound packages, each containing thirty-two pieces. That sounds something like 21,000,000 brews. A lot. Franklin County, Virginia, has a population of 24,000. The city of Richmond, with 189,000 people, used 2,000 pounds of yeast during the same period. There were said to be single families in the county that used 5,000 pounds of sugar a month.

There were other startling figures introduced by the government. These, totaled by government statisticians, revealed purchases of commodities useful to illicit liquor makers as follows: sugar, 33,839,109 pounds; corn meal, 13,307,477 pounds; rye meal, 2,408,308 pounds; malt, 1,018,420 pounds; hops, 30,366 pounds; and miscellaneous grain products, 15,276,071 pounds.

Someone had invented a five-gallon non-gurgling tin can. That was an idea. Most of the liquor made in this Virginia mountain county had to be run out to some distant city, and one of the pests to the rumrunner is the gurgling sound arising from containers on rough roads. The non-gurgling cans apparently worked.

And they sold. Into this one mountain county during a four-year period there were shipped 205 carloads of 516,176 pounds. One witness testified that a carload runs about 3,000 cans, which means that the county consumed more than 600,000 of the five-gallon cans.

That would account for some 3,501,115 gallons of moon liquor pouring down out of this one mountain county, being rushed at night in fast cars into the coal-mining regions of West Virginia, to the big Virginia towns along the valley, to Roanoke, Lynchburg, Norfolk, and on into eastern cities. The business, once organized, kept growing. They were at it up to the moment when some thirty-four of the more prominent citizens of the county were brought into the United States Court.

In this mountain country in the very heart of America, the government in its recent wholesale raid didn't pay much attention to the little moonshiner ("blockader" is the local name for the illicit liquor maker). He exists everywhere but he doesn't count. On the witness stand at the big trial some of the big makers spoke of these little picayune makers, and always contemptuously. "These little cobwebs," they said, meaning the poor little hillside farmer, the poor mountain white, who creeps off up some mountain stream, under the deep twisted laurel, with a home-made still, to run himself off "a leetle run" for his own use, or perhaps to sell a gallon now and then.

In Franklin County the little fellows were out. The officers, it seemed, had to make a show now and then, a few stills captured and cut up. So they got the cobwebs. Any number of the little fellows testified at the trial. "I tried making a little run but I got caught."

Sometimes one of the big fellows, or a county or state officer, came to call on such a little cobweb.

"Howdy, Jim."

"Howdy, Jake."

"You been making a little now and then, eh, Jim?"

"You know I have, Jake. But I ain't had no luck."

"You got your still cut up, eh?"

"I sure did, Jake."

A smile from Jake. "Suppose, Jim, you go see Jeff. You know who I mean. You talk to Jeff." (Jeff would be one of the big shots.) "I think, Jim, you might have you a little better luck than you been having."

It was the contention of the government in the conspiracy trial that the little fellows, the old-fashioned rifle-toting mountain moonshiners of romance, had been quite put out of business in this section.

The county had been divided off into sections, a big blockader and a state officer for each section. Some of the really big operators didn't make any liquor at all. They let out the job to other mountain men. "Jim, I'll be up your way next Wednesday night at about ten. Where'll be a good place to leave the stuff?"

Witnesses at the big trial, testifying:

"So I was working for Jeff" (or "Henry" or "Peg"). "I was hauling. So I hauled the yeast out, the sugar out, the meal out."

"Where'd you leave it, Ed?"

"I left it just where I was told, sometimes by a bunch of trees or laurels just off the road—maybe ten, fifteen, twenty hundred-pound bags of sugar, so much meal, so many cans, so much yeast."

"You just dumped it down there in the dark? And there was no one there to receive it?"

"There may have been some one there. I dunno. It was black night. I didn't see no one."

"And what did you get for this, Ed? Bear in mind, Ed, you were running the risk of going to prison every trip you took."

"Yes, I know. I got maybe a dollar, maybe a dollar and a half."

There was plenty of testimony of that sort. Men running stills, back in the mountain laurel, for the big fellows, working for the big fellows— some of them testified, turning out moon at ten cents a gallon.

There should have been money in that for the big fellows! There was.

There were plenty of romantic figures at the trial. The government had two attorneys and the county men had some ten or twelve. In a United States Court the judge can question witnesses. He can make comments.

One of the lawyers pleading to the jury for a mountain man: "Men, send him back where he came from. Send him back to his mountain home."

The judge: "You mean, send him back to keep making the same kind of mean whiskey he was making."

There was Willy Carter Sharpe on the witness stand. She is a rather handsome slender black-haired woman of thirty. It came out, when she was questioned, that she had been a mountain child from a neighboring county, and as a child had gone down into a Southern industrial town to work in a cotton mill. Then a spell in an overall factory and a job in a five-and-ten-cent store. She met and married the son of a big shot.

"I began selling liquor around town, drumming up trade."

She had, however, a passion for automobiles and developed into a fast and efficient driver. A Virginia businessman at the trial, full of admiration, whispered of her accomplishments: "I saw her go right through the main street of our town and there was a federal car after her. They were banging away, trying to shoot down her tires, and she was driving at seventy-five miles an hour.

"She got away," said the businessman. He liked her, as did everyone in the courtroom. She told her story frankly, as did many other witnesses. It was evident that something new had sprung up in the mountains—big business, mass production, introduced by a few shrewd determined men, the plan being to make the little fellows work at a dangerous occupation—prisons staring at them—for little more than a day's wage.

There were mountain boys and men working nights at the still—big stills some of them, 1,000- or 2,000-gallon capacity. Men hauling the meal, sugar, yeast, and containers back up into the hills at night.

"What did you get?"

"Oh I got a dollar a trip."

The lawyers for the defense didn't even cross-examine Willy Carter Sharpe. She told a story of mountain men become big-time promoters, convoys of cars on the roads at night, herself in a fast car acting as pilot, government men, not fixed, coming in from Washington, the chase at night, cars scattering, dashing through the night streets of towns, the big business carried right on after prohibition ended.

Men in the crowd in the courtroom whispering: "This is the biggest it's ever been in the mountains. This'll clean things up."

One of the men accused—he had pleaded guilty and faced prison: "I'm glad it's over. It had got too big. We don't want our county to be like that."

After she had been on the witness stand and had told her story, Willy Carter Sharpe talked freely. "It was the excitement got me," she said, and spoke of other rumrunners employed by the big shots. "They were mostly kids who liked the excitement." There were women, some of them of respectable families, who came to her—this after she had been in jail, had been in the newspapers. "They wanted to go along with me on a run at night. They wanted the kick of it," she said. She refused to tell who they were. "Some of them had in their veins what you call the best blood of Virginia," she said.

The trial was extraordinary. Even some of the big-shots—mountain men who had gone into the outlaw liquor business in the new big way—

came down out of the hills to testify for the government. The jury was made up pretty much of mountain men from neighboring counties. The mountain men came down, some of them, to convict themselves. They seemed to want it stopped. They seemed to want to go back to the old ways.

The big way was too cruel. It brought out too many ugly things in men.

## Kit Brandon: A Portrait, Chapter 5

There were all kinds of fellows in with Tom Halsey, more or less under his orders, some bold ones, some sly crafty ones, some brutes. They talked, whispered among themselves. "What the hell?" It was because of Tom Halsey's son, young Gordon Halsey. He had got stuck on the skirt—Kit Brandon.

There was that other woman, Kate, a good deal older than Kit. She was all right. She knew how to keep her mouth shut.

But just the same. It was an old, old idea—*cherchez la femme.* "They gab. You get in a jam and you are mixed up with some dame and, sure as hell, she runs out on you."

The old war between men and women. Many of the mountain men who worked with Tom Halsey . . . Tom was a pioneer, a bringer of a new and modern world into the mountain life . . . they were of an older order.

You saw a mountain man coming into some little mountain town afoot. He strode along the road ahead of his woman, did not walk beside her. Many of the mountain men had big families. The children walked in the road behind, the girl children at the end of the little procession. When a son of the family had reached maturity, began to think of himself as a man, he stepped ahead of his mother and walked just at the heels of his father.

The women submitted. A mountain man did not do any work about the house. He did not milk the cow, feed the pigs, carry firewood into the house. He crept away to the woods to make himself a run of liquor; he worked in his few hillside fields.

But the new world had come, even into the hills. Paved roads were being pushed through. They twisted and wound along little river bottoms, under majestic hills, occasionally climbed over a hill and went on down into another valley. Industrial towns had come, some of them growing swiftly, towns of North Carolina, eastern Tennessee, eastern Kentucky, southwest Virginia. Tourists in Fords, Chevrolets, Buicks, Packards went whirling along roads and through the hills. The industrial towns had come because of power in the rivers of the hills and because of cheap labor. There were still hundreds of square miles of country in the mountains apparently uninhabited, but not uninhabited. The tourist going along in his car looked about. "What a desolate country!" He was mistaken. There were many thousands, even hundreds of thousands of people, hidden away, in little hollows, on mountain sides, in mountain cabins no car could climb up to. The mountain people had lived thus for many generations. Books had been written about them, tales of mountain feuds . . . the Hatfield-McCoys of West Virginia, stories out of Breathitt County, Kentucky . . . sentimental yarns . . . "Trail of the Lonesome Pine."

There were garages strung along the new big highways and these were often gathering places for Tom's men. How quickly they had taken to the automobile. They gathered before such places, sat about, some in overalls. A surprising number of them could not read or write. They were outwardly listless enough looking men. They talked slowly and quietly. As always happens, the mind of the man out of another world too much influenced by the reading of newspapers, popular magazines and novels, could not differentiate. The mountain men were thought of, by tourists passing swiftly through the hills, as all of a type. They were dangerous, secretive, sly. They spent their time hunting "federals" or shooting at each other. It was of course all nonsense. They were of every type, incipient poets, honest hard-working men, killers, horse traders, liars, men faithful to friends unto death, stupid ones, smart ones, God-seeking ones. It is true that in lonely isolated places things did happen. What Kit's father had, she thought, intended doing to Kit was not a too unusual thing. They lived in a country long out of the path of so-called American progress, a country long forgotten. The westward drift of population in America in earlier days had been along rivers and across the plains, over the Alleghenies from the East and down the Ohio, or along the upper lake region.

Then out into the fat rich plains, the prairie country, the great American agricultural empire. A man of Tom's crowd took a load of liquor into Ohio. He came back and talked. During the Civil War Mosby's raiders[21] cut across river from Kentucky into the North. They would have been southern boys, for the most part Poor Whites, fighting they did not know what for. They raided through Indiana and Ohio and some of them came back.

They came back shaking their heads. Talks at night by Confederate camp fires. "Boys, we can never lick that people. Why, look how our fields are desolated. Up there the barns are groaning, towns are growing, even while this war is going on. They are too big, fat, and well-fed for us."

Mountain man, of Tom Halsey's crowd, in a garage, talking to other mountain men. "Good God, Jim, Fred, Joe, Harry, here we are. We scratch the ground on one of these hills to raise a little corn. It gets up shoulder high and we think we've got a crop. Little scrawny corn stalks as big as my finger. Up there the corn is like trees and you should see their towns, the way their women dress, the houses they live in."

It was no wonder that the money crop of the hills, moon liquor, had, under prohibition, got so important. Tom Halsey, in organizing, drawing together under one head, a scattered industry of thousands of small units, had but followed in the footsteps of others in a modern world— organized steel, the oil industry, tobacco, the woollen industry. Control the illicit liquor business, control and organize crime. Although Tom Halsey did not have an office in an office building, board of directors' room with mahogany table, etc., he was ambitious. He felt himself in the American business tradition. He had thought about it, had his own pride. He felt that American business men, captains of industry, were really big men and that he was on the road to bigness.

The mountain empire in the very heart of America was long forgotten. In Old Virginia the big families, the F.F.V.'s,[22] are nearly all in the Tidewater country. The Washingtons, Jeffersons, Madisons all lived in Tidewater. They forgot the mountain country, the mountain men. Daniel Boone lived out there, Abe Lincoln's people came from the hills. The mountain men were the adventurers, openers up of Kentucky, of Tennessee, of what is now West Virginia—land of coal. Once the mountain men tried to get out from under the overlordship of Tidewater Virginia. They organized the state of Franklin, a purely mountain state, elected a governor and United States senators. They didn't get away with it.

The men of Tom Halsey's crowd, bringers of the new era into the hills, whiskey-making organized, put on a business basis, on their hours off loafing before a roadside garage, looked out over a lovely country.

The garage, let us say, is high up, near a mountain top, where one of the new paved roads sweeps up out of one river valley to pass over and into another. The men's eyes are accustomed to the sight before them. However, and although the mountain folk do not often speak of it, not being given to flowery talk, there is in them a deep love of their hill country. Some of the men of Tom Halsey's liquor-making, liquor-handling, liquor-running crowd, men who under Tom began suddenly to make money, to drive automobiles, to take trips down out of the hills and even into the rolling hill country of southern Ohio and Pennsylvania . . . some of them had been as far away from their home hills as Detroit . . . belonged to families that had been in the hills since before the Revolutionary War. They were sons and grandsons of men who had got the hill country love, love of isolation and independence, into their blood. They were poor men but they were no time-clock punchers. They didn't become clerks in stores and banks. "I am poor but be careful. Do not tread too hard on my toes." When a stranger came into the hills he was watched, but the mountain men were not necessarily suspicious lest he be a federal. The poorest mountain man, living in the most isolated hollow of the hills, in the greatest poverty, often in a one-room cabin with a dirt floor, when such a stranger came to his door invited him into his house, invited him to eat, to spend the night, to stay, if he wished, in the poor hovel for a long visit.

A surprising number of the men in the American Southern Highlands are Scotch-Irish, so-called. It does not mean, however, that they are half Irish. It means that, in old Europe, an English king once sent mountain Scots into Ireland and gave them free land there but mountain people are like the French. They hate paying taxes. The English king tried to tax them and great hordes of them came to America. They were always whiskey makers. Their ancestors had made pot liquor in Scotch hills. They came through Pennsylvania and down through the valley of Virginia, the "Shenandoah," and to the hills because they were hill people. They were in the Whiskey Rebellion in Pennsylvania in early days. "What was all this business about taxes? What has government done for us that we should pay taxes?" For generations the material growth of America had gone on, a great boast, a great wonder, railroads built, later highways built, schools built, cities built. It hadn't happened in the hill country, in all the great sweep of mountain country, starting in the East, almost within sight of the capital at Washington, and sweeping westward, through Virginia, touching North Carolina, taking in a great part of West Virginia, Tennessee, northern Alabama, and Georgia, Kentucky, and Missouri.

It is true that modern industry had done something to, if not for, the hill country. The great lumber kings had invaded the country. There had been thievery of great boundaries and ruthless cutting and slashing. An old story, the whole country may some day realize what a tragic story.

In the early days the mountain men, families, drifted into the hills one by one and settled there. They knew little of courts of law. Titles for land when acquired were often not recorded in the courts. After all Daniel Boone, at the end of all his exploring, his daring penetration into unknown places, when he was old and had settled on a piece of land, to enjoy in peace his old age, was gypped out of the land by some big land company. The big land companies were one of the earliest forms of American graft. Even the immortal Washington got in on that racket.

The early mountain man, coming in, picked himself a place with a bit of creek or river bottom. Hundreds and even thousands of cold mountain streams flowed down out of the hills. They were alive with trout. The forests were full of game. There was enough grass . . . the nutritious blue grass in the limestone hill . . . to feed a cow, a team of oxen or a horse. Pigs could be marked and turned loose to roam in the forest and in good years they grew fat on the fallen acorns.

A life that would have seemed barren to many Americans, in a land where riches came so rapidly, so much flat land, easily farmed, land to be had for the taking in an earlier day. Mark Twain's writing of the Tennessee land in "The Gilded Age"[23] . . . queer creatures, the mountaineers, so listless, so ignorant . . . nothing said about the beauty of Tennessee hills. Would they produce coal, would they produce iron? What other use is there for such land?

To city men, town men, men of fat middle-western farms, such a land would seem of no use. But there was something else to be said. Did not Thomas Jefferson declare that the best government was the least government? There was independence. Your mountain man did not bend the knee. "Treat me with the respect due to my manhood or . . ."

"Or, or, or."

Life was hard but good, too. A mountain man, grown lean and hard in a hard land on hard fare, thought nothing of walking twenty-five miles over mountain trails, through the thick laurel, under the great trees, to some tiny settlement, to bring home tobacco, salt and sugar. He went with his "passel of ginseng," called "sang," or with a few hens in a "poke," slung over his shoulder. There was something mysterious about the wild sang. It was wanted, a good price would be paid for it, by some far-off people. The people who wanted it might have been living in Mars. The mountain man didn't know, didn't ask. In many of the mountain cabins, mere huts, the doors were left swinging open winter and summer. Hens came indoors and laid eggs on the beds or under the beds. The mountain man's children had fixed a place for hens to set in a corner of his one-room house. His pig wandered in and out at the open door. You can housebreak a pig, too.

Suspicion of government deeply rooted. Again: "What right has government to say my children shall go to school? What do we need of book-larnin'? What has government done for me? I myself have no book-larnin', cannot read or write, but am I not a man in my place?" Tom Halsey, the man who became a mountain gang leader . . . he was a rather small compactly built quiet man . . . blue-black hair, black sharp eyes, an upshoot out of his people, more cunning, perhaps cruel, determined, ambitious. How he got his power over other men and, when he wished it, over women, no one knew. He could remember when, as a boy, he went, for the first time, with his father and other men to a town.

They went, the little caravan of mountaineers, some sixty miles, over stony winding mountain roads, half trails. The men carried axes to cut underbrush away. Up and down mountains they went, a team of oxen pulling a covered wagon, a few dozen jugs or kegs of whiskey in the wagon. They made good whiskey in that day, let it mature, didn't hurry it, didn't load the beer with sugar to hurry it, didn't make the later stomach-destroying stuff Tom got rich handling. The whiskey would be buried in straw in the wagon and a man with a gun walked on a mile or two ahead. If a federal appeared . . . they existed at the time too . . . he was to fire the gun. The whiskey was quickly hidden in the near-by brush. At night, when the little caravan camped by some clear mountain stream, it was again carried into the brush, hidden for the night under the thick laurel and rhododendron. When the men got down, near the town, it would be again hidden while they went on into town.

The caravan took all of three long days making its way down to the town where there was a store. There was a branch railroad that came up to the town. It was another three days getting home.

Could a man, several men, come over such roads, for such a great distance, merely to sell a few hens, a little sang? It was too difficult to haul the corn down. Whiskey was the distillation of the corn. Men wanted it. A man and his family wanted sugar, salt, tobacco, snuff. The women and children had to have clothes.

The little pilgrimage going down camped at night by a mountain stream. Tom Halsey remembered that. He remembered the mysterious darkness of the great forests, the cry of owls at night, the talk of the men. The men who would be so silent in town, among town men, now talked freely. When they got near the town the whiskey would be hidden and the smartest, shrewdest one among them . . . it would be Tom's father . . . pride in the boy in that fact . . . would be appointed the one to make the trade for the liquor. "We are mountain men, cannot read or write, but when we speak we tell the truth. It is good liquor. If you think we are dull and stupid, come, try swapping horses with one of us.

"The whiskey is hidden in such and such a place. Come, I will show you." Tom's father spoke of good times when he was a boy. His people lived in the hills of Tennessee. There was a war . . . it was the Spanish-American War . . . and thousands of young men from the North came to camp at a place called "Chickamauga Park." [24]

And did they want whiskey? Did they buy it? It was good times for the liquor makers in the hills. It may be that later, when Tom became a big business man, he remembered his father's talk of that time.

In the town something to be seen. There was, for example, the railroad locomotive. It was really a cheaply constructed bit of railroad that ran up to that mountain place, a mere branch road. There was to be a big lumber cutting started there. But, to the boy, the railroad engine had seemed wonderful and terrible enough. To Tom's mind it may have suggested something. Organizers of big business must have imagination too. They must be born with imagination. The business, the acquisitive instinct, that enables a man to grow rich and powerful, may be, after all, but a perversion, a twist of some finer instinct. Oh, the great world, off there in the distance somewhere, down along that poor little mountain railroad, great rich plains opening out down there, broad rivers flowing! Oh, the great cities being built! Oh, the great forests that still covered so much of a hill country!

The mountain country lay between the North and the South. It had long been the middle-land, the border-land between two civilizations. How many battles of the Civil War fought in the hills, mountain men on both sides in the struggle. Birds from the North, going South, stopped their flight for a time in the hills. Some from the South stayed there, in the high cool places; from the North, in the warm valleys. Southern and northern flowers and trees grew along mountain trails. There was snow falling on the mountain tops, far South, warm days in winter far North.

The forest that once covered the whole land to be remembered by all those who had known it. Tom's father became a lumberjack when the lumber kings came. He talked, sometimes, when Tom was a young fellow, growing up at home, of the forest. It was something mysterious. You felt strange sometimes. Tom's father could not find words for what he wanted to say. He did not know that man had got his notion for the cathedrals, for the Gothic, from the forests. The great aisles, leading away mysteriously under the trees. It was dark overhead, the branches of the great trees intertwined. "You didn't want to speak loud."

There was no underbrush in some places, on upper plateaus where the biggest trees were, and the ground underneath was soft. You walked always on a deep thick carpet of moss.

It was a great sponge. You sank in it to the boot tops.

An idea Tom Halsey never got, that his father never got. This great middle-ground between the North and the South, the Southern Appalachian Highlands, meant something terribly important to the whole country. It was the great stream source. What great rivers having their source in the hills. Once Pinchot,[25] in Theodore Roosevelt's time, was trying to make the idea of forest preservation clear to a group of senators. He took a board and held it on a table, at an angle of forty-five degrees. He poured a glass of water down the face of the board and then took the same board and covered it with blotting paper.

Again he poured the water down the face of the board but it did not run off. The water trickled, a few drops at a time, slowly out at the base of the board.

To see the country as a whole, understand it as a whole, a faculty that, as statesman, Lincoln had, as warrior, Grant had. The lumber kings going into the Southern Highlands and stripping the timber away, often destroyed timber they could not get out. Whole mountain slopes were often destroyed to make a runway for tall timber on some upper plateau . . . the washing away of the good soil beginning, going on year after year, floods in the Tennessee, the Cumberland, the Ohio. Floods down the Mississippi . . . fair lands made deserts . . . countries have been destroyed thus . . . towns destroyed, farms destroyed. A lumber baron has made a million, two million, five million. It is a sweet picture. Kill the TVA! Kill the CCC! These things embarrass private enterprises. Suppose it were possible that, some day, a new impulse be carried to the point where all men, in youth, were compelled to spend perhaps three years, working in the forests, or in any work that would benefit the whole country, getting thereby a sense of the country as a whole.

The dream of a new conception of life and the land.

---

## The Ivanhoe High School Graduation Speech

The address that Anderson delivered to the graduating class of Ivanhoe High School in southwestern Virginia on June 1, 1938, fairly summarizes his feelings and concerns about his region and the world at the time. Nonetheless, he emphasizes the familiar world that the graduates know and will likely occupy in the future, reminding them that one must reconcile oneself to life in the particular before turning to the general. Although his mention of new forms of hatred is a veiled reference to imminent hostilities in Europe, he has praise for the town of Ivanhoe and contends that one has as much chance of finding the good life there as in the larger world. His affirmation of democracy as a belief in the ultimate goodness in humanity suggests an optimism that he might not have so freely expressed just a few years before. Finally, his emphasis on love between individuals as a sustaining force for individual and collective happiness echoes one of his most consistent themes.

The text is edited from Anderson's typescript. It was first published in the *Winesburg Eagle* 15 (Summer 1990): 11–12.

You people here in Ivanhoe will have to be patient with me if I am compelled constantly to look at my notes here. In this attempt I am going to say a few words to this graduating class and to you. Now that I am here I am a little puzzled as to why I am here. It may have been something in Mr. Hicks'[26] letter, asking me to come over here and address you, that induced me to come and it may have been just the name of your town. Your town has a very literary name and I am a literary man. When a man has been sitting at a desk for 25 years and writing, writing comes much more natural to him than speaking and that is the reason I have had to write out my speech.

But after all you cannot be a writer as I have been for so many years without thinking a great deal about people. To be a writer you are compelled to observe, to learn to listen, to think about what you see and what you hear. You listen to people talk but sometimes do not hear their talk. You are trying to think what they are really thinking. The lives of people, their acts and thoughts, their secret desires, their relationships, one person to another person, of their loves, their friendships, their hatreds, their jealousies, their generosities. People are the materials with which a writer works.

After I had told Mr. Hicks that I would come here and that I would try to say a few words to the youths graduating here from this school and to the friends and parents of these youths, I got nervous. A man naturally thinks of the graduating exercises in schools as a time of giving advice. At this time older men commonly stand up before young men and women and tell them how to do it, how to achieve success, how to find happiness, how to find the road to the good life, and I remember many just such talks by older men to the youths that graduated in the schools of my own town when I was a boy.

Now you all know that here in America for a long, long time it was presumed that the road to happiness in life, to the good life, was to be found by doing what we call succeeding. It usually meant getting into some big position in life, getting rich, getting into the newspapers, being an outstanding figure. You all know well enough what we meant. It used to be talked of so much—it is I believe talked of a little less nowadays. It has come about that nowadays there are so many of us who, by force of circumstances or because of lack of some particular type of talent or perhaps even because we like it best, are content to lead rather humble lives, but there are others who are ashamed of leading humble lives. They are afraid they haven't made good. They feel a little apologetic about the matter. But I would like to say here, in fact I would like to make the whole point of what I say, that what is commonly called success among us Americans is not what it is cracked up to be.

It has happened that in my own life I have known a great many people. I am a professional writer and have been one for nearly 30 years and during all of this time I have also been a passionate traveler, and being a writer I have been all my life intensely interested in people. It happens that I have known pretty intimately a good many prominent men, men in high stations of life. I have known a good many men rich and powerful in industry.

We all know that too many men who have got into high positions, for example, in American politics, have got there largely by blah-blah. They haven't said what they really thought. They haven't dared to and if any of you want to know about many of our great American fortunes, how they were got together, it is easy enough nowadays to find out. Nowadays we are all getting somewhat disillusioned about such matters. The histories of these great fortunes, how they have been acquired, and how many men have often been made to suffer in acquiring them, are now being written. As a people we are getting more and more aware.

I do not believe that I need to say to you here that the youth of today is going out into a strange kind of world. Old ideas are everywhere being set aside and new ideas are springing up. In almost half of the civilized world new dictators have been set up. As a driving force in the acquisition of power, hatred has taken the place of tolerance. Certain races are being hounded, old beliefs in the brotherhood of man denied. We see whole nations of people apparently giving up almost overnight what men have for centuries struggled to achieve, that is to say tolerance, freedom of speech, the right of man to find his God in his own way, the belief in the final good intent of humanity, that is at the bottom of the belief in democracy. Understanding and tolerance are being cast away. And all this for what? For the building up of new hatreds. Queer fantastic figures of men are being thrown up as dictators. Sword rattling is in vogue again. More and more millions, even billions, are every year being spent for this kind of power worship, the kind of power worship that is taking the place of tolerance.

Now this is the world into which youth is coming now. Why blink the matter? Every young man and woman has now to decide where he stands. Is he or she going to go in for new hatreds or for tolerance, democracy or dictatorship? The whole substance of the impulse to surrender the liberties of men to the dictator is after all simple enough. It comes down to "letting George do it," to the shrinking of responsibility. It is a throwing up of the sponge, nothing less. It is a wide-spread human cowardice.

So you see what youth is up against now, and what is the answer? It is a little complicated I admit but it seems to me that for youth in America it comes to these certain points. First to stick to democracy at all costs, not to believe in miracles to be achieved by short cuts. For every young man and woman to try to find somehow a kind of work to do that he or she can enjoy doing, to cultivate more and more human relationships, try to make your lives filled with friends, not to be afraid to believe in others, to try to think about others as well as yourself.

We are in a mechanical age and the problem of what we, as a people, are going to do with it, whether or not we can make it benefit more and more of us or only a few, is going to be the big problem in the future in all our lives.

But over and above this problem I think that it would be well for us to remember that men and women are always the same. Even in the face of these new problems, in our greatest factories, in our cities and towns, no matter what happens, or how very complicated life becomes for us, there is always love springing up between man and man, man and woman, woman and woman, there are the hills, the sky, the river, the forests. There is plenty of work to be done. Sometimes it seems to me absurd that there should be anybody out of work. To build America into what it really should be would keep all of us busy for at least another thousand years.

Now for myself I like to see men and women learn to play as well as to work. I think there are millions of us who will likely never be great outstanding figures in life, so-called successful men, cutting a big figure, filling the pages of newspapers—there are millions of us for every one of the other sort, and not only is this true but I think also that, life being set up as it is, there is even likely to be more real satisfaction, more real happiness, a better chance for the good life, just being men and women going along, more and more aware of others, being good sports about disappointments when they come to us, than there is being so-called big shots. This I really believe. Life has taught it to me. My own powers of observation have taught it to me. It is absurd to talk, for example, of loving your country until you can learn to love and respect your own town, your own street, the people of your own town, of your own street, the people you see about you every day. These new hatreds that have come into the world cannot always dominate even in the countries of the dictators. Hatred is too self-destructive. I even believe that the world will get over the passion for war, for killing, and I sincerely believe that every youth now has his or her part to do in bringing us back to this sanity.

So that is about all I can say to you. I was nervous after I had told Mr. Hicks I would come over here and try to speak to you, but as I have been standing up here before you I have got over my nervousness. I think that we in Southwest Virginia live in a pretty gorgeous country and I enjoyed the drive over here. I have been in Ivanhoe before and I like your town. I like the looks of these graduates. I like your Ivanhoe baseball team, and to the graduates I certainly wish luck in life—that both the young men and women among you will find lovers and people to love, that you will laugh more than weep, that you will be good sports, that you will in short find for yourselves the good life and help others to find it.

# Notes

## Preface

1. Southern materials appear in varying amounts in Anderson's own collections: *Hello Towns!* (1929), *Perhaps Women* (1931), *Death in the Woods and Other Stories* (1933), *No Swank* (1934), *Puzzled America* (1935), and *Home Town* (1940); and occasionally in the two posthumous editions of his memoirs (edited by Paul Rosenfeld in 1942 and Ray Lewis White in 1969) and *The Sherwood Anderson Reader* (1947) edited by Paul Rosenfeld. Three of Anderson's novels are also related to the South: *Dark Laughter* (1925), *Beyond Desire* (1932), and *Kit Brandon: A Portrait* (1936).

2. Often this recognition has taken the form of editions of scattered writings from the period. Two such examples are *Return to Winesburg* (1967) and *The Buck Fever Papers* (1971), both consisting of columns from his two Virginia newspapers. They supplement *Hello Towns!*, Anderson's own journalistic sampler, gathered from his first year as a small-town editor and publisher. New editions of *Dark Laughter, Beyond Desire,* and *Kit Brandon* have also appeared, as has a reprint of *Death in the Woods and Other Stories.* Southern-related selections also are included in *Sherwood Anderson: The Writer and His Craft* (1979) and *Certain Things Last* (1992), the most recent edition of Anderson's short stories.

3. Works edited from manuscripts and published here for the first time include: "How I Ran a Small-Town Newspaper," "O, Ye Poets," "Night," "Moderating the Ransom-Barr Debate," "Lumber Camp," "Sugar-Making," and "This Southland."

4. Christopher Sergel, introduction, *Kit Brandon* (New York: Arbor House, 1985) viii.

## Introduction

1. In Pendleton Hogan, "The Big White Portico of Sherwood Anderson," part 2. *Winesburg Eagle* 6 (November 1980): 4.

2. *Letters to Bab: Sherwood Anderson to Marietta D. Finley, 1916–33*, ed. William A. Sutton (Urbana: U of Illinois P, 1985) 122.

3. *Sherwood Anderson's Secret Love Letters: For Eleanor, a Letter a Day*, ed. Ray Lewis White (Baton Rouge: Louisiana State UP, 1991) 222.

4. *Secret Love Letters* 175–76.

5. *Letters to Bab* 133.

6. "In New York," *Marion Democrat*, June 19, 1928, 8.

## 1. Discovering the South

1. *Letters to Bab* 118.

2. *Sherwood Anderson: Selected Letters*, ed. Charles E. Modlin (Knoxville: U of Tennessee P, 1984) 29.

3. "New Orleans: A Prose Poem in the Expressionist Manner," *Vanity Fair* 26 (August 1926): 36, 97.

4. The *Double Dealer* was edited at this time by Julius Friend and Basil Thompson.

5. On February 1, 1922, Anderson wrote to his brother Karl that the French Quarter of New Orleans was "surely the most civilized spot in America. . . . Where else in all America could one spend a day, as I did yesterday, working steadily all morning, going to see the oyster opening championship of the world settled after lunch, walking on the wharfs among singing Negro laborers in the late afternoon and seeing Panama Joe Gans whip his man in an out of doors arena in the evening. And at that I missed the horse races. Do you not suffer of envy?" Modlin, ed., *Sherwood Anderson* 29.

6. Wells, known for his science fiction and satirical novels, published *Outline of History* in 1920. Villard at the time was editor of *The Nation*.

7. Quoted from Song of Solomon 5:4–6.

8. An offbeat author, translator, and world traveler, who lived in New Orleans from 1877 to 1887.

9. In the early 1920s Anderson, like many other writers, sometimes used the term "nigger" not intending to offend African Americans but, rather, to refer to a free, natural approach to life that he (or in this case his character, Bruce Dudley) admired and envied. Later, however, he became critical of writers from the North who played upon this racial stereotype—"the nigger craze," as he puts it in "The South," p. 29; see also "A Meeting South" and "Paying for Old Sins."

10. The list is ironically eclectic. White was a famous longtime editor of the Emporia, Kansas, *Gazette*; Broun was a columnist and newspaper critic, at the time on the staff of the New York *World*. Brooks, Crowninshield, Bankhead, Mencken, Loos, Young, and Lardner were all friends of Anderson's. Brooks

was a literary critic and biographer, author of *America's Coming-of-Age* (1915); Crowninshield was editor of *Vanity Fair;* Bankhead was a famous movie actress; Mencken at the time was editor of the *American Mercury;* Loos was a prolific author of screenplays; Young was drama critic, author, and an editor of the *New Republic;* Lardner was a sports writer and author of *You Know Me Al* (1916). Le Gallienne was a prominent actress in American and British theater. Johnson, a famous black boxer, and Haywood, a radical labor leader, were both convicted of crimes and were living abroad. For Wells, see p. 3, n. 6.

11. The *Literary Digest* was a weekly magazine of news and commentary. "The Dial Book of Modern Art" is probably a reference to the *Dial's* portfolio of modern art, *Living Art* (1923), a copy of which Anderson owned. Wills was an outstanding black heavyweight boxer whom Jack Dempsey was reputed to have avoided fighting.

12. New Orleans newspapers.

13. John McClure, a member of the editorial staff of the newspaper as well as one of the founders of the *Double Dealer.*

14. From "Negro on the Docks at Mobile, Ala.," published in Anderson's *A New Testament* (1927) 84–85.

15. From "The Red-Throated Black," in *A New Testament* 42–43.

16. An art museum that exhibited the work of several of Anderson's friends, including Alfred Stieglitz, Georgia O'Keeffe, and Arthur Dove.

17. Paul Gauguin (1848–1903), who lived for two years in Tahiti. The English translation of his autobiographical novel, *Noa Noa,* appeared in 1924.

18. Fredrick O'Brien, a journalist, author of *White Shadows in the South Seas* (1920), and friend of Anderson's.

19. See, for example, H. Edward Richardson, "Faulkner, Anderson and Their Tall Tale," *American Literature* 34 (May 1962): 287–91; and Walter B. Rideout and James B. Merriweather, "On the Collaboration of Faulkner and Anderson," *American Literature* 35 (March 1963): 85–87. For another contribution by Anderson, see Ray Lewis White, "Anderson, Faulkner, and a Unique Al Jackson Tale," *Winesburg Eagle* 16 (Summer 1991): 5–8.

20. *Letters of Sherwood Anderson,* ed. Howard Mumford Jones and Walter B. Rideout (Boston: Little, Brown, 1953) 162–64. The editors speculatively date the letter 1927; however, in "The Collaboration of Faulkner and Anderson" (*q.v.*), Rideout revises the date to 1925.

21. See Walter B. Rideout, "The Break Between Sherwood Anderson and William Faulkner," *Winesburg Eagle* 13 (Summer 1988): 2–5.

22. Boots with elastic sides, frequently worn by U.S. congressmen in the nineteenth century.

23. See Judy Jo Small, *A Reader's Guide to the Short Stories of Sherwood Anderson* (New York: G. K. Hall, 1994) 413–23.

24. The narrator of *Moll Flanders,* a novel by Daniel Defoe, first published in 1722.

25. Heavyweight boxing champion, from 1882 to 1892.

26. Famous impresario of nineteenth-century tours and exhibits, most notably his circus, "The Greatest Show on Earth."

27. One of Anderson's numerous references to his father's alleged southern background. See Introduction, p. xv.

28. Lincoln in a speech in 1858 said, "I do not understand that because I do not want a negro woman for a slave I must necessarily want her for a wife," a passage Anderson would likely have read in his favorite book on Lincoln, *An Autobiography of Abraham Lincoln,* ed. Nathaniel Wright Stephenson (Indianapolis: Bobbs-Merrill, 1926) 162.

## 2. The Southern Highlands

1. There are two editions, both posthumously published: *Sherwood Anderson's Memoirs,* ed. Paul Rosenfeld (New York: Harcourt, Brace, 1942); and *Sherwood Anderson's Memoirs: A Critical Edition,* ed. Ray Lewis White (Chapel Hill: U of North Carolina P, 1969). The text that follows is from the Rosenfeld edition.

2. Elizabeth Anderson with Gerald R. Kelly, *Miss Elizabeth: A Memoir* (Boston: Little, Brown, 1969); Caroline Greear, "Sherwood Anderson as a Mountain Family Knew Him," *Winesburg Eagle* 14 (Summer 1989): 1–12. See also Robert F. Williams, "The Great Train Ride," *Winesburg Eagle* 1 (April 1976): 4–5.

3. Julian Harris and his wife, Julia, edited the Columbus, Georgia, *Enquirer-Sun.* His father was the author of the popular Uncle Remus stories, Joel Chandler Harris.

4. When Anderson knew him, Wallace was U.S. secretary of agriculture; he visited at Ripshin in 1933. From 1941 to 1945 he served as vice president.

5. English author (1803–1881), whose stories, frequently involving gypsies, were favorites of Anderson's. *Lavengro* was published in 1851 and *The Romany Rye* in 1857.

6. Dave became a good friend of the Andersons; see "Lumber Camp," p. 170.

7. Formerly the wife of Jerome (Jerry) Blum, an artist and good friend of Anderson's in Chicago. Swan lived at Ripshin during the summer of 1927.

8. See p. 28, n. 27.

9. Liveright was the owner of Boni and Liveright, which in 1925 published *Dark Laughter.*

10. W. O. Gant is the proprietor of a tombstone shop in Wolfe's novel, which was published in 1929.

11. After the Andersons' trip to Europe during 1926–27, they spent the summer of 1927 at Ripshin prior to his purchase of the Marion newspapers and their move to Marion in the fall.

12. See Welford Dunaway Taylor, ed., *The Buck Fever Papers* (Charlottesville: UP of Virginia, 1971).

13. George Daugherty, who is the subject of "The Feeders," in Anderson's *Memoirs*, ed. White, 376–81.

14. Published in Paris in 1922 but banned in the United States until 1933.

15. "Country Squires," *Vanity Fair* 33 (October 1919): 63, 128.

16. From a manuscript of "Country Squires."

17. "A Mountain Dance," *Vanity Fair* 29 (November 1927): 59, 110; reprinted in *Hello Towns!* 40–47; "These Mountaineers," *Vanity Fair* 33 (January 1930): 44–45, 94; reprinted in *Death in the Woods and Other Stories* 161–71.

18. The present text appeared in *Vanity Fair* 29 (January 1928): 46, 118; and in *Hello Towns!* 265–72. The other appeared in *Death in the Woods*, 175–86.


## 3. A Country Editor

1. See, for example, "Nearer the Grass Roots," *Outlook* 148 (January 27, 1928): 3–4, 27; "I Will Not Sell My Newspapers," *Outlook* 150 (December 5, 1928): 1286–87 (reprinted with changes in *Hello Towns!* 333–39).

2. All were famous newspaper editors: Franklin (1706–1790) with his *Pennsylvania Gazette;* Charles A. Dana (1819–1897), the *New York Sun;* both James Gordon Bennett (1795–1872), and his son of the same name (1841–1918), the *New York Herald;* Horace Greeley (1811–1872), the *New York Tribune;* Henry Watterson (1840–1921), the *Louisville Courier-Journal.*

3. A small town a few miles west of Marion.

4. Charles H. (Andy) Funk, commonwealth attorney of Smyth County, and Burt Dickinson, also an attorney and former mayor of Marion, were good friends of Anderson's.

5. An imaginary cat whose travels around the area were frequently reported on in Anderson's papers.

6. See "Virginia" in chapter 2.

7. One Confederate veteran, William C. Pendleton, wrote a political history of Appalachia, which Anderson praised for the loyalty it expressed toward the region (*Marion Democrat,* November 22, 1927). Another was Uncle Steve Groseclose, a Confederate veteran who sold Bibles in his later years. He is the subject of a humorous Buck Fever sketch (see *The Buck Fever Papers* 173–75. Also, see "On Being a Country Editor").

8. John C. Breckinridge, U.S. Vice President (1857–61).

9. Ambrose E. Burnside, Union general, had taken over command of the Army of the Potomac from General McClellan but, following his defeat at Fredericksburg, was replaced by Joseph Hooker.

10. Oliver O. Howard, Union general.

11. See for example, "Jim Carter Says," *The Buck Fever Papers* 229–30, and "Conversation with Jim Carter," *The Buck Fever Papers* 233–34.

12. County superintendent of schools and father of Eleanor Copenhaver, who in 1933 became Anderson's fourth wife.

13. The state's second-highest mountain, located near Ripshin.

14. Virginia Polytechnic Institute in Blacksburg, Virginia, then the state agricultural and mechanical college.

15. Henry Staley was the owner of a mill near Marion. Anderson is being facetious.

16. An imaginary club comprised of local citizens, whose purported activities Anderson frequently mentions in the newspapers.

17. This view is on the road from Marion to Ripshin.

18. The first of these entries appeared on February 12, 1929. The opening letter to Bockler was published with the same title in *Outlook* 151 (February 13, 1929): 247, 278, 280.

19. American artist living in Paris, whose popular paintings were frequently of women in the outdoors.

20. Metaphors Anderson often used about these cities, probably inspired by Carl Sandburg's poem "Choose" in *Chicago Poems* (1916): "The single clenched fist lifted and ready, / Or the open asking hand held out and waiting."

21. The opening lines of a hymn by William Cowper (1721–1800).

22. Max Eastman was a political writer and lecturer. Floyd Dell was a journalist and novelist. In earlier years they were editors of radical magazines, the *Masses* and the *Liberator,* and were friends of Anderson's.

23. Anderson lived in an apartment in the Upper Pontalba Building when he moved to New Orleans in 1924.

24. Wharton Esherick, a wood sculptor from Paoli, Pennsylvania, whom Anderson had met during his stay in Fairhope in 1920.

25. Anderson frequently made this claim, although it is apparently without foundation.

26. Hall, an eccentric painter, lived in a restored antebellum home near New Iberia, Louisiana.

27. Gutzon Borglum had begun the monument in 1923, but two years later his contract was cancelled, and Augustus Lukeman took over. In the summer of 1929, the project was suspended for lack of funds. It was completed in 1970 with Lee in front and the others on each side.

28. Published as "Small Town Notes," *Vanity Fair* 32 (July 1929): 48, 110.

29. Anderson also wrote an account of the harness races at Lexington, Kentucky, in "Here They Come," *Esquire* 13 (March 1940): 80–81.

30. On May 18, 1929.

31. Col. E. R. Bradley of Lexington, Kentucky.

32. Inscribed on the base of the statue is the text of King George's proclama-

tion establishing the colony of Georgia. See *Sherwood Anderson's Love Letters to Eleanor Copenhaver Anderson,* ed. Charles E. Modlin (Athens: U of Georgia P, 1989) 42–44.

33. A former owner of the Marion newspapers.

34. The pseudonym for Elizabeth M. Gilmer, a journalist, whose columns of advice to readers were carried in newspapers for more than a half century.

35. Gregarious residents of Marion.

36. The staff of the newspaper with whom Anderson socialized included Mark Ethridge, Aaron Bernd, and Ben Johnson. The owner of the *Telegraph* was William T. Anderson.

37. Owner of a laundry in Washington, D.C., and a good friend of Anderson's.

38. The house of Wharton Esherick at Fairhope.


## 4. Southern Labor

1. *The Nation* 128 (May 1, 1929): 526–27.

2. Elizabethton was incorporated in 1905.

3. Alfred Hoffman, a representative of the United Textile Workers.

4. In *Perhaps Women* (New York: Liveright, 1931) 9–17.

5. See *Sherwood Anderson's Love Letters to Eleanor Copenhaver Anderson,* ed. Charles E. Modlin (Athens: U of Georgia P, 1989) 53–59.

6. Ed Geers, famous harness-racing driver at the turn of the century, whom Anderson admired and frequently referred to in his writings.

7. The opening lines of "The Happiest Heart," a poem by John Vance Cheney (1848–1922).

8. Anderson embroiders his account of this incident at the end of *Perhaps Women.* Several men ask, "Me?" and the woman responds, "No, not you [ . . . ] I want a man" (143–44).

9. See *Letters* 227.

10. See Ray Lewis White, "Sherwood Anderson, American Labor, and Danville, Virginia," *Winesburg Eagle* 15 (Summer 1990): 1–9.

11. *Winesburg Eagle* 15, 9.

12. Woodrow Wilson, Georges Clemenceau, and David Lloyd George, the representatives of the United States, France, and England at the Paris Peace Conference in 1919.

13. A war drama by Stallings and Maxwell Anderson, first produced in 1924.

14. See *Sherwood Anderson's Love Letters* 83–97.

15. That is, letting them slide.

16. Additional versions were published as "'Sold!' to the Tobacco Company" in *Globe* 2 (July 1938): 30–35; and "Sold" in *Youth Today* 2 (September 1939): 28–30.

## 5. A New South

1. Published posthumously in the *Squib,* May 6, 1941.

2. George W. Chamlee Sr. and Samuel Leibowitz were attorneys for the defense in the Scottsboro, Alabama, case of eight black youths convicted in 1931 of the rape of two young white girls. In 1933 Judge James E. Horton overturned a conviction and ordered one of a series of retrials of the case.

3. Vice president of the Confederacy, congressman, governor of Georgia, and author of *Constitutional View of the War Between the States* (1868–70).

4. See, for example, *Selected Letters* 42–43, 52–54.

5. English professor, author, and journalist from New York State.

6. Born in Missouri, known principally for his poetry in such collections as *The Weary Blues* (1926) and *Dear Lovely Death* (1931).

7. "A New Chance for the Men of the Hills," *Today* 1 (May 12, 1934): 10–11, 22–23.

8. Harcourt A. Morgan, Arthur E. Morgan, and Lilienthal were appointed by Roosevelt in 1933 to be the directors of the TVA.

9. That is, those taking inferior timber, fit for woodpeckers.

10. Anderson disliked the sentimentality of John Fox Jr.'s popular novel *The Trail of the Lonesome Pine* (1908). Caldwell's *Tobacco Road* appeared in 1932.

11. Anderson wrote about the CCC (established in 1933 as a part of the New Deal) in "Tough Babes in the Woods," *Puzzled America* 69–83.

12. Roger L. Sergel, president of the Dramatic Publishing Company and a close friend of Anderson's. He had formerly taught English at the University of Pittsburgh and published a novel, *Arlie Gelston* (1923).

13. The National Recovery Administration was formed in 1933 to establish standards of fair practice in industry.

14. A contract by which miners agreed not to join the union.

15. Edward Bellamy's utopian novel, *Looking Backward,* was published in 1897; Robert Ingersoll (1833–1899), attorney and lecturer, was noted for his agnosticism and criticism of Christianity.

16. Sanger (1883–1966) was a noted advocate of birth control.

17. As defined in the popular 1927 movie *It,* starring Clara Bow, *it* is "that quality possessed by some which draws all others with its magnetic force."

18. See Sherwood Anderson, "Man and His Imagination" in *The Intent of the Artist,* ed. Augusto Centeno (Princeton: Princeton UP, 1941) 39–79, and Welford Dunaway Taylor, "Kit Brandon: A Reidentification," *Newberry Library Bulletin* 6 (July 1971): 263–67.

19. Carter Glass served as a U.S. senator from 1920 to 1946.

20. Governor of Virginia (1926–30) and U.S. senator (1933–64).

21. Confederate cavalry led by John S. Mosby, famous for its guerilla attacks.

22. First Families of Virginia, a designation for Virginia aristocracy first recorded in the nineteenth century.

23. A collaborative novel by Twain and Charles Dudley Warner, published in 1873.

24. As a soldier in 1898, Anderson had camped at Chickamauga Park, Georgia, the site of the Civil War battle near Chattanooga, Tennessee.

25. Clifford Pinchot, formerly a member of the National Forest Commission, governor of Pennsylvania, and author of books on forestry and conservation.

26. H. P. Hicks, the school principal.

# Index